VOICES

VOICES

Trula Michaels LaCalle, Ph.D.

DODD, MEAD & COMPANY • New York

1 2 3 4 5 6 7 8 9 10

Library of Congress Cataloging-in-Publication Data

LaCalle, Trula Michaels.
Voices: a psychologist's journey.

1. Kincaid, Christopher—Mental health.   2. Multiple
personality in children—Patients—United States—
Biography.   3. LaCalle, Trula Michaels.   4. Clinical
psychologists—California—Biography.   I. Title.
RJ506.M84K565 1988   616.85'236 [B]   87-20109
ISBN 0-396-08974-7

To Christopher,

*who wanted his story to be told so that the
shocking truths about child abuse will
not remain a secret.*

CONTENTS

ACKNOWLEDGMENTS

My thanks to the many teachers who have guided, informed, supported, and inspired me along the way; to Jane Jordan Browne, my agent, friend, and incredibly skilled trailblazer; to Mary Bowen Hall, writer, who helped me produce the manuscript in its final form and whose sensitive optimistic spirit kept me going; to my collegues in the multiple personality study group; to my mother, who entertained my children while I sat at the typewriter; to my friends, who critiqued the earliest drafts; and my deepest appreciation to the real-life Bob Slater, Paula Reynolds, Jerry Swenson, and Sue Costello, who shared this true drama with me.

Finally, I wish to thank my husband for his tenacity, his undying hope, his willingness to grow, and his courage in allowing me to tell his story as well.

FOREWORD

The year is 1980. A thirty-four-year-old psychologist discovers that one of her patients is suffering from a rare psychiatric illness—multiple personality disorder. She seeks consultation, reads all she can on the subject, unsuccessfully tries to refer her patient to a more experienced practitioner, acquires special training, and is eventually forced to "wing it"—to fall back on her generic training as a psychotherapist. She refuses either to give up on her patient or to discharge him to the care of professionals obviously less informed about his illness than she has become.

In her tenacity, she jeopardizes her marriage, her relationship with her children, her practice, reputation, income, and health. At times she compromises her own emotional well-being. She is ultimately transformed by her adventures and misadventures from a life of relative security and complacency to the life of a maturing and growing psychotherapist.

Dr. LaCalle has no way of knowing that her stressful experiences are being repeated throughout the United States and Canada. Psychiatrists, psychologists, and clinical social workers are finding their marriages dissolving before their eyes. They are being rebuffed by their colleagues, facing malpractice suits by their patients, having their hospital staff privileges revoked, watching their licenses to practice being suspended or subjected to sanction, being forced to resign from professional organizations, receiving notice of investigation by ethics committees, finding their patients stripped from them by hospital or university employers while official notices of reprimand are being placed in their personnel files. Patients with Christopher's diagnosis—multiple personality—are even being barred from admission to psychiatric hospitals on the grounds that they are "too disruptive . . . too difficult to treat . . . lead to too much staff conflict. . . ."

She also has little way of knowing that, just as she is discovering Christopher's illness, two revolutionary papers on multiple personality, authored by independent researchers, are appearing. At the time Dr. LaCalle is searching the professional literature, these writings are still too new to have yet been included in referencing services.

These events are at the very least perplexing. Why is a widely known psychiatric illness, which almost no professional has ever encountered, suddenly being identified with almost incredible frequency? Why is the diagnosis of even obvious cases so controversial during these times? Most of all, why are highly trained clinicians from the best schools experiencing so much grief and turmoil in attempting to treat these patients? The answers to these questions provide the context for this book.

The quarter century from 1955 to 1980 was one of the stormiest periods in psychiatry's already unsettled history. The extent to which mental illnesses were primarily seen to be the result of faulty learning or experience, or as the result of subtle disorders in brain chemistry, came to be argued as never before. As in all specious forms of argument, that which follows is ultimately incomprehensible. These nonconnecting debates, each bolstered by its own premises and systems of logic, each consuming thousands of pages of exposition, and each leading to contradictory public policy as to how best to treat the mentally ill, moved the American Psychiatric Association to publish the most extreme redefinition of psychiatric terminology and diagnostic procedures in its history. The year was 1980.

The appearance of the third edition of the *Diagnostic and Statistical Manual of the American Psychiatric Association (DSM-III)*, a 494-page text that went into seven printings with 200,000 copies within two years of its initial appearance, challenged many time-honored ways of looking at mental illness, multiple personality included. No longer viewed as a sub-form of hysteria, patients who failed to display hysterical symptoms could now be considered as candidates for the disorder, so long as they met specific criteria. At least one reason multiple personality was being more frequently diagnosed, therefore, is that the vivid descriptions of the dissociative group of disorders in *DSM-III*, of which multiple personality is an example, made these patients easier to recognize. Much of the subsequent controversy over this diagnosis can be traced to a conflict between those who have readily embraced the concepts of *DSM-III* and those who have clung to traditional views. Authoritative training and standard reference texts that continued to identify multiple personality with hysteria were still appearing five years after the publication of the new diagnostic manual. Old ideas, especially treasured ones, die hard.

To give the devil his due, however, it must be admitted that therapists identifying these supposedly rare patients were having their hands full in attempting to treat them. By 1980, it would not be inaccurate to argue that no more than six mental health professionals in North America really knew what they were doing with these patients, and even this select group had to rely on a lot of trial and error before they eventually learned workable approaches.

Whether Dr. LaCalle made "mistakes" in her treatment of Christopher by today's standards is moot, for no accepted canons of treatment for these patients existed at the time. What is important about the experiences she presents is that they are the experiences of many therapists at the time and of many more to come. For even as we came to understand this illness and to develop useful strategies of treatment, one factor will never change: that of the profound emotional impact these patients initially make on their therapists—powerful feelings the therapist needs to learn to manage for the good of both. No other patients as a group had been subjected to as much child abuse as these—often heinous abuse—taking the form of repeated physical brutality, neglect of affection, long-term incest, sexual molestation, and abject humiliation. Dealing with this material easily provokes a response in many therapists to make things right, to become the good parent the patient never had. Stated this way, the goal is impossible, and those who have literally tried to fulfill the healing-parent role have often become hopelessly enmeshed with those they are trying to treat. What has happened has happened; the ultimate goal of therapy must be the transcendence of the past. This is painful and difficult work. The way Dr. LaCalle struggles with these issues in her own emotional life often makes for dramatic reading.

In 1982, the International Society for the Study of Multiple Personality was organized from a small group of eleven persons in five states and from Israel. By early 1987, membership had grown to 700. Three highly successful scientific meetings have now been held in Chicago, with Dr. LaCalle as one of the presenters. She has also been active in forming one of the first and largest chapters of the Society in California.

Finally, thanks to Christopher for allowing his own story to be told.

> George B. Greaves, Ph.D.
> Adjunct Professor of Psychology,
> Georgia State University;
> Founder and President,
> International Society for the
> Study of Multiple Personality
> and Dissociative States (ISSMP&D)

Chapter 1

DISCOVERY

Christopher stood looking out at me through the large picture window at the front of his apartment. His forlorn expression was diffused by the rain on the window, as if a torrent of teardrops were splashing down his cheeks. In the split second that I saw his look, I knew I'd done the right thing by coming. Yet the knot in my stomach wouldn't go away. I still had nervous doubts about Christopher.

He moved closer to the window, touching his nose and fingertips to the windowpane. I had seen that look before. Christopher, at this moment, reminded me of my five-year-old son. I had the sense of a small boy—lonely, waiting for his mother to come home.

Why was I feeling so motherly toward a man only seven years younger than I? As his psychologist, I had to be on top of such feelings. He had done nothing to encourage these feelings in me, and had, in fact, always kept his distance, as if afraid to trust me or be dependent. But I was bothered by my impression of déjà vu, as well as by this particular look of Christopher's. None of this was making sense.

Pulling my open umbrella closer to me, I watched my step as I maneuvered the slippery wet walkway to his front door. I was suddenly anxious, aware that I was about to enter Christopher's apartment—alone. Maybe I should have told my husband about this, just in case. But just in case of . . . what? There was no time to have second thoughts about my decision, I reminded myself. Christopher was my patient; he'd tried to kill himself, a second attempt. I was doing what I had to do.

When was I going to be able to take risks on my own? I was irritated with my tiresome insecurity. I'd been in practice six years, I told myself, with plenty of successful outcomes under my belt. I lifted my hand to knock at the door, but hesitated. Christopher opened it without my knocking and greeted me with a faint grin.

"Hi," he said softly, and motioned for me to come inside.

His pale blue eyes shook me with their sadness. Though he wasn't a tall man, I felt small looking up at him from my five-foot-two perspective. He was attractive. His thick blond hair and square jaw line framed his face nicely, but his soft lips and delicate features took away any sense of rugged masculinity.

"I couldn't believe you'd come," he said, looking at me with childlike awe.

"I told you I would."

He'd said on the phone he felt too shaky to drive to my office. And I'd left in a rush after he'd called—cancelling an appointment, giving up my time for lunch. I felt I had to come. I didn't want Christopher to be my first suicide. I felt shaken. This second attempt had been such a close call. My fault, I thought. I hadn't gained Christopher's trust. I imagined him, alone on Halloween night . . . the bottles of pills . . . slowly taking them. He could have phoned me, but didn't. He'd called Bill Jefferson at the outreach clinic instead.

Christopher's small apartment was stark, with beige carpet and sterile white walls. There was a white brick fireplace, but no fire on this chilly day. The walls were decorated with a few framed film posters from the 1930s. The mantel held a collection of photo-portraits, and I moved toward them as if the smiles could warm me.

"Are these pictures of your family?"

"No, they all belong to my roommate."

Christopher's little-boy quality had vanished. He spoke with total disinterest—a flat, vacant response that had me absolutely baffled. What could I draw out of him? I was in his home; there must be something to learn from being here.

"You seem to like nostalgia," I said, indicating a poster

of W. C. Fields wreathed in cigar smoke.

"That's Luke's."

"Is there anything here that belongs to you?"

He nodded toward an onyx chess set.

"That's mine."

"Then you like to play chess?"

"Not really. I just had it, so I set it up."

What was it about Christopher? Why was he so different from my other patients, so . . . inexplicable? I traced back over his many strange and unpredictable mood shifts—darkly somber, sociable and talkative, maturely logical, coquettish—and then there was that cold, callous, unsettling side. How could I forget that? Remembering it unnerved me.

When Bill Jefferson had called me the day after Halloween, he, too, had been startled and shaken by the second suicide attempt. He told me that Christopher had seemed enormously frightened. And I'd sensed there was something more, something Bill could not describe.

I remembered that first call from Bill, when he originally had referred Christopher to me.

"He's in his late twenties, nice-looking, clean-cut, very polite, but a little shy. No family around here, lives with a roommate." Bill had hesitated a moment. "And . . . he's homosexual."

"And?" Bill knew I'd had gay patients before. I couldn't understand his hesitation.

"He seems really frightened. . . . I don't quite know what to make of him." Then Bill told me he'd promised Christopher he would try to find a warm, motherly type for a therapist. That made me pause. Why had he made Christopher that promise? And how could Bill think of me as motherly? I was only thirty-four, and I felt even younger. Pleasant looking, I'd hoped. Blond, with a little help—but motherly?

Christopher interrupted my thoughts, speaking in that same disinterested tone.

"Would you like to see the rest of the apartment?"

"Just the part you use." Maybe this sterility didn't reflect Christopher at all.

"Then I'll show you my room." He shrugged. "That's all there is."

His room was like a prison cell. One high window let in a

shadowy light, filtered through the rain-drenched trees outside. A white chenille spread covered a frameless mattress set, and a nondescript dresser, painted beige, sat beneath an empty bookshelf.

"Pretty bad, I know," Christopher said. "I suppose I should do something with it, but . . ."

I suppressed a shiver. The room—and Christopher—were so cold and colorless at that moment.

Bill had referred Christopher to me after the first suicide attempt. He had full confidence that Christopher would be in good hands, but I was all too aware I didn't understand my patient. Bill had sent Christopher to the hospital, where I met him for the first time. For the three weeks that Christopher was there, I'd had plenty of time to get to know him. Yet despite psychological tests and repeated interviews, I was left with a confusing clinical picture. I could be certain only that he was intelligent, ambivalent about his sexuality, and had had a rough childhood. Then there were those strikingly varied moods of his.

I had ignored my vague apprehensions and let Christopher convince me, convince the hospital staff and the psychiatrist, that he was ready for release. There had been no evidence that he was still suicidal. He was a voluntary patient, worried about his job. He had a right to leave. But why couldn't I have predicted he'd try suicide again? At least, now, I had a reprieve, another chance to do it right. I'd have him admitted at a hospital close to my office, so I could see him more frequently. And this time I'd enlist the help of a different psychiatrist—another opinion might help. But the hospital wouldn't be ready to take him until tomorrow. The task now was to help him wait this out safely.

We had moved back into the living room.

"I'd ask you to sit down, but . . . there isn't any furniture."

"Don't worry about it."

I looked out the sliding doors. The rain had stopped. "Why don't we go out on the balcony? You seem to have a view from here."

I pulled my jacket snugly around me, and we stepped outside. I breathed in the rain-fresh air, a welcome relief after the stifling feeling of the apartment. Christopher propped himself against the rustic wood railing and stared blankly out over the grassy

4

hillside that gleamed wetly from the rain. His soft lips and delicate features were etched with sensitivity. He seemed lost in thought. Dressed in T-shirt and tight jeans, he cut a nice figure, muscular and lean, narrow in the hips. He had the body of a gymnast, I thought, though his hands seemed much too fine and fragile.

It was a matter of waiting this out until tomorrow, I reminded myself. I knew, when I'd learned of this new suicide attempt, that I could have sent him to the county hospital. They'd have taken him immediately, but the county facility was crowded, chaotic. It was important that Christopher be in a private hospital.

For me, that was a good enough reason to take this more risky approach. But that wouldn't have been explanation enough for my husband. No matter that José is a psychologist, too. He would have reacted like a husband. He would insist I was running an unnecessary risk with an unpredictable patient. How could I be certain he wouldn't attempt to harm himself—or me—while I was alone with him? Of course, I could have argued that social workers in ghettos take worse chances. But, still, I would have seen his worried look. I didn't want to be dissuaded from something I felt impelled to do, so I didn't tell José where I was going. I told only my secretary, Liz, and acted as nonchalant as I could.

I was getting involved, I had to admit it to myself. Maybe my judgment wasn't the best. Once again, I was going out on a limb for someone. Surely my Florence Nightingale style would cause me trouble someday. José liked the sensitive side of me, which coincided with his own sense of compassion for people. But I suspected that he thought of me as a bit naive and gullible. As long as he was there to protect me, he could be comfortable with my missionary spirit.

What was it about Christopher that made me react like this? He didn't act as if he needed my help, although at times I felt that he was calling to me from some deep reaches within him. Yet, at this moment, I wasn't drawn to him at all. In fact, I felt downright uneasy.

I studied him. He'd shifted his gaze from the hillside to the ravine below. No more little-boy quality. That was it! The little boy, that was the look that had seemed so familiar. Now I realized I'd seen that quality before. It was in my office, the day after his hospital discharge last week. I'd been looking absentmindedly at the photo collection on my office wall, focusing on a picture of several little boys like those in the "Our Gang" comedies. One had flaxen hair and vacant eyes, a lonely little boy who stared straight into the camera as if he might find a comrade behind the lens. I found myself commenting to Christopher that he must have been a lonely child.

His response was immediate.

"Why do you say that?"

"I'm not sure why." I paused, then some instinct told me to keep on. "I just get a lonely feeling from looking at you. Your father was drinking and reckless. You had a little baby brother to take care of. It doesn't seem, from what you have told me, that anyone was taking care of you."

Silence.

"I'm also thinking," I continued, "that you weren't protected when your father's friend sexually molested you."

Christopher squirmed in his chair, startled. Could he have forgotten he told me about that? I stopped myself from saying anything more. I was operating on instinct again, using a conditioned response I'd learned as a mother. I knew when to back off with my five-year-old son, when his feelings were too tender.

Christopher shifted his weight on the balcony railing.

"I've been feeling a little better," he said guardedly, "but I know you're right about the hospital. I don't think I . . . trust myself."

"Has Luke been here with you a lot as he promised?"

"Yeah. He'll be back any minute. My friends Diane and Sylvia were over here this morning." He sounded chagrined. "It makes me feel like I have to have babysitters."

"Well, the hospital is set for tomorrow morning. It won't be long."

Touch and go, I thought. Wait it out.

Christopher said nothing further. I became uneasy as he looked back out over the ravine. He seemed hypnotized, drawn to the depth below him. One quick twist of his gymnast's body, I thought, and he could hurl himself over the top of the railing.

"Christopher," I said softly.

He appeared not to hear me.

6

"Christopher," I repeated in a slightly louder voice.

There was no response, so I touched him on the shoulder to gain his attention. Apparently startled from a deep reverie, he stared at me.

"Let's go inside."

He didn't move. His soft blue eyes looked through me, beyond me. He turned his head as if he heard something—but what?

"Let's go inside," I persisted. I took him gently by the arm and brought him back into the living room. He settled down cross-legged on the carpet in a dejected posture, his chin resting on his hands, his arms folded across bent knees.

The phone rang.

Christopher reached from his spot on the floor to pick it up. He listened intently, then murmured a few indistinguishable words. His face was still expressionless, but as he continued to listen he started to shake. First his hands trembled, then his forearms, and finally his shoulders and entire upper torso were quivering. He was shuddering as if caught in an icy wind. The telephone receiver slipped out of his hand and I could hear a voice saying, "Hello? Hello!"

"I'm sorry," Christopher stammered, "I have such a headache."

"What's happening, Christopher?" I tried to stifle the alarm in my voice.

"My boss . . . I'm fired."

Christopher must be mistaken, I thought. I'd talked to his employer earlier and had been told he was waiting for Christopher's return.

"Let me have the phone, Christopher."

He sat stone-faced, hopelessness in his voice. "It won't do any good."

"You never know. It might make a difference. I've talked with your boss before, remember?"

I reached over for the telephone, then took a moment before saying anything. I remembered Mr. Woods all too well. He was brusque, aggressive, abrasive—a company-first, produce-or-else type. This man lived in a world apart from mine, and I knew he wouldn't speak my language of feelings and concern. But I mustered my composure and plunged in, attempting to meet him on his own ground.

"Hello, Mr. Woods. This is Dr. LaCalle. I am the psychologist who talked to you about Christopher being unable to go back to work. He's quite upset and can't talk right now."

"Sorry he's upset." Woods spoke abruptly, impatiently. "He had to be told."

"Then Christopher really has been fired?"

"Yes." When Woods spoke again he sounded sarcastic. "He no longer has to ask for time off."

I calmed myself.

"Mr. Woods, as you know, Christopher has been unable to work. In fact, he was unable to drive to my office today, so I felt it was necessary to come here to see him. He'll be going into the hospital again tomorrow morning."

"Uh . . . don't misunderstand me, doctor, don't get me wrong. Christopher's been reliable—an excellent supervisor for the last four years." He seemed to be floundering. For a brief moment, I thought I might be able to change his mind. Then he became assured, businesslike again. "You see, we have to put somebody in his position. There's a thirty-day sick leave allotment, and Christopher's already used it. We were told he'd be gone only two weeks."

I tried to put him back on the defensive, but Woods's voice remained coldly factual. Christopher had used up his thirty days. That was that.

I gave up.

"Will Christopher be able to reapply for his job when he's able to work again?"

"We'd be happy to interview him and consider him among the applicants."

He spoke the words mechanically, as if he'd said them many times before. I fought back annoyance and the urge to be more aggressive.

"I'm glad you'll consider rehiring Christopher. Will your company's insurance cover him for another thirty days?"

"You'll have to call the central office and talk to the person who takes care of the group insurance. There's nothing further that I'm assigned to handle."

"Aren't you calling from the central office?"

A pause.

"Yes."

I waited, exasperated. He did not say anything more. It was all I could do to remain civil as I asked to be transferred to the insurance section. I learned that Christopher had insurance coverage for another sixty days.

The desolate look on Christopher's face told me to give him the news in the most optimistic way I could.

"Your boss said he'd be happy to consider rehiring you, and your insurance policy covers you for another sixty days."

"I didn't think about the insurance." He sat dejectedly, his head turned toward the balcony. "Thanks for talking to him for me. I . . . just . . . can't think too straight right now."

"I can see that. Just take one day at a time."

My words fell on deaf ears. Christopher again had the look I'd seen when we were on the balcony. His gaze was focused on the bluff outside.

I got up slowly, positioning myself between Christopher and the balcony. I was overly anxious, I told myself. He was making no threats. As casually as possible, I made conversation with him about ordinary topics—the distance to the beach, the summer temperatures, the local shops. I kept my voice soothing until he seemed a little more responsive.

"Tell me about your roommate, Christopher. How's he doing these days?"

As if on cue, Luke burst through the door, a grocery bag under each arm.

"Sorry I'm so late, Christopher," he said, ignoring me. I was struck by the lack of eye contact that belied his outward confidence. He set the bags down, introduced himself to me as quickly as he could, then kept right on talking.

"I stopped by the grocery store to get some food I thought Christopher might like," he said. "He's hardly eaten a thing."

His behavior was a combination of authoritative father and clucking mother hen.

"How about some chicken soup, buddy?"

There was no response from Christopher.

"Come on, kid, I'll even fix it for you."

"No. Not right now, thanks." Christopher's answer was listless, but he appeared to be less anxious now that Luke was home.

"Hey, you've got to eat! What could be so terrible that you

9

can't eat? Remember, I'm the best Irish-Jewish cook in town!"

"I've just been fired from my job."

Luke's response was explosive.

"That son of a bitch! I knew he'd pull something like this. Well, he won't get away with it. He can't fire you because you've been sick. It can't be legal." Without a break in his heated talk, Luke picked up the phone. "I'm going to call my attorney. You remember him, don't you? If anybody can fix this for you, he can."

Christopher did not protest, but I intervened.

"Luke, perhaps Christopher needs a chance to consider this before you call."

"No point in waiting. It's better to get right on it. He'll do a good job. I'm one of his best clients."

Luke's take-charge attitude made it easy to understand why there was nothing of Christopher's presence evident here in the apartment they shared. Why did Christopher allow Luke to dominate him? It seemed to me that Luke was Christopher's alter ego, the one who would act out Christopher's hidden aggression. Didn't Christopher know how Luke would react to the news about his job? And wasn't he tacitly encouraging Luke by remaining childlike and passive?

By now Luke had gotten his lawyer's office on the phone.

"Luke Schwartz. Yes, Schwartz. S-C-H-W-A-R-T-Z." Luke, looking embarrassed, put his hand over the mouthpiece. "Must be a new secretary."

He kept right on talking but shortly hung up.

"Have to wait until tomorrow. He won't be available until then."

I watched Christopher breathe a sigh of relief, then turned my attention to Luke.

"I stopped by to see how Christopher was doing," I told him. "Now, because of his job, I think he's more depressed than ever. Can someone stay with him until he's admitted to the hospital tomorrow morning?"

"Oh, I planned to be with him. I'll take good care of him." Luke made sure I knew who was in charge. "Don't worry, I even flushed all the rest of those pills down the toilet."

That would have been my idea, exactly.

"Babysitters," Christopher said softly.

"Then you're not feeling suicidal, Christopher?"

"I don't know." His voice was lifeless.

"I felt uneasy when you kept staring at the balcony. Can you tell me what you were thinking?"

"Nothing. I wasn't thinking anything. I was just sort of listening."

Listening to what? I decided not to ask.

Christopher would not admit to suicidal thoughts, but I was glad I'd gotten the message across to Luke that the balcony could be a danger. Luke and I exchanged a knowing look. He promised to drive Christopher to the hospital the next morning before he went to work, and I left the apartment with his assurance that "everything's under control."

The next day, I happened to send my secretary on an early-morning errand near the hospital. When she came back, she told me she thought she had seen Christopher wandering around looking lost and dazed. In a panic, I called the hospital.

But Christopher had checked in, apparently in a perfectly routine manner. He'd also already been interviewed by Dr. Swenson, the psychiatrist who had agreed to admit him for me. I hurried to the hospital. As soon as I entered, I thought of how psychiatric wards reminded me of old hotels, musty with the mixture of smoke and closed-in people. I went to the central nursing station and checked the psychiatrist's notes. But Swenson had reported that Christopher was alert and well-oriented to his surroundings.

There seemed to be no end of surprises. After having observed Christopher for a month, first in the other hospital after his suicide attempt and then in that one puzzling office visit afterward, I was still playing catch-up almost every time I saw him. Now that we had a chance to talk, I was determined to waste no time.

On the way to Christopher's room, I decided to check the day room, but it was occupied only by worn-out stuffed furniture and a blaring television. I quickened my pace, detouring around a laundry cart in the hall and an immobile young woman in a flannel nightgown who stared into space. I found Christopher in his room, sitting on his bed, composed and neatly dressed.

"What happened this morning, Christopher?" I asked. "I thought that Luke promised to bring you to the hospital."

"He got angry. He wouldn't drive me here."

Angry? Now what?

"What made him so angry that he would change his mind on something as important as this?"

"He said I insulted him. He left me a nasty note this morning."

Christopher handed me a typewritten note.

> I'm not driving you to the hospital. You're crazy all right, but you don't need to be taken care of. You need to be taught a lesson. I told you in July that it would kill me to lose your friendship. Not anymore. That note you left has to be the worst slap in the face I have ever experienced. Without any regard for my feelings, you wrote one of the most unfeeling and insensitive pieces of work I have feasted my eyes upon. Just look around my house at the love and warmth and everything in here and you will see what I have done.

I nearly choked on that. Love and warmth! Only Luke's dominance was evident. Perhaps Christopher had finally said something about the way Luke made decisions for them both.

"What did you say in your note to Luke?"

"I don't remember," he said blankly. "I was very upset."

"Surely you remember something."

"Not much. I was very tired and sort of falling asleep. I brought my note with me. Luke left it in the kitchen, along with the note he wrote me."

"You didn't reread it?"

"I didn't have time."

"Where is the note now?"

"It's still at the nurse's station with the rest of my things. I'll go get it."

When he returned, he handed the note to me without looking at it. I passed it back to him.

"Why don't you read it to me?"

"No, no, that's okay," he said, brushing it aside. "You read it."

As I began to read the note to myself, I noticed that Christopher's handwriting appeared different and clumsy.

> I will not tolerate being reprimanded in front of my friends. Do not insult my friends.

I was incredulous.

You have never helped me financially, so please don't offer.

The writing became bolder, the words more angry.

I will smoke anywhere I want in my house. Your gluttonous appetite must be controlled (there are others at the table). You are a conniving manipulator and you offer help only when it is convenient or good for you.

This was incredible! Had someone else written the note for Christopher? The message on the paper didn't fit any side of him I had seen.

"No wonder Luke got angry with you!"

"What did I say?" He looked surprised. What kind of a game is he playing? I wondered. How is it he doesn't remember?

"You wrote that he is gluttonous and manipulative, and you implied that he is stingy, selfish, insulting, and insensitive."

"Well, he is all of those things, but I can't believe I wrote that and then let him see it. It's a good thing I'm here. I must be getting spacey."

"Could be." I reflected for a moment. "It may be, too, that this is one of your first attempts to be truthful about the way you feel. We've talked about how you seem to let others influence you too much. Of course, that note came out pretty aggressive."

"I don't know why. I really don't want to hurt Luke." Christopher seemed quite earnest about this.

After a pause, I changed the subject. I wanted to find out how he had responded to the psychiatrist who would be handling the medical aspects of his hospitalization.

"What did you think of Dr. Swenson?"

"I didn't want to talk to Dr. Swenson. I didn't want him to help me. I didn't like anything he said." He shrugged. "So I just shut up and acted as if everything was fine."

"But Christopher, this isn't like you."

"I don't know. For some reason, an angry voice inside me just said, 'Don't tell him anything.'"

I let this statement slip by me. I was more concerned about whether Christopher would be able to relate to Jerry Swenson. I had always thought of the psychiatrist as friendly and quick-witted, someone who got along well with his patients. He was a good diagnostician, and I valued his clinical opinions. I wanted him to be more involved with Christopher than the previous psychiatrist had been.

We talked the next morning.

"I've seen him twice now," Jerry told me. "He doesn't seem depressed, and he's well-oriented. In fact, he seems to be feeling just fine."

Just fine? Just fine! The words echoed in my mind. Here we go again! My neck felt stiff, and I realized more than ever how much tension I was feeling over Christopher's case. What was going on here? I had seen Christopher severely depressed and confused at his apartment. Then there was the puzzling business with Luke and the notes. Now Swenson was coming across as if I'd made a mistake in hospitalizing him. Was this some sort of malingering? No. No one could fake depression that well. And what would the payoff be?

"I've decided against using any medications," Jerry was telling me.

"Okay, no meds," I agreed, "as long as he is able to get some sleep. It may be better that we don't cover up any symptoms."

Late that night, a nurse called me from the hospital.

"Christopher's been transferred to the intensive care unit," she reported. "I've already called Dr. Swenson."

What could have happened to put Christopher in I.C.U.? Why would he need to be put in that one-room cell?

"Christopher told one of the staff that he hears a voice talking to him, telling him to do destructive things. Tonight the voice was telling him to break the glass with a chair and throw himself out the window."

I shuddered at the image of Christopher leaping to his death six floors below. So this was why Christopher had trouble sleeping! But what did this mean, this business about a voice?

When I got to the hospital, I questioned Christopher.

"Tell, me, Christopher, what is it you told the nurse last night."

He looked away, then down at the floor. "It's crazy. I know it's crazy. It can't be."

"Christopher, you're censoring something before it can be

viewed objectively."

"Well, there is this voice," he began tremulously. "It's really me. I know . . . it's coming from inside my head. But he keeps telling me to do things—mean, angry, awful things. Things I would never do. I could never . . . but he won't drop it. He won't let go. I get so tired, listening. I try to ignore him, but sometimes I can't."

"When can't you?"

"Mostly at night, when there's nothing else to do but sit around or try to fall asleep."

"Is that why you drink at night?"

"I can't hear him so loud when I drink. Then it's easier sometimes to ignore him, but sometimes I still give in. Like on Halloween night when I took the pills. He kept telling me to take them. I tried to resist. I didn't take them all at once. He kept insisting. He's always insisting." Christopher paused and took a deep breath. "I took them slowly, one at a time, so that he had to force me to take each one. Finally, I was so out of it that I couldn't get the pills in my mouth. That time I won."

"When I was in your apartment, when we were on the balcony, Christopher, was the voice talking to you then?"

"Yes. He was telling me to jump off the balcony. Since you were there, I knew he wasn't going to win that time either."

What would have happened if I hadn't gone to Christopher's apartment? And I'd very nearly decided against it. Thank God I had gone! But my protective husband wouldn't have seen it that way. José would really have had a fit if he'd known what a chance I'd taken. And, in a way, he'd be right, as usual.

"Tell me, Christopher, have there been other times when you've just barely won?"

Christopher paused.

"Yes, once right after my parents divorced." Pain was evident in his voice. He was hunched over, staring downward. I had to lean forward to catch his words. "He kept telling me to cut my wrists, and I wouldn't make the cuts deep enough. And then another time, after I came out as gay."

He was silent then. There were no scars on his wrists that I could see, but I believed his story. I had to prompt him to continue.

"That's when you were discharged from the military because

of a suicide attempt?"

Christopher nodded, looking uncomfortable and ashamed.

"How long has the voice been there?"

"For a long, long time. I can't remember how long. I can't remember never hearing it."

"Even when you were a child, you heard that voice?"

"I think so. Maybe since I was seven or eight."

I was stunned. I couldn't imagine how Christopher could have lived with this tormenting voice all his life. Most schizophrenics start hearing voices during their early adulthood. And every psychiatric patient I'd ever seen had had long periods without any auditory hallucinations.

"Did he ever cause you to hurt someone else?"

"Yes," Christopher said thoughtfully. "Once I had a fight with a lover, while we were in a truck. My lover was driving and he, the voice, began to make me kick and hit until we ran into a brick wall."

"Have there been other times like that, when the voice made you violent?"

"One more maybe . . . I'm not sure. I was told I did it, but I don't remember. It was while I was stationed in Virginia and I had just come out. This guy was driving me in a car. I don't remember. . . . After I kind of woke up, he told me I'd shouted obscenities. . . . I just don't ever do that! He said I had completely changed, as if I were another person. I still don't understand that one because I don't remember the voice telling me to shout. But it must have been him making me do it."

"Had you been drinking or using drugs?"

"No. I used drugs up until I was seventeen, and then I quit. I started drinking just a few months ago."

"Have you ever had that sort of amnesia again?"

"Yeah. A lot lately, but I think it's because I've been drinking too much." He was obviously embarrassed.

"Have you told all of this to anyone before?"

"No. I was afraid to. People would think I was crazy. But it's probably better that I tell you."

It was hard for me to believe that Christopher had lived twenty years with this. Yet now that his secret was out, he was willing to tell me everything. He wanted to stop the persecuting voice, and I wanted to help him. But how? By this time I at last had a hunch what I was up against—and this was no ordinary hallucination or delusion.

Christopher leaned forward, searching my eyes with anxious anticipation.

"Am I crazy?"

"There are lots of kinds of craziness, Christopher," I replied as steadily as I could. "If you are asking me if I think you are psychotic or schizophrenic, the answer is no."

"That's good." He breathed a deep sigh of relief.

I called a nurse to take Christopher back to the I.C.U. I felt wobbly and weak-kneed. Could I be seeing what I thought I was seeing? As quickly as I could, I hurried back to the office so I could call Dr. Swenson in private.

"Jerry," I said, "I think it's dissociative. He hears a menacing voice, coming from inside his head rather than externally. I'm glad we're not giving him any medications because I don't want to reduce any of the symptoms yet."

"I agree."

"Jerry . . ." I was apprehensive. "If it's dissociative—dual or multiple personality—I'm in way over my head."

"So am I."

"Oh, that's a great comfort!" It was a relief to laugh, but I was only half-kidding. "So it's the blind leading the blind," I said. "Do you know anyone who's worked with dissociative disorders?"

"No, but I think there was someone who worked for the county department of mental health who was doing research in that area."

"Okay. I'll have to see if I can track down a name."

I had to find someone with the experience I needed, but I wasn't looking forward to the search.

I hung up the phone feeling pressured. I already had too much work to do, and this search for a consultant was going to take up a lot of time. How was I going to fit this into my schedule? Five patients that afternoon, not to mention the paperwork. On top of the stacks of papers on my desk was my "to do" list: write lecture notes for Women's Center, report on rape case, conference with Eddie's kindergarten teacher, pick up José's suit at cleaners, find a good washer repairman, appointment for Carmen's twelve-month checkup—the last item underlined and followed by "overdue."

I pulled down the rolltop on my desk as if hiding the clutter would make it all go away. At least my patients wouldn't be able to see my disorganization, although they usually were so self-absorbed that they rarely even commented on the cozy look of my office with its warm earth tones and country classic charm.

I needed to talk to José. I sighed and pushed back my chair to get up. José would make me feel better with his predictably sound advice and comfort. Yes, I'd start my search for an expert on dissociation with him.

Just then, a light rap on the door was followed by José's entrance. He didn't ask permission, the privilege of a husband. And after ten years of marriage, I still found myself admiring him as if he were a new man in my life. A three-piece charcoal suit, impeccable. Reddish-brown hair, graying at the temples, a neatly trimmed mustache. The distinguished professional. He smiled at me, and the devilish twinkle in his eyes lit up his face.

Maybe José knew something about dissociation that I didn't know. He was my best source of information about things in general, even outside the field of psychology. I'd come to rely on his knowledge and wisdom for nearly everything.

"Dissociation?" he said, raising his eyebrows. He gave a long pause. "Are you talking about a fugue?"

"No, nothing as straightforward as temporary amnesia." I was disappointed to realize he probably knew no more than I did. "I'm trying to figure out why one of my patients hears a voice, but he's not schizophrenic and not psychotic. I'm guessing it must be a dissociated part of his consciousness."

"A split personality?"

"Maybe."

"Well, there's not much in the textbooks about that, you know."

"I was never taught anything about it in my doctoral courses. Were you?"

"Very little. Too controversial as a diagnosis, and too rare. In all practicality, we'll never see one of those cases."

"But what if my patient—"

He looked at me with his let's-be-reasonable expression, and I quickly sought a way to bolster my position.

"Jerry Swenson also thinks the patient might be dissociative."

"Chances are you'll find out he's a borderline personality disorder with the voice stemming from psychotic depression."

José's tone of voice told me he thought I was wasting my time. He still didn't think that I could have come across a multiple.

"How can you say . . ." I started, then gave up. "Maybe you're right." I meant it. His explanation seemed feasible. He usually was right, even when his comment was a shot-in-the-dark guess, like this one. "In the meantime," I continued, "I'm going to call around to see if I can find someone who has some expertise in this area."

"Well, if you think you must," he said reluctantly, and then gave me the names of a few people I should call. I added them to the mental list I already had started.

First, I wanted to try to find the unnamed person Jerry Swenson had mentioned. Each call was a dead end, so I searched among private clinicians. I started by calling the most prestigious psychiatrists I knew. I didn't really expect that they would know more about dissociation than the best psychologists, but I wanted to know their opinions about whether or not to use medications. I got nowhere, except to be given more names to call. Then I turned to my fellow psychologists. Like the psychiatrists, they were sympathetic, but as call after call yielded no results, I felt cold desperation welling up in me. The only positive outcome of the calls was the confidence that I was not alone in my ignorance.

At long last, one psychologist was able to give me the name of the former employee of the county mental health department, the person I had been searching for. And the expert turned out to be someone I already knew, Dr. Paula Reynolds.

I gave in to a momentary feeling of smugness. Not only was Paula a psychologist rather than a psychiatrist, she was a woman! I nodded to myself, acknowledging the smugness, and then I called her. After we'd finished with greetings and explanations, she asked me a series of questions.

"Does he complain of frequent headaches?"

"Yes."

"Has he ever lost track of time, not been certain of what elapsed during a given period?"

"Yes, but only once when it absolutely was not alcohol- or drug-related."

"Then he has a history of alcohol or drug abuse?"

"Both."

"That's often the case. Was he abused as a child, especially sexually?"

"Yes. He was physically abused, beaten, I should say, by his father. He suffered psychological abuse from both parents, and was sexually molested by a friend of his father when he was seven years old."

"Okay. There might be more there that you'll uncover later."

That I would uncover later. Yes, I suppose I would. After all, I was Christopher's psychologist. The reality that Christopher might actually be a multiple personality was slowly dawning on me. This would be a rare opportunity.

It was also an enormous challenge, and I wasn't sure I was ready for it. After all, I had no special qualifications. Although a wall in my office was filled with hard-earned credentials, not one of them was outstanding. I was just an average, workaday therapist with an ordinary general practice. For hours each week, I listened to depressed, anxious, angry, or confused people tell me their problems—marital conflicts, job stresses, personal losses, sexual worries, mid-life crisis, troubled childhoods, alcoholism—a full range of life's troubles. And I'd seen people who were not just upset, but truly mentally ill. But as I listened to Paula, I couldn't seem to think of anything in my experience that would equip me to deal with a multiple personality.

Paula continued. "Does he have many physical problems that could be largely psychosomatic in nature?"

"Besides the headaches, a stomach ulcer and lots of gastrointestinal problems."

"Has anyone ever told him that he behaves in strange, bizarre, or unpredictable ways?"

"I've witnessed it myself. He has contradictory and disparate moods. Also, his handwriting changes. He's never used another name for himself, though."

"Does he have any psychosexual disturbance?"

"He's very unhappy about his homosexuality and has only begun to think of himself as gay in the past three or four years."

"Has he made suicide attempts or suicidal gestures?"

"Three that I know of. The voice tells him to do it."

Tension mounted inside me. Paula was narrowing in on Christopher's diagnosis.

"Does he seem extremely distrustful, evasive, guarded?"

"That depends. At times he's very aloof and distant, other times more trusting. Overall, I would say he's been extremely cautious about opening up."

"Does he have any runaway history or unusual impulses to escape?"

"He has been leaving everything he owns with a series of lovers. He just walks out unannounced and never goes back. I suppose that would qualify as a runaway pattern."

"It sounds to me as if you have a multiple there."

She spoke so matter-of-factly! I wished I could be as composed. But she gave me absolutely no time to mull over my apprehensions.

"The next step is to interview him under hypnosis and see if any other personalities come out."

"Paula, I'm not feeling at all confident about how to proceed." I knew I could confide in her. "Would you be willing to come over to the hospital? Would you be willing to do a consultation, including the hypnosis?"

"Sure. Give me a call when everything is set up. In the meantime, I'll copy what few journal articles I know of that might help you."

I hung up the phone, relieved at Paula's offer of help, yet more apprehensive than ever. Then I called Jerry Swenson. He was as eager for the consultation as I, and so I set up the session with Paula at the hospital.

When I caught sight of Paula in the doctor's parking lot, I realized how quickly the years had gone by. She had lost weight, and her hair had begun to show just a little gray. She wore a beige knit suit, set off with a single strand of pearls. Altogether, she looked very distinguished. But what I remembered best about her, that calm and confident style, hadn't changed. She'd always had the air of someone who knew where she was going and what she wanted.

"Christopher has been prepared for your visit," I said as we walked through the hospital's double doors together. "He's looking forward to meeting you."

We stepped into the elevator, and she handed me a packet of materials.

"The paper you'll find most helpful is this new one by Watkins and Watkins on ego state theory. Some other new literature is due to come out this fall or winter. Right now, not much is available."

"So I noticed!" I'd had a computer search of the literature done, and practically nothing had turned up. "It's 1980—I can't believe it—twenty-three years after *Three Faces of Eve,* and so little information is available! The first case, Mary Reynolds, was documented in 1811. Incredible, how slow the research has been and how little help I found!"

The elevator stopped, and we walked out onto the psychiatric floor.

"I've never been in this hospital," Paula said. "What made you choose it?"

"Convenience. My office is close by." I told her I generally prefer psychiatric hospitals instead of general hospitals with a psychiatric unit, but the easy access to medical services would be helpful in Christopher's case. "Most of the doctors whose patients are here are psychiatrists," I said. "You know it's harder when there are not many psychologists, because we're still a novelty on medical staffs like this one."

"You're designated as the primary therapist?"

"If I didn't have that kind of arrangement, I wouldn't use this hospital."

We stopped to pick up Christopher's chart, and Dr. Bernstein, head of the psychiatry department, came over to greet us.

"You must be Dr. Reynolds." As usual, he was officious. He extended his hand to Paula in a civil but not quite friendly manner. "I understand you've been working with multiple personality patients."

"I've been treating one for the past two and a half years." Paula held his gaze. Inwardly, I cheered her on.

"You must be very energetic," he said. He seemed to be implying that he knew all about multiple personality disorder, but nobody had asked him. "I'll be interested to find out what happens here today."

"I'm sure Dr. LaCalle will keep you informed."

I suppressed a grin. He'll make sure of that, I thought, as we headed down the corridor.

"Dr. LaCalle!"

It was Sue Costello, tagging behind us. She was the energetic young nurse who reminded me of an Italian Raggedy Ann doll. She had been assigned to Christopher a few days before.

"I'm glad I caught you in time, Dr. LaCalle!"

She spoke with excitement.

"Christopher asked me if I could sit in on the session with Dr. Reynolds. He's been talking to me a lot and says he would feel more comfortable if I were there, too. I'd really like to learn about this, especially if I'm to continue to work with him."

Paula and I looked at each other. I thought how important it would have been to me to have two older professionals take me into their confidence. When we were Sue's age, we had so few women as good role models.

Paula nodded. There seemed to be no question about it.

"We'll double-check with Christopher," I told Sue. "If he still agrees, you're welcome."

Please, I said to myself, no more interruptions.

After I showed Paula into the conference room, I sent Sue to get Christopher. When he came in, I could see he'd had little sleep.

"I had a terrible dream last night," he told me immediately. "I dreamed I was stabbing someone with a knife. I don't know who the person was, but the dream was so bad it woke me up. I've felt awful ever since. I just don't trust myself. I feel like I could really get violent, but I don't know why."

I chose not to talk about the dream right then. Instead, I introduced Paula, and reminded Christopher of the purpose of our conference. When I asked him if Sue could stay in the room, he agreed without hesitation.

Paula began by telling Christopher that she had reviewed his symptoms, including the voice he said he heard, and told him it seemed likely he was suffering from a dissociative disorder.

23

"Every person has different aspects of himself and takes on different roles depending on his moods or the situation," she explained. "But with some people, there are parts that are separate and unique, so unique that they don't fit together comfortably. The person has a very difficult time feeling whole."

I took note of her succinct and clear explanation and felt envious of her authority and confidence. She'd paused, as if to assess what Christopher's response might be.

"Each aspect may be so separate," she continued, "that one part doesn't even know about the other. Something we call amnesia barriers exists between the parts. Each part may even become a separate personality, and a person who functions this way is called a multiple personality."

"You mean like a Sybil?"

"Yes. Have you read that book about Sybil, Christopher?

"Yes."

"What did you think of it?"

"I thought it was very interesting, but it didn't seem like those things could really happen." Disbelief showed on his face. "I mean, I can't see how someone like that could be real."

"Well, not all multiples are just like Sybil. Some people have separate parts that know about each other but still tend to function somewhat independently. Others have stronger amnesia barriers. These barriers can cause a loss of memory for one of the parts, sort of a blackout. Have you ever had a blackout, Christopher?"

"No!"

To my surprise, Christopher denied he had ever had a blackout. He was implying that his diagnosis of multiple personality was not in order. I looked at him closely. He'd begun to tremble. Christopher's denial that he was a multiple, I knew, made it all the more likely that he was one.

"Do you find these ideas frightening?" Paula asked.

"Kind of. It's just that I don't think I'm a multiple personality."

"You may not be," Paula was saying. "It may simply be that your case is less extreme. We believe you do dissociate." She tilted her head upward in an authoritative way. "But we just don't know how much yet. That's what we're hoping to learn more about today."

She gave him time to consider this. "Christopher," she then asked, "have you ever been hypnotized?"

"No."

His trembling had increased. I feared he would refuse to continue.

"Have you ever seen anyone hypnotized?"

"Only on television, nightclub-act stuff."

"Is there anything about being hypnotized that worries you?"

"I'm not sure of what I would do." He paused, then added cautiously, "Maybe I might get violent."

"We'll work out a method you can use to come out of the hypnotic trance any time you wish," she said. "If you feel you may become violent, you'll be able to stop the impulse." She continued with her reassurances and explanations. "Hypnosis can help you become more aware of your innermost thoughts."

"But maybe there is nothing inside."

There has to be something inside, I thought. No one has a void! But how would Paula convince him of this?

"Many people who have been abused as children feel empty," she said gently, "and have said the same thing."

After Christopher had agreed to proceed, Paula began a relaxation induction, leading him to relax and turn his attention inward. With surprising ease, he slipped into a hypnotic state, his face and body peacefully at rest.

Paula set up the means by which he would return to a waking state if he became violent.

"Bend your left arm at the elbow and keep your hand elevated," Paula instructed. "You will immediately come out of the trance simply by lowering your arm."

I knew the elevated-arm technique was an excellent safety measure. If Christopher indeed became violent and attempted to leave his chair, his arm would automatically come down.

Paula repeated her instructions soothingly. "You are to remain comfortable, relaxed, peaceful. If you feel uncomfortable in any way, you may come out of the trance by lowering your arm."

Christopher breathed calmly, rhythmically, his body limp in the chair.

"I want to speak to the part of you, Christopher, that can tell me the most about what has happened to you."

Christopher was in a deep trance. His response came slowly. With effort, as if his eyelids were very heavy, he opened his eyes just a crack and averted his gaze to the floor.

We waited for a response. No response. I looked at Paula quizzically, not understanding what I was witnessing.

"You may talk now if you wish," she instructed.

Still no response. She waited again a few more moments.

"In the future, you will find it increasingly easy to talk, and you will be able to assist Dr. LaCalle with the therapy."

Oh, God! The thought overwhelmed me. That's right! Next time *I'll* be the one in Paula's place.

"Since you are not ready to talk with us yet," Paula continued smoothly, "you may close your eyes and go back to the relaxed state you were in."

Christopher closed his eyes. His breathing became slower. Paula's voice guided him deeper into the trance. Would there be so much resistance in Christopher that she would have to bring him out of the trance with nothing accomplished? What would I do then? Christopher stayed quiet, as if asleep. No new personality was surfacing. Had we been wrong about the diagnosis?

Paula tried a different approach.

"I would like to speak with the part of you that can be most helpful to you and Dr. LaCalle right now."

Again it seemed as if nothing was happening. Then Christopher's eyes suddenly began to move rapidly under his eyelids, as if he were vividly dreaming. His body became restless and fidgety, and he opened his eyes with a startled expression and looked about the room.

Wordlessly, Christopher searched Paula's face as if trying to recognize her. His gaze was direct and alert, and he didn't seem to be in a trance at all. Nonetheless, his movements lacked their usual smooth coordination. To me, it seemed that his body was awkwardly large for him, as if he were a child who had gone through a growth spurt and was still getting accustomed to the size of his limbs.

Christopher's body had taken on a different aspect, but his

posture and facial expression looked vaguely familiar to me. He twisted in his chair and opened his mouth as if to speak, but said nothing. Paula took the lead.

"Hi," she said.

"Hi," he answered in a small meek voice that didn't sound at all like Christopher. He pulled up his knees and crouched in his chair as if attempting to hide.

"It's okay," Paula said. "We are here to help you."

"I know. I . . . I've been watching."

"Who's been watching?"

"Me." He dropped his feet to the floor with a thud.

"Me?"

"Yeah. Me, Timmy," he said shyly, swinging his foot.

2

TIMMY IS NOT ALONE

I was stunned. I thought I was prepared for this, but I wasn't. Nothing could have prepared me. In every aspect, except for his body, Christopher was gone, vanished. I looked over at Sue, who was staring dumbfoundedly at Timmy. But Paula kept on confidently, as if nothing unusual had occurred.

"Pleased to meet you, Timmy," she said. "You have an awfully small voice, Timmy. I can hardly hear you."

"I'm sorry," he said meekly. "I'm not big enough."

"How old are you, Timmy?"

"I'm four,"

"Ohhh. You're four! Four is a very nice age." She'd switched instantly to the way one talks with very young children. "What have you been doing, Timmy?"

"Riding my tricycle," he answered timidly.

"Where, Timmy? Where do you ride your tricycle?"

"In the field where Mommy tells me to play, but I don't like it there."

"Is there anyone there with you?"

"Just Richard." Timmy scowled. "I don't like Richard."

"How old is Richard?"

"I don't know."

"Is he the same size as you, or is he bigger?"

"He's bigger, but not as big as Daddy."

"Does Richard play with you?"

"No. I'm afraid of Richard." He pouted. "I play by myself."

"You seem to be all alone."

"There's nobody to play with."

"Where's your mother?"

"She's busy. She's *always* busy."

"She leaves you all by yourself?"

"Yes." He gave an angry kick with his foot.

"Where's your father?"

"He's gone." His voice had become mournful. "I want him home. He's been gone for a long, long time."

I wondered why his parents couldn't have seen how lonely their child was becoming. Didn't they care?

Paula brought her line of questioning back to the present. "Do you know Dr. LaCalle, Timmy?" As she spoke, she glanced in my direction.

"I know her, but she doesn't know me."

"Where have you seen her, Timmy?"

"In her office," Timmy answered. "I was watching her. I was hiding in the chair and she couldn't see me. But she told me I was lonesome." He paused, his expression pensive. "How did she know that?"

I felt a lump in my throat at the recognition of the lonely little boy whose presence I had sensed in my office, and a familiar sadness pervaded me once more. Timmy had been there all along, but it was as if a veil had just been lifted so that I could see him more clearly. This unique, childlike personality was sharply in focus.

"Dr. LaCalle understands a lot about little boys," Paula said. "Do you like Dr. LaCalle?"

"She's a nice lady, but she doesn't know me."

"She knows you now."

Timmy looked over at me with a frightened, wistful gaze, then quickly looked down. I, too, looked away, trying to hide the tears that were welling up. What a strange sensation! I was moved by compassion for a little boy who existed in a man's body. But in that moment the boy was altogether real. I knew his feelings were as real as those of any four-year-old.

"Would you like Dr. LaCalle to be your friend?" Paula asked Timmy.

He nodded. "I cried after I left her office," he said. Then his voice dropped to a whisper. "I didn't want to go home. I wanted to stay there. I wanted to tell her I was there, but they wouldn't let me."

"Who wouldn't let you?" Paula asked.

Timmy shook his head. "I'm not supposed to tell."

That angry voice probably won't let him, I thought. *More* personalities, but how many?

"They can't stop you now, Timmy," Paula said. "You're out, and you can make Dr. LaCalle your friend if you want to."

Timmy nodded, but he wouldn't look in my direction. Paula gestured for me to come over and take a place next to Timmy. What would come next? None of my training fit this situation. I would have to trust my instincts. I knelt beside Timmy's chair, and I could see his eyes looking trustfully up at me under the hair that covered his brow. Those tearful eyes searched mine, but he said nothing. Paula broke the ice by introducing us as if we were meeting for the first time.

"Dr. LaCalle, this is Timmy. Timmy, this is your doctor lady and very special friend. You will be able to have lots of time together to talk and to play."

"Hello, Timmy," I said. "May we shake hands?"

I took his hand in mine. He acquiesced, but his response was tentative. As I took his fragile hand, I thought it was as delicate as a child's. I held it gently, and my heart reached out to him.

"I'm glad we finally met. I sort of knew you were there all along."

Timmy now held tightly to my hand and nodded wordlessly, tears flowing down his cheeks. He gripped my fingers and rubbed his thumb over the back of my hand as if trying to tell me something that words would not say.

"You seem to be really frightened, Timmy," I said. "You told us you're afraid of Richard. I'll help you with Richard if you would like me to."

Was I saying the right thing? I glanced at Paula, and she smiled and nodded agreement.

Timmy looked at me raptly through wet lashes, and his quiet weeping began to subside. With one last sniffle, he let out a deep breath and relaxed the grip on my fingers.

Slowly, I withdrew my hand, and then let all the warmth I genuinely felt come into my voice.

"I'm really glad you finally came out to talk with me, Timmy."

He looked back at me unwaveringly, trustingly.

"Now we will be able to have lots of time together, talking and getting to know each other. You won't have to sit quietly and just watch me any longer."

I thought fleetingly of children's games that a four-year-old would love and, surprisingly, I could easily envision Timmy playing them. Gradually I backed away and let Paula take over to bring Christopher out of the trance. I felt suddenly tired and enormously relieved that my part in this session was over. Timmy gently closed his eyes. Actually, he disappeared. His presence was completely gone from Christopher's face, and no trace of him was left in Christopher's limp body.

Paula brought the session to a close, and I let Sue know I'd explain what had happened later. Then Paula and I left the conference room together. Sue stayed behind, talking quietly with Christopher, giving him a few more moments to collect himself before she took him back to his room.

I was still weak-kneed and shaken, and I found myself clutching Paula by the elbow as we walked down the hallway.

"Dear Lord, Paula, I don't believe what I just saw. It can't be true!"

"But it is. You have a bonafide multiple personality, and you've only begun to discover what is there."

She stopped and faced me squarely.

"You heard him after he came out of the trance. He was able to detect the presence of other personalities, even if he does not know more than the fact that they're there."

I recoiled from what she said, all the while knowing I would have to come to terms with it.

"I didn't understand what was going on with the one who wouldn't talk. Christopher didn't mention it afterward, although he recounted everything that Timmy said."

I was still trying to tie all the pieces neatly into place, as if pigeon-holing all the details would somehow make everything easier to face.

"I don't think he remembered anything about that ego state," Paula said. "The amnesia after the trance simply indicates how that part of him resists becoming known to his primary conscious personality—as well as to us."

"Do you think you'd be able to bring that ego state out further?"

"Very likely, with time, increased trust, and perhaps a deeper level of trance." She paused, gazing straight into my eyes with that confident gaze of hers. "*You'll* know more about that later."

There was no possibility of missing her slight emphasis on the pronoun. She wouldn't be investigating that ego state. I would.

"Me." I gulped. I was in a state of panic. "Gosh, Paula, I don't feel that I can continue with this case. Look at me! I'm shaking. My stomach feels queasy."

"That's how I felt the first time, too," she said sympathetically. "You'll get over it."

She started walking down the corridor again. Her reassurances were inadequate in the face of my doubts.

"You're a good therapist," she continued. "You catch on fast. And from what I just observed, you have some instinctive abilities that will carry you far." She stopped walking again and confronted me face to face. "Besides, who else around here is more qualified than you to handle this?"

"You are, Paula," I replied.

"Oh, no you don't, old friend! I just agreed to take on a second multiple, and I've already got my hands full with Trisha. No more, thanks!" She turned away.

Paula was too smart to over-extend herself, I thought. I learned she had already made an extraordinarily self-sacrificing commitment to Trisha. Paula's time was taken up with Trisha, but she had more time to give than I did. She had no husband or children who made demands on her. I'd be over-extending myself by taking on even one case of multiple personality.

"I knew you would turn me down, Paula. I knew this case was mine and there was no way out. And I've already promised Timmy I'd be his friend. Although," I let my voice become a little snippy, "you certainly helped set me up for it."

"Do I detect a note of hostility?" she asked in a teasing voice. "Or is that just panic?"

"Both," I admitted. "I don't want to direct it at you, but I'm getting the 'Why me?' feeling. I want to run like hell! This case is exciting, but when I really think about it, about handling it, being responsible, the commitment . . ."

"I know the feeling. The intensity of the first discovery dies down, but there's still curiosity. Mostly it's tinged with that fear. It comes back at times, and keeps coming back."

We walked in contemplative silence for a moment.

"At least, Trula, you have me to talk with."

"I know, and I appreciate that," I said gratefully. I tried to relieve the intensity of our conversation by going back to a lighter tone. "Believe me, I have a hunch I'll be calling you a lot!"

"That's fine, but don't forget that no one really knows the most effective way to treat a multiple." I marveled at how she could state such an unsettling thought so matter-of-factly. "Maybe we'll know more a few years down the road." She paused thoughtfully. "By the way, how skilled are you in hypnosis?"

"Not skilled enough for this, I'm afraid."

"It doesn't take more than the basics to put him into a trance. He puts himself in trance every time he shifts personalities. But knowing what to do with each of the altered states—that's what's difficult. I went to Bob Slater for help with this when I first started to work with Trisha. He's the best around here when it comes to hypnosis."

I was impressed. Bob Slater's reputation was longstanding—and excellent.

"I've been meeting with Bob once a month, and I'd be happy to share the time with you, if he says it's okay. Do you want to sit in with us?"

"I'd appreciate the help," I said, beginning to feel a bit more hopeful.

"Well, we've just had our meeting, so we won't be getting together again until next month. But, Trula, you've gotten off to a good start with Christopher." She put her arm around me in a gesture of reassurance. "You know, he was even more surprised than you to find Timmy there. Yet he seemed to accept the discovery and the diagnosis fairly well afterward."

"He was flabbergasted, to say the least," I told her. "I think Christopher and I will both need a few days to let this sink in."

Paula's positive attitude helped, and I began to consider what lay ahead. What I wanted was to have a whole month to get ready, but I had to deal with reality. I had twenty-four hours—just twenty-four hours to adjust to the idea that I was to become the so-called expert in a purely trial-and-error treatment plan!

That evening, I shared my apprehension with José.

"Don't panic," he advised me. "Maybe Paula knows what she's doing, but your patient could have had a spontaneous age regression during hypnosis."

"That's not what I saw." I took offense at his thinking I wouldn't know the difference between a regression and a personality switch.

"I didn't mean to offend you, Trula. I'm just thinking that you're still in the evaluation phase, and you could see something tomorrow or the next day that could cause you to change your mind."

"Well, maybe there is some comfort in that thought," I conceded. I would have been happy to discover that Paula had been wrong and there was some simpler way to treat Christopher. But no, I had to believe my own eyes. I saw what I saw.

The next day came too quickly. I had made only minimal gains in my confidence, but I mustered all the outward assurance I could on my way to the hospital. Christopher had had twenty-four hours to mull over the impact and emotions of the session with Paula. I couldn't help but wonder what a shock the discovery must have been to him.

I checked in at the nursing station, delaying a moment in order to relax, and then found Christopher in the music room. He sat by the window, staring down at the cars passing on the freeway below. Another patient was playing the piano, "Laura's Theme," and an air of seeming calm pervaded the room. I stopped and listened, taking the opportunity to observe unnoticed during the brief moment before my presence was felt by the two of them.

The musician self-consciously folded his sheet music and left. Christopher and I were alone. The radio had been left on a classical music station at a nearly inaudible volume. I clicked it off and took a seat on the piano bench. Christopher's chair was turned away, and he did not rotate it in my direction. He glanced at me, and then his eyes went back to the movement of the traffic. His body was totally relaxed, his face placid. He appeared to be in a semi-hypnotic state simply from watching the monotonous movement of the cars.

"Christopher, how are you feeling today?"

"All right, I guess," he answered dully. "Timmy is feeling pretty upset, though. He's really afraid."

I sighed with relief that Christopher not only remembered the discovery of Timmy, but he had been able to stay in touch with him somehow.

"Can you hear Timmy talking to you?"

"I can now, but I never could hear him before, just the other voice."

"What's Timmy afraid of?"

"He doesn't know. He's just afraid. I think he must be afraid of the others." I tensed up again at the mention of the "others." I wasn't ready for more revelations. "I'm having a hard time, too, getting used to this idea of multiple personalities. I just don't want to believe it."

Well, I thought to myself, that makes at least three of us! At least I could manage an inward chuckle.

"Did you sleep well last night?"

"No. There were voices talking all night long. I listened as hard as I could but I couldn't really hear what they were saying or who was saying it. It's like they're far, far away . . . but I know they're there. I think they've been there for a long, long time."

"How long? Do you remember now?"

"I'm not sure. I know they were there when I was a teenager." He frowned, trying to remember. "I think they were there when I was eleven or twelve. Before that I can't tell. It seems like I can't remember anything at all about when I was younger than ten, except I can remember stuff from when I was really little, like before I was four."

"You have a blank spot in your memory from age four to age ten?"

"I can remember a few things, but not very much. I always thought that most people didn't remember things from those years."

Startled, I looked at him keenly. He had spoken blankly, without acknowledging the absurdity of such an idea.

"There must have been a lot of things happening to you between ages four and ten that your mind wants to erase. But all

35

of the memories are still there, and we can get to them with hypnosis."

"I'm not sure I want to remember."

I felt a sudden rush of sympathy. From what Christopher had already told me, I had every reason to understand his reluctance to rediscover the miseries of his childhood.

"Something very traumatic must have happened to you to have created other personalities." I wanted to put Christopher at ease, and spoke with as much gentleness and warmth as I could. "I can see why you would not want to remember that trauma. But if you are to get better, it may be necessary to remember and come to terms with the past."

Listening to my own words, it sounded so simple—"remember . . . come to terms"—but I knew it was a monumental task, one that I wouldn't want to have to do if I were in Christopher's place.

"I want to get better. I do want your help." These were courageous words, I thought, yet I wondered if he would have the tenacity and strength to see it through the long process of therapy.

His voice was quite sincere, but even as he said this, his body was showing resistance. He had become rigid in his chair, stretching out his feet in front of him as if trying to dig his heels into the floor and apply the brakes to any further movement in our conversation.

"If you want to get better, you will get better." I knew how simplistic this sounded, but I was trying to be reassuring, not profound. And I was reassuring myself as well that Paula's predictions of success would come true.

"No!"

Christopher's voice broke abruptly into my thoughts.

He shook his head, again and again.

What had provoked this? Had I said something wrong?

"No! No!" he shouted.

He was clenching his teeth, and he clutched the chair with a force that turned his knuckles white. His body quivered. He dug his feet harder into the floor, and the chair creaked as his trembling increased. His face was livid. I looked into his eyes. A wild, terrified glare stared back at me.

"No! No!"

"Christopher, what is it?"

My heart pounded at the terror in his eyes, his struggle for control. I'd never seen such a terrified look before. What did it mean? I made ready to run, if need be. Violence, I thought with sudden panic. He had talked about the violence in him.

"Back! Back!"

I stepped backward, toward the door. I remembered the emergency ring button on the wall. My eyes stayed fixed on Christopher. He spoke no further. My arm was lifted, ready to push the button, but I hesitated.

It was important that I handle this on my own. I'd lose his confidence in my ability if I called for help.

Christopher was doing everything he could to fight whatever was within him, and his eyes stayed fixed on the traffic below. Would he try to break through the window? He was in a trance-like state, I now realized, but without the benefit of a guiding voice. He had no therapist to help him remain in control.

"Christopher, look away from the window," I ordered firmly, keeping my voice as calm as possible. "Look away from the window. Look at the wall to your right."

I could see the muscles in his neck strain, as if having to overcome a physical resistance to following my command. He was struggling to pull his eyes away from the traffic.

"Turn your head away, Christopher. Face the wall to your right." I kept reinforcing my commands—despite my doubts about my own authority in this matter—and at last he obeyed.

"Now, Christopher, look at the wall carefully. Notice everything you can about it. Notice every mark, every crack, every imperfection."

I watched. His eyes roamed about the wall, and his body tremors began to subside.

"Now look at the piano. Pay attention to the room you are in. I'm going to turn on the radio."

I turned away from the emergency button and reached for the radio. I made a guess about the volume, and was relieved when the music flicked on softly.

"Listen to the music, Christopher."

His body relaxed even further.

"Now stand up. Go over to the drapery cord and pull the drapes shut across the window."

Robotlike, he completed the task, then turned to look at me. I could see that the terror was gone.

"It's all over," I said, as relieved for myself as for him. "You're okay. You can take a deep, deep breath."

I waited, and took a few deep breaths myself. I thought of José's strong, protective arm around me and calmed down further. I'd be able to go home to him later.

"Now tell me what happened."

"I don't know . . . don't know what happened." He shook his head slowly in bewilderment. "Everything in the room just started flying around—the chairs, the piano, everything, like a tornado was in here. I couldn't control it. I couldn't make everything stop spinning."

"Why did you tell me to get back?"

"I was afraid you would get hit."

"Hit by the flying objects?"

I was trying to determine the nature of his hallucination. I was touched by his concern for me, but immediately brushed this emotion aside as I tried to determine the nature of his hallucination.

"No. They were flying only for me, not for you. In my mind, the things were flying."

I knew that Christopher was not psychotic. He was aware that the hallucination was of his own making, not an external reality. He knew things were not actually flying around the room.

"I might get hit by what, then?" I went on. "By you?"

"No, not by me." He looked hurt that I would even think such a thing. "I would never hit you."

"By what, then?" I persisted.

"I don't know. I was just afraid you would get hit." He paused and rubbed his forehead. "What happened to me? I don't understand."

"You were in a sort of trancelike state in which you could hallucinate. My guess is that your hallucination is symbolic of your own internal conflicts, your chaotic feelings. It seems that you can self-hypnotize, almost by accident. You just slipped into it, watching the movement of the cars. But, unfortunately, this can't help you. At this time, you need my help to use the hypnotic state for your benefit."

"I didn't feel out of control when Dr. Reynolds hypnotized me." He seemed perplexed.

"No, that's what I mean. She was guiding you, helping you stay in control."

Christopher looked exhausted. He rubbed his head and complained of a headache. I walked him back to his room, numbed with my own reaction yet pleased that I had made my point about the advantages of hypnosis, and pleased as well that he seemed to trust my ability as his therapist. I was glad he didn't know about my self-doubts, which would only have made him more fearful just when he needed hope.

Christopher had trust in me as a person, too, I thought. That was more important than ever now. He was ready to use hypnosis and get on with the work to be done. I knew I was not, but at least I'd give this challenge my level best.

I gathered up books on hypnosis from the medical library at the hospital and from the bookshelf in my office. I took them home, determined to be as prepared as I could for the next day. I shut myself in the study and began poring over the chapters as if I were cramming for an exam. But I had a difficult time concentrating. I was eager to learn—had to learn. Nonetheless, I felt guilty. My family needed me, and I knew I was stealing precious time away from them. It wasn't long before I heard my fifteen-month-old daughter trying to get into the study. The door to the room was closed, but Carmen had learned that Mommy was likely to be inside when that door was shut. Feeling guilty but resolute, I tried to keep my mind on my reading, but I could not keep Carmen out of my awareness. For a few minutes, she struggled with the door. Then, after a moment or two of silence, I heard her voice, wheedling her older brother for help. Nothing would have dissuaded her from seeking out Mommy.

Soon she was in, but I kept on sitting with my feet up in the chair, hunched over the book on the desk in front of me. I forced my mind to stay on the meaning of the words on that page, foolishly trying to search out and absorb just a few more scraps of information. But I read and uselessly reread the same passage. I'll ignore her, I told myself, and not reinforce the behavior. Maybe she'll give up.

No.

She touched my arm to get attention. She did not say a word, but stood there patiently patting my arm. I had to look at her.

She won.

I turned away from my book and picked her up and kissed her. She giggled with delight, and she felt good in my arms. I sighed. "Oh, Carmen, how I love you!" I said aloud. I took in the smell of her silky skin and hair, and thought of how long I had waited for parenthood. I sighed. I'd postponed having a family. Having children had had to wait. José had been in agreement that it was up to me to decide when we'd start a family. He wanted me to finish school, but I became pregnant during my internship. I was glad I hadn't waited until graduation, even though I just barely finished my dissertation and oral exams before the baby arrived. I'd waited, first for my son, and now for this red-headed, green-eyed little goddess—after I got my license, after my career was on the road.

But now she will have to wait, I thought sadly. I would play with her later, after I had a chance to prepare my course of action with Christopher.

"Lupe!"

My Mexican housekeeper came quickly into the room and swooped up the baby. I told her I would be studying until supper, and then listened enviously as she went off with my daughter, talking to her in that warm and caring special voice. What would I have done without Lupe and the others who had come before her? I was thankful I'd learned Spanish, with José's encouragement, since it was easier to find Mexican household help in southern California. I could never have juggled career and home life without someone to help with the house and provide care and nurturing to my babies. And what about all the mothers who worked at jobs that didn't pay well enough to afford this kind of help with their infants and preschool children?

Even with a housekeeper, my juggling act was a constant source of conflict. Something or someone usually got short-changed. Like most men, José never fully understood the amount of emotional drain this mother/professional conflict put on me. Guilt-ridden, I turned back to my books for the time being. I would pay attention to the family at dinner, then go back to my reading after the children were in bed.

If I took time away from my husband, I didn't think he'd mind. He was always so self-contained, so accustomed to acting on his own, never seeming to have to depend on anyone. I envied that. It wasn't just that he was eight years older than I. José was a bachelor until he was thirty-two, and he was already established as a psychologist when I met him. Ten years later, I still lagged behind him in our profession, while he had made a name for himself through being appointed by the courts for difficult legal cases. Surely, he'd understand my need to dedicate myself to this.

I had a hard time concentrating on the reading, and it wasn't altogether helpful. It afforded me only a review of the general principles of hypnosis. In no way did it come close to giving me the guidance I needed. I also found a harsh warning on the use of hypnosis with multiple personalities—but no supporting facts to explain why or to substantiate it. And worst of all, just as I had expected, I could find nothing that could even begin to tell me how to proceed, what to do to protect Timmy, how to reduce Christopher's fear, how I could discern what other personalities might exist.

After some deliberation, I decided on some general guidelines. My reading had reminded me of my obligation to be a cautious behavioral scientist. I would take a neutral stance, like a researcher intent on not contaminating the data that resulted from an experiment. I felt there was a possibility that Christopher would begin to develop more personalities if he sensed I was fascinated with their presence, so I would not act too interested in finding them. Further, I would tape the sessions to review what I had done and to be able to seek guidance from others.

Even after this, I began to ask myself questions about whether it was ethical to proceed. Was I going beyond the bounds of my expertise? Even with help, would I be able to learn fast enough?

Desperation and doubt were eroding my sense of self-confidence. How could I reassure Christopher, make him feel safe, when I was so unsure of myself? I called Paula that same night.

"You are taking enough ethical precautions," she assured me. And she persuaded me that I was competent enough to carry on the hypnotherapy.

"Remember," she said soothingly, "he's become an expert at

hypnotic trances. He's been doing it spontaneously for years. Just go slow." She paused, then repeated her advice. "When you're in doubt about uncovering material, just go slow." Easy enough. It wasn't my style to be invasive or overly confrontive as a therapist.

She also told me about a technique to help Christopher feel more secure. We could use guided imagery, she explained, and she told me how to help him create in his mind a "safe room" where he could escape from anything he did not want to deal with during hypnosis.

I hung up the phone, grateful for her help but still skeptical of my ability. What would I find? Would a violent part of Christopher take over? What other personalities would pop out at me as I sat there unprepared to meet them?

Christopher had spent the next morning waiting for me to arrive at the hospital for our two o'clock appointment. I could see that he wanted to begin. He responded well to the composed, reassuring manner I was portraying, but at the same time he was hesitant.

I could sense a growing anxiety in him. Was I projecting my own apprehension onto him? No. I was sure I was not misreading him. He had confessed to worrying about the potential for violence within himself. On the other hand, I had to keep myself from picking up on his fear and letting it escalate my own anxieties.

Because we both needed to feel as safe as possible, I suggested we ask Ben, a burly psychiatric technician, to sit outside the door. This was a last-minute idea, but it certainly felt right at the moment.

Christopher readily agreed. "I'm glad Ben is a big guy," he said.

As I talked with Ben, I wondered if I was overcompensating for my own fear and uncertainty. When I told him that Christopher was potentially violent and might need to be restrained, he looked at me quizzically.

"Christopher?"

I understood his disbelief. The shy, passive, depleted personality of Christopher hardly seemed the type to require this precaution. Nevertheless, Ben obediently took his seat outside the door.

Christopher went into a deep trance very readily, and I summoned Timmy.

"Timmy, I need to talk with you again. Christopher tells me you have been really frightened. I want to help you so you won't have to be so afraid. I have an idea that is special and nice, and I want to talk with you about it. Are you there, Timmy?"

"I'm here," he said meekly, but his eyes were closed.

The voice was Timmy's, but the body had not changed dramatically. Timmy was not fully out. I waited. Then he began to shift his weight in the chair, much as he had done before, and his body slowly took on a different aspect. His legs seemed more awkward, and he held his head askew. It was as if I could see Timmy getting closer by the second.

"If you are there, and ready, come out to talk with me."

The eyes opened. Timmy, completely there, squirmed uncomfortably in front of me.

"What's the matter, Timmy?"

"I don't like coming out."

"You'll be able to go back in right away. I just wanted to ask you something. Where is your favorite place to play?"

"The room at the church that has toys in it. I play there when my mother goes to hear the man talk." Then he frowned. "But I have to share the toys with all the other kids."

I decided he must mean the room where preschoolers went for babysitting during the church service.

"What is your favorite toy in that room?"

"It's a great big red top," he said gleefully.

"That's wonderful, Timmy. I can just see you playing with a big red top. I'll bet it's lots of fun."

Timmy was smiling.

"Where do you play with the top, Timmy?"

"When the boys and girls are outside playing, I have the top, and I sit in the sun and see it shine." I could imagine a tow-headed Timmy sitting with a red top to spin away his accustomed boredom. His life must have been completely barren if this brief moment with a toy meant so much! "Then they come back inside." He frowned. "They take it away from me."

I tried to make my voice as comforting as I could.

"Timmy, soon Christopher will help you to have a playroom all to yourself, and you'll be able to go there whenever you like.

Would you like that?"

Timmy didn't say anything, but I could see by the look on his face that he seemed entranced by the idea.

"You'd like that, wouldn't you, Timmy, having a nice, safe place all your own?"

He nodded.

"You can go back inside now if you wish."

I waited to see what he would do. Timmy closed his eyes, and his characteristics simply faded into Christopher's adult body. The slow, heavy breathing of the hypnotic trance returned.

"Christopher," I announced, "you are going to take Timmy by the hand now and take him to a secret playroom. This secret playroom is far away, and only you and Timmy will know where it is. It is a wonderful room, just like the one at the church, except Timmy is going to have this room and the toys all to himself. He won't have to hear or pay attention to anything that will be said or done during our session here today. He will be able to leave the room whenever he wants, or whenever you tell him it is safe to leave."

Christopher remained in the peaceful, deep trance. His slow breathing continued, but the movement under his eyelids suggested he was envisioning the scene with Timmy. I waited for a few moments.

"Is Timmy in the room now, Christopher?"

"Yes."

"Will he stay there for a while?"

"Yes, he wants to stay for a while."

"Good. Now I want you to find a safe room for yourself. Find a pleasant, comfortable place for you to be. It can be any place at all, but just the kind of room that you like best. Put all your favorite things in it."

I waited.

"Have you done that, Christopher?"

"Yes."

"Very good. Now describe the room to me."

"It's upstairs, like a loft, but it has a fireplace and a window seat. It has a big white bear rug on the floor and lots of oversized pillows on the window seat. There's a leather couch in front of the fireplace. I can look out the bay window to the green valley below."

What rich visual imagery! This fantasy room of his was far afield from the reality of the cell-like cubicle I'd seen in his apartment.

"Do you feel safe and comfortable in that room, Christopher?"

"Yes."

"Good. Now you will stay in that room with that same comfortable feeling." I wished I could give him a safe room in real life, a place where Christopher could go to escape his constant, tormenting confusion. "Your room will be locked from the inside so that no one and nothing can get in to harm you, but if you wish, you will still be able to hear very distinctly everything that is said in the session today. Just relax . . . in that safe . . . warm . . . restful place."

A safe room . . . I'd like one, too, I thought—a quiet spot with all my responsibilities locked outside the door.

I continued, my voice droning on in a hypnotic tone. I watched Christopher's rhythmic, restful breathing.

"Do you hear anything, Christopher?" I asked after a while.

"Yes, I hear voices."

Good! I thought. We're on target. Now, if I can get him to tune in on one.

"Listen very carefully to just one of them now. Are you listening?"

"Yes."

"I want to speak to the voice that Christopher is listening to right now. The part of Christopher that is this voice he is listening to, come forward."

I watched Christopher's lips move slightly, as if he were struggling to say something. Several moments passed, yet no words escaped from his lips. I was confused. What should I do now? Should I simply repeat the instruction? Then I remembered my former instruction to Christopher. He might be able to help.

"Christopher, can you tell me what is going on here? Have you been paying attention, listening or watching from your room?"

Christopher's voice and face were flat and expressionless. His words came slowly and painstakingly.

"He doesn't . . . want to come out. He doesn't . . . want to have anything to do with this."

"Why not?"

"He's angry. He's *always* angry."

Christopher had already talked about such a voice. I knew that this voice was a male, and the "he" was angry. I was almost certain Christopher was referring to the same voice that told him to take the pills and to throw himself out of the window. If this was the same "he," I was in for an encounter that was more of a confrontation. This would be very different from the tender meetings I'd had with Timmy. I thought momentarily of Ben sitting outside the door. I couldn't back away now. My only recourse was to do as Paula had said: Go slowly.

Maybe I could learn something about the "he."

"Have you told me about him before?"

"I'm not sure . . . don't remember."

I had hoped for more. I was still trying to put the pieces together, but nothing seemed to fit.

"What else can you tell me about him, Christopher?"

"Nothing. He won't talk."

Frustrated, I wondered what to do next. All of my questions seemed to be leading me down blind alleys, but I had to keep trying.

"Are there other voices there besides his?"

"Yes."

"Maybe one of them will be able to tell me more about what is going on with this angry one. Relax in that safe room for a while, Christopher. Just sit back and listen to a different voice for a while. The angry one can fade into the distance."

Christopher followed the suggestion readily. Without further instruction, his eyes were opened. A different personality looked about the room with a face that was expressionless and unfamiliar to me. He looked almost catatonic.

"Hello," I said.

"Hi," this new presence replied feebly.

"How are you feeling right now?"

I wondered if I could trigger more response from him.

The eyes darted back and forth, but his expression was still flat. "I'm . . . okay."

"Have I talked with you before?"

"No."

I knew, somehow, that I had not been in contact with this ego

46

state before. This personality certainly seemed more reclusive than angry, but I wanted to be absolutely sure I was not talking with the angry "he."

"Has Christopher told me about you?"

"You don't know anything about me."

"What's your name?"

The eyes continued to dart back and forth as if searching for an answer. I pressed the question another way.

"What shall I call you if I want to ask for you again?"

His answer came slowly. "I don't know."

"Well, tell me about yourself. Maybe then you'll think of a name for yourself. What do you do mostly?"

Silence, then, "I watch."

"You watch." I reflected. "What do you watch?"

Another long pause. "Everything. I see everything."

I was feeling frustrated by this person who was giving me slow, one-word answers and telling me practically nothing. I began to feel that I was a pawn being moved, rather than the player. I would have to switch to another tactic. Clearly, this part of Christopher would not be self-revealing, not even with so much as a gesture. But maybe this ego state could serve as an informant.

"Do you know about this angry person who doesn't want to come out and talk with me?"

"Yes. That's what I came out to tell you. He's always complaining." The even drumbeat of his words now came more rapidly. "He doesn't like anything. He hates Christopher."

"He does? Does he hate you, too?"

"Oh, he doesn't know about me. . . . At least, I don't think he does." The eyes darted uneasily from side to side. "I don't think anyone knows about me." His pace had slowed again, but, at least, he was telling me something.

"You mean you just observe what goes on, and no one knows you are there?"

"Right."

He wouldn't tell me more about himself, I knew, yet I sensed he could tell me about the angry voice.

"Tell me, who is this angry person? Since you observe everything, you ought to be able to tell me."

"His name is James. He's the one who tries to get Christopher to hurt himself."

My hunch had been right. I would be dealing with the voice that told Christopher to throw a chair through the window and hurl himself six floors below.

"Oh, yes, Christopher has told me about the angry voice."

"Yeah. Christopher knows a lot about him. James talks to him all the time."

"What does James talk to Christopher about?"

"Nasty things."

"Are you referring to vulgar and sexual things?"

"Yeah. He's mean about it, too."

"Well, I've heard vulgar and nasty words before," I said, careful to make my voice as nonchalant as possible. "I'm sure I can manage if that's all there is to be afraid of. Do you think James will talk to me now that I know he's there?"

"I don't know."

"Well, I'd like to give it a try," I said, putting every bit of confidence in my voice that I could. "How can I reach you if I need your help again?"

"I think I'm going to go now." He had become rigid and reclusive again. "I don't want to talk anymore."

"Okay, but what shall I call you?"

I was growing weary of having to pull everything out of him, yet I had to be able to identify this ego state again. "May I call you 'The Watcher'?"

"That will be all right for now." The eyelids began to flicker. "I want to go back in now."

"All right." I had little choice. "Go back in. Close your eyes and go all the way back in and rest."

The eyes settled shut and The Watcher faded quietly.

I gave Christopher further instructions, guiding him, telling him to relax, deepening the trance. I listened to the sound of my own voice and was lulled by it. I, too, needed a chance to relax and think for a moment.

What was the answer to the puzzle of The Watcher? There had been something in his flat, vacant look that seemed familiar to me, yet The Watcher said we had not met before. Of course! I hadn't met The Watcher before, but Paula had. He was the first ego state to appear. She had asked to speak to the part of Christopher that could tell her the most about what had happened to him. The eyes had opened as if an ego state were present, but whoever was that silent presence would not talk. This had to be the same one! After the trance, Christopher had had no memory of the appearance of any personality other than Timmy. What ego state, other than The Watcher, would know the most about what had happened to Christopher? But I'd have to set these questions aside now, and go back to discovering more about James, the angry and dangerous one.

I decided to check with Christopher, who had been listening from his imaginary loft. Pleased with myself, I knew I was beginning to get the hang of how I could persuade these co-conscious parts to work with me.

"Christopher, were you listening?"

"Yes," he replied distantly.

"I want to talk with James, but he doesn't need to come out all the way. He can come just as far as is comfortable."

I was hoping James would stay "in" with his eyes closed. This would make me more comfortable, if not him. I was not eager to meet this hostile character, and I took time out to glance toward the open door to make sure Ben was still outside and hadn't decided he wasn't needed.

The angle of the shoulders became more square and the face tightened slightly. I knew instantly that James was there, hidden just under the surface. I watched in silence for a moment. To my relief, he did not open his eyes.

I continued cautiously. "I understand, James, that you're pretty angry about something. Is that right?"

"Yes."

The voice was gruff. I cringed slightly. It was my spur-of-the-moment decision to ask the risky question first. I took a deep breath and plunged forward.

"Are you angry with *me*?"

"I wanted to hit you . . . not right now. I was angry."

Even with closed eyes, Christopher's familiar face now had a cold and uncaring expression. I leaned away, repulsed.

"I wanted to hit you in the mouth."

There was a quiet venom in his voice. I drew farther back.

"When do you mean?"

"Yesterday, when you were saying that stupid stuff about Christopher getting better."

"Why?" I was astounded at the ferocity in his voice.

"I didn't want you messing around with him."

"You mean you thought I was just fooling around carelessly with Christopher?"

"Hell, no! I don't give a shit if you mess him up. Just don't help him. Christopher doesn't deserve any help!"

It was all I could do to keep my voice free of the fear I felt. "Does it make you angry that I like Christopher?"

"Not anymore. I'm beginning to understand the little creep. I figure it wasn't always his fault he didn't do what I wanted. What pisses me off now is I don't know who's been telling him things I don't want him to hear. There's somebody besides me and Timmy. I don't know who it is."

Our interchange had a surrealistic quality. James was expressing his passion with closed eyes, and I was piercing the veil between us with my probing questions.

"You don't know the others? You just know they're around?"

"Isn't that screwed? I just found out about them."

It was hard for me to empathize with James. Although his words and tone told me he felt a fiery frustration, I had nothing within my own experience to help me relate to it. It was easier to imagine what Christopher might have felt when he discovered that another part of himself took over during his blackout periods. I have, myself, sometimes been surprised to discover the influence of my subconscious mind. I could not imagine how James might experience the realization that he was not the only alter personality inside Christopher's body.

"Do you want to meet them, the others?"

"No! No! Hold it," he ordered fiercely. There was a touch of panic in his voice, and the muscles just above his jaw had begun to twitch and tighten. "I don't want to meet them. Not now, anyway."

"That's fine." I was glad to withdraw from the idea. "That's fine," I repeated to calm him down. "Whenever you are ready to meet the others, perhaps we can arrange it." The clenching of his jaw ceased, but he remained tense and motionless. Still repulsed by the look Christopher's face had taken on, I wondered at the fortitude it must have taken to live constantly with this inner voice. It was so unlike the gentle, clean-cut Christopher.

Somehow, his expression and body conveyed a restlessness, though he had not moved. But I paid little attention. I was concentrating, trying to think of how I could learn more about James and his relationship to Christopher.

"Why are you so down on Christopher?"

The body came alive. Veins and muscles on his neck bulged. Suddenly, the previously fragile hands looked as if they could rip me apart. His eyes opened very wide, and I found myself confronted with the full force of James's malevolent stare.

Chapter 3

KNOCK, KNOCK, WHO'S THERE?

My heart was pounding. "Maybe I shouldn't have insulted you by saying you were down on Christopher," I said. I sized James up as quickly as I could, and it was obvious he was doing the same to me.

James was someone to be reckoned with. In an instant, I had recognized those cold, glaring eyes. I met him when I first interviewed Christopher, and his malignant stare had been just as unsettling. Schizoid personality, I had thought then, unable to establish rapport. And all the while I had been wondering why Bill Jefferson had described Christopher as shy and polite.

"I don't believe in shrinks," he had told me in that interview during his first hospitalization.

"Then you've never been to one?"

He looked away and said nothing, drew slowly on his cigarette, and then exhaled over his shoulder.

"Look, Christopher, I know it's hard, but you'll have to talk if I'm to help you."

"I can talk to you. I just don't—"

Want to. I'd finished the sentence in my head.

And now I felt just as I had then. An icy chill ran through me, as it had the first time.

"I didn't mean to insult you." I said. "I'm just trying to understand your relationship with Christopher."

"What relationship? Just because we're the same age, it doesn't make us brothers."

By now James had taken a bold position in the chair, erasing the last traces of Christopher's passive posture. Put up a tough front, I told myself.

"So what is it with you and Christopher?"

"Hell if I know. I get so damned depressed sometimes. He'll never do what I tell him to. Then the dumb shit gets depressed because I'm depressed—but he's so dumb, he doesn't know what's causing it. I wish he'd get depressed enough to kill himself," James said, as dispassionately as a Mafia hit man, I thought. James's brutal manner put me at a disadvantage. I was no match for him. "He never listens to me about that, either. Too chicken to jump out the window. I'd love to be rid of him."

"Then what would happen to you?"

"Me? I'd be fine. I'd go out and pick up all the little tricks at the gay bars. He couldn't interfere."

I was astounded that James failed to realize that if his wish came true, he'd die along with Christopher. I now understood that James wouldn't direct his anger at me as long as I didn't take sides in this matter. In any event, I was determined to be even-handed with all the personalities. I felt my breathing slow down.

"Listen James, I don't want to take anybody's side. I'm not saying that you *shouldn't* be disappointed in Christopher."

"I'm just looking out for Number One. But damn! All my life I've been forced to look out for him, too. He can't look out for himself. When we were kids, he was such a skinny runt. He'd never go and play ball or other stuff with the rest of the kids." James spoke with disgust. "Damn sissy! I told him, 'Get in there! Be like the rest of them!' But no—he'd never listen. Little fool! He'd be afraid, afraid of what they'd think and afraid they'd laugh at him."

Hold it! I wanted to tell him. Not every boy is meant to be a ruffian. I wouldn't want my son, Eddie, to be picked on for not being an athlete.

"So you kept trying to get Christopher to be more confident, more strong, more active?" I was attempting to understand and not fall into the trap of taking sides among the personalities.

"Now you're getting the idea," James said. He seemed to be calming down, but was still filled with contempt.

By the end of the interview with James, it became apparent that he was not a violent part of Christopher. James might have had the impulse to hit me, but he would not have carried it through. His anger was toward Christopher. It was Christopher he wanted to harm. He might persuade Christopher to hurt himself.

There had been no need to have the psychiatric technician sitting outside the door that day to protect me. I was spent and grateful our session was coming to an end.

As Christopher came out of the trance, he had difficulty re-orienting himself to waking consciousness. Confusion clouded his face.

He looked around the room. Late-afternoon shadows graced the cold, angular institutional furniture, and the crimson sky cast a warm hue on the barren walls. He settled back in his chair.

"How much time has passed?" he asked.

"Almost two hours," I said quietly.

"It seems like ten minutes," he said with suppressed astonishment. "Is Ben still sitting out there?"

"No. While you were in the trance, I got up and told him he could leave."

"That's strange." He hesitated. "I felt like there was someone else listening in when James was talking. I was afraid of James, but the other person wasn't and really wanted to come out. I think it's a she. A girl. No—it's her and somebody else—maybe a couple more." He paused for a second. "I think . . . I've only begun."

"Do you remember The Watcher?" I asked, wanting to double-check my conclusions.

"Who? No. I don't know what you are talking about." He fidgeted. "But just thinking about it now makes me feel really anxious."

After finishing with Christopher, I found it very difficult to return to my office for my last two late-afternoon appointments. Compared to the anxious anticipation I had felt that morning prior to the session, I was feeling confident and relieved now that the hypnosis had been successful. Nevertheless, I wanted time to get over the effect of meeting James again, this time knowing I was speaking to a different personality. I had forgotten about that brief first encounter with James. Christopher had changed so completely, it escaped me that he had had this other side of him. And I had been in his apartment! I wanted to be alone, to think all of this over. Instead, I was face to face with another patient who needed my help and deserved my full attention.

After several years of practice, I'd learned to compartmentalize my thoughts and feelings temporarily until I could get back to them later. I had my transition between patients down to a science: a few notes in the chart, a check at my message spindle, a trip to the filing cabinet, and I was ready to move on to the next person. But I could not put Christopher out of my mind so easily. I sorted through some mail and then lingered near the coffee pot, hoping that a few extra minutes would make a difference.

Liz, my secretary, noticed that I was stalling.

"Can I pour you some coffee?" she asked.

"No thanks," I said distractedly. I knew I was straight-arming her, but I didn't have the resources to go beyond politeness.

I walked away and stepped into my husband's office, closing the door behind me.

"Hi. What's up?" José asked curiously.

"Nothing I can talk about now. I just came in for a kiss." He obligingly reached up from his chair as I bent over to receive his hug. It felt good, but did not have the same soothing effect as usual. José noticed my tension.

"Are you having a rough day?"

"Actually, I don't know how to describe it." I felt a stiffness in my neck and back as I moved away from him, without saying more. He looked a little hurt and was puzzled by my remoteness. "Well, listen, I better get back to work," I said. "I've got another patient waiting."

I put my own concerns aside and listened with every ounce of concentration I could muster. I had to fight to suppress thoughts about Christopher. I was successful in moving forward, but the strain on me took its toll. I arrived home exhausted and irritable. I hardly spoke during dinner. I wanted to collapse in a heap. I wanted time to myself. But I had to wait until the children were in bed. At the first opportunity, I escaped into the seclusion of our bedroom.

At last I could think! I sat cross-legged on the bed, staring silently into space.

My husband came in and began to change into his pajamas. Frowning at me, he said, "What are you doing?"

"I'm thinking," I said, annoyed at having been intruded upon.

"About what? I can see the smoke coming from your ears."

"About a patient." I was defensive, knowing I was breaking an agreement. For years, we had done our best to comply to a verbal pact about not bringing work home from the office. We had especially agreed not to think about other people's problems after nine o'clock at night. I sat on the bed indulging myself. "It's really an unusual case." I was trying to justify breaking our agreement.

"You're not talking about that so-called multiple personality case you mentioned last week?" he questioned suspiciously. "You don't really believe you have a multiple personality patient, do you? Just because he went through an age regression during hypnosis? Next thing you know, you're going to tell me he has half a dozen personalities."

I felt myself becoming angrily defensive—and all I really wanted was to be alone to think. I didn't feel like explaining, but I thought an explanation might help.

"Look honey," I said with as much control as I could gather, "I'm just beginning to explore this fellow, and I'm not sure what is there yet. Today it looked as if there are three more personalities besides the one little boy. Possibly there are even more than that."

José shook his head, disgruntled. At this moment, he was the very picture of Basque temperament, just what one would expect of a man from the mountains of northern Spain—fair-complected, dark-eyed, willful, stubborn, and never dominated by any woman. Thankfully, his European education had taught him reserve and refinement, a balance to a sometimes fiery temperament.

José brushed the air with an exasperated gesture, his characteristic way of indicating he was dismissing all that I had just said.

"Anything you say. But you aren't going to be in this kind of mood every night, are you?"

I thought this sounded offensive, but he didn't seem to realize it. I bit my tongue, knowing I was tired, preoccupied, and overly sensitive.

"No, I hope not," I said, knowing it wasn't the truth.

"Good," he answered sarcastically.

That did it!

"I wouldn't exactly call this a *mood*, you know. It's more like exhaustion, and I'm certainly getting no sympathy from you!"

No answer. He wasn't going to give me any support, and, worse, I was going to have a cold war on my hands. He turned and left the room without a word. I felt desolate. Why was he responding this way? I didn't understand, and I was too tired to try to figure it out.

As I walked through the psychiatric unit the next day, I noticed that my perception of the other patients had changed. Their pathologies seemed mundane. They grouped around the television, played pool or Ping Pong, or hammered their initials into pieces of leather. None of them compared with Christopher. None could have caused me to disrupt a night's sleep with anticipation of what I might encounter the next day.

Christopher was standing at the nurses' station, leaning against the wall. He looked the worst that I had yet seen him. His hair was disheveled, and he wore his gray robe and slippers, but still he had a grace that distinguished him from the others. As usual, his skin looked freshly showered, but he had not shaved, and I could tell he had not slept.

Christopher's head rested against the wall, his vacant sky-blue eyes stared blankly at the floor. It's like the hush that stills the forest after a storm, I thought. He stood motionless, scarcely breathing, oblivious that I was observing him from only a few feet away.

Sue bustled over to me with Christopher's chart. "I just called your office," she whispered. "I was hoping you were on your way."

"How long has he been standing there like that?"

"Quite a while, twenty or thirty minutes. He's been asking for you all morning."

I felt myself respond to the enticement of being intensely needed by such a wistful and fawnlike young man. Christopher and his problems were seductive in so many ways, I thought. Attractive, intelligent, needy, appreciative—he'd have no trouble commanding any doctor's attention.

Sue and I quietly approached Christopher. He smiled faintly when he saw me.

"I'm sorry I look so grubby," he apologized. "I couldn't sleep. I couldn't escape the voices. I fell asleep for a little while and had a nightmare. I was being chased by a pack of wild dogs, and I was trying to climb a cliff to get away. I couldn't escape. People were holding my feet. A couple of girls and two guys were hanging on to me. I could hear them shouting at each other and at me. I woke up and then sat up in bed, but I could still hear them in the distance."

This had to mean there were three other adult personalities I had not met: another man—and two women!

"Are you ready to find out about the other voices?" I asked.

"Yes, I suppose so," he replied reluctantly. "I do have to learn about them, don't I?" He seemed to be speaking more to himself than to me.

I turned to Sue and asked her to sit in on the session that day. I was doubtful that Christopher would become violent, but I was still uncomfortable about being alone with him until I knew more.

Christopher slipped into the trance especially quickly this time. He was eager to have me guide him into his loft where he could find emotional respite from his internal conflicts. And no sooner did Christopher settle into his imaginary sanctuary than I could see a switch and the eyes popped open.

"Well, it's about time I got out!"

I was startled at this quick entry. I could tell immediately that this was the female Christopher had mentioned the day before. There was an effeminate flair in the tone and gesture, in astonishing contrast to Christopher's passive stillness. Her gestures were flamboyant.

Her voice was a notch above Christopher's, but not falsetto. The tones simply came out softer, with an uplift in pitch at the ends of sentences. And when she gestured, it was of course Christopher's arm, but limp-wristed.

"I tried to come out yesterday, but he wouldn't let me—the old fuddy-duddy." She made a face and giggled.

"Who wouldn't let you come out?" I asked, still astonished.

"Ernest! He's always telling us what to do." She made the same face again, screwing up her features in mock disgust.

"Who's us?" I asked, wondering how much more I'd be dealing with.

"Me and Jackie." Her voice took on a slightly more serious, but nonetheless intense, tone. "I don't know where he gets off bossing us around. I could easily have broken in on one of the conversations you were having with James, but Ernest said I must wait my turn or it would have been too hard on you."

Well, well, I thought. One of them is aware of the effect these rapid-fire appearances were having on me. And I made a mental note of the name "Ernest." I would assuredly have to deal with him later. For the moment, I studied the personality sitting in front of me.

"It's true that I have about all I can handle with one of you at a time," I said frankly. "So you know about James? I thought James told me he didn't know about any others but himself and, now, Timmy." There seemed to be an inconsistency in their stories, and I was on the lookout for any flaw in this increasingly intricate system.

"I'll tell you how it works," she said pertly. Her original flashes of impudence seemed to have been replaced by a more businesslike manner. I was dealing with her in a forthright manner, and not responding to her more impish qualities.

"Ernest and Jackie and I know about James, but James doesn't know about us. Well . . . he does now, because he's listening. Ernest and I didn't know about Timmy until last week, then I found out that Jackie knew about Timmy all along but just didn't tell us about it. I don't get along with her at all. The only thing we have in common is that it takes both of us girls to gang up on Ernest."

She took a breath.

"Listen, I gotta go. I can't stand being out like this, all crumpled." She made another face. "I can't really be myself." Then she gave me a nod, indicating she was talking female to female, but her voice had a saccharine insincerity. "That's a real nice dress you're wearing today."

Without closing her eyes this feminine scamp disappeared as Christopher's face took on a vacant, glazed look. He stared into space. I relaxed for a moment. She'd been interesting, almost a show, but I couldn't feel the woman-to-woman camaraderie she'd been trying to establish.

A second later, a new personality looked up at me.

"Hello, Dr. LaCalle," he said. "I'm Ernest."

So soon? I thought to myself. The voice had changed to a low, slow-paced intonation. There was a look in his eyes that I had never seen in Christopher.

"She took me by surprise," he said. "Sometimes she's very uncontrollable." His voice was bland.

"Who is she?"

Ernest—calm, relaxed, confident—folded his arms in front of him and got more comfortable by crossing his outstretched legs. He leaned back in his chair and appraised me, his chin tilted slightly upward. His mannerisms reminded me of a minor business executive in a settled, comfortable position. In contrast to Christopher's intuitive intelligence, Ernest had an air of ploddingly methodical logic.

"Her name is Sissy. I wanted to be the first one out so I could explain this whole thing to you, but she's so impertinent she thought she would take charge."

Impertinent? That's not a word Christopher would use. It had a stuffy, old-fashioned ring.

He was still talking. A complacent tone had crept into his voice. "I didn't let her out all the way, though."

"Does that mean I haven't seen Sissy in 'full bloom,' so to speak?" I was incredulous. Sissy seemed already quite dramatic.

"Not yet. I hope you never do, at least while Christopher is in this hospital. She's rather wild and impetuous."

And he's rather smug, I thought.

"All she wants to do is party and pick up men." Despite the flat even tones, he spoke disdainfully. "She keeps wanting to leave the hospital, complains that she's bored."

I learned from Ernest that Sissy was a nineteen-year-old heterosexual who liked excitement and adventure, and, in fact, seemed intent on being as hedonistic as possible.

"I have to work hard to get her to be reasonable about her expensive tastes and reckless lifestyle," Ernest told me. "She'd like to spend money in beauty salons and wear sexy clothing."

Wait a minute, I thought. Hair salons? What kind of sexy clothing?

"She drives her car like a maniac and chases after men just as fast."

At least I could envision this happening—Christopher behind the wheel of a speeding car, or Christopher paying attention to another man.

"And she's attractive, flirtatious, and particularly seductive on the dance floor."

Ernest, still with that same satisfied-with-himself air, leaned back farther in the chair when he'd concluded his description of Sissy. He'd apparently been oblivious to the double-take I had done when he mentioned beauty salons and sexy clothes.

I considered that Sissy was only nineteen, and an immature nineteen at that. "Is she prepared for the fruits of her seductivity?" I asked, falling more or less into Ernest's style of speaking.

"After she has lured a man into her grasp," he said, "she has always fled the premises."

"So . . ."

"So that leaves him in the hands of James, who carries out and completes the sexual seduction."

I recalled Christopher's "Nellie" behavior at the other hospital. That must have been Sissy, but I didn't know it at the time.

He'd been there a week, and one day I watched him while he was talking with another male patient in the courtyard. I'd never heard his voice so excited, high-pitched, and animated. He tossed his head to one side as he spoke, coyly eyeing the other fellow. He was dressed in a bright new T-shirt that showed every contour in his chest. His jeans were much tighter than the pair I had seen him in previously.

These gestures and coquettishness in certain gays were not surprising to me; I was only surprised to find this behavior in Christopher. From the first day I'd seen him, he'd behaved just the opposite in front of me. And I fully expected him to drop these mannerisms as soon as we started our session, but he didn't.

"Well, hi, Dr. LaCalle! How are you today?" he chirped.

"I'm fine, thank you, Christopher," I said with some interest. "You seem to be in good spirits today."

"Oh, I am! I'm feeling just great." There was a melodic pitch to his voice. "I've been having a wonderful time."

"What have you been up to that's so enjoyable?"

"Nothing in particular. I just decided I wanted to have some fun."

He kept on behaving that way, and the remainder of the time I spent with Christopher that day was not what I would call productive. Yet, still, I had attributed his flippant mood to the fact that he was delighted to find another attractive gay man in the hospital. His style had become increasingly exaggerated and theatrical, and I'd been only too happy to leave and stop being his audience. I assumed the mood would pass as soon as the fascination with the other fellow had subsided.

Remembering how obnoxious I found the saucy—even competitive—behavior of what I now knew to be Sissy, I wanted to turn the conversation back on Ernest so that he would have to talk about himself.

"You haven't said a word about yourself, Ernest."

"There's not much to say."

"What do you do with yourself?"

"I keep things organized, make sure that the important things get done," he answered drably. "I try to keep out of trouble—try to keep Sissy and Jackie out of trouble—but I'm not very successful. Neither of them listen to reason, and reason is all I have."

"How long have you been around?"

"I haven't been able to figure that out. I know it was about the time Christopher got out of the drug scene."

"How old are you, Ernest?"

"Same age as Christopher."

"Are you homosexual or heterosexual?" With Ernest, because of his stuffy manner, my clinical inquisitiveness seemed more like impudence. His stodgy outlook was certainly in sharp contrast to Sissy!

"Neither," he said with a touch of pomposity. "I can't be bothered with such base needs."

Ernest's tone was particularly monotonous. He never deviated from his position in the chair, and his facial expression had taken on an almost snobbish aspect. Altogether, Ernest had turned out to be quite a boring creature. I searched for a way to comment on that.

"You remind of Mr. Spock from *Star Trek*," I told him. But even Mr. Spock, despite his "logical" approach, had more pizazz than Ernest.

"Never thought of it that way, but I suppose you could say I'm a bit like him."

"Maybe you can help me with something, Ernest. You know that Christopher has had quite a drinking problem the last few months. Who or what is responsible for it?"

Ernest quietly listened to voices he was consulting inside his head.

"I'm not really sure who is responsible, but Sissy is telling me right now that Jackie is causing it. It's probably true. Teenagers these days . . ."

Ernest had begun to sermonize, but then he jumped in the chair and sat bolt upright. His face and body had changed instantly and completely.

"That bitch!" came a shrill shout. "Sissy is putting you on. She thinks she's such tough stuff!"

Wait! I'm not ready for this, I thought. Ernest was correct, I would have a hard time with more than one at a time. And he apparently had not been able to hold this one back.

"Are you Jackie?"

"Yours truly, so what's it to you?" Her voice switched to a growl, and she put one fist on her hip and raised the other. She clenched the fist tightly and—keeping her eyes locked on mine—shook it as if she were ready to cuff me on the chin.

My head was reeling with yet another mental adjustment to make. Jackie, I thought, how could I placate her? "It's just what Ernest said . . ."

"Yeah, he don't like nobody who isn't"—she paused—"*mature*." She gave her head a debonair sweep. "And Sissy, Miss Prissy, don't like no 'punk dykes.' " She focused her gaze directly at me, a challenge, and then spoke with venom. "I'll get her ass!"

"What did you mean, Sissy is putting me on?"

"She knows perfectly well who is making Christopher drink. All of us are. James especially don't leave him in peace."

"You're doing it, too?"

"Sure! And I give Sissy a lot of shit. She's always trying to quiet me down, but I won't." She thrust her chin forward in defiance. "I refuse. Her and her prissy behavior," she snapped.

"You and Sissy are always competing?"

"Compete with her?" She puffed herself up indignantly and squared her shoulders. "She's not even in the same ball park. Even the 'fems' I know aren't as piss-ass as her. Naw, she's just always putting me down. She thinks she's so much better than anybody."

And she made a mocking caricature of Sissy's limp wrist.

"Are you a homosexual?" I asked hesitantly.

"Jeez, you *are* something!" she taunted. "Yeah, I'm a dyke, at least as much as I can be for my age. Most people just think I'm a tomboy!" She smirked, and her voice was mocking. "Isn't that cute?" she asked. "But I know the difference. I figured it out a year ago."

"How old are you?"

"Fourteen."

"Then you're not really an *active* lesbian yet."

Her boldness softened, as if I had called her bluff.

"Had no chance. Christopher tried to make it with a woman once. But he didn't feel anything. Me? I just don't think about it much. It's not a big deal. What do you expect?"

"I don't expect anything. I've got the message." I paused to let her know I'd back off. I was beginning to get a glimpse of a scared kid beneath that tough exterior. "Is there anything else you want to tell me?"

"No. Except when I'm around, you'll know it. I make sure of that."

Jackie was absolutely right. The next morning, Sue spotted Jackie immediately. Jackie woke up grouchy, dressed herself in a plaid shirt with rolled-up sleeves, loose jeans, and a pair of sneakers. She stomped out of her room and threatened to break the bathroom mirror with her fist. Then she threatened to throw her roommate out of the room, because his snoring had kept her awake all night. "I'm 'The Evil One,' " she proclaimed, trying to scare both staff and patients. But when Sue took her into the isolation room and handed her a pair of foam rubber Batakas so she could pound the walls as freely as she wished, she was unable to let loose of her anger. She could not even pick up the foam rubber bats. Her rage was frozen, paralyzed. She became tired and depressed. Finally, fully spent, she fell asleep.

A while later, Christopher woke up. He sought out Sue and thanked her for her part in controlling Jackie.

"She's really scaring me," he confided. "I don't trust her. She can really get out of hand. What must my roommate think? He can't help it if he snores."

When I came in that day, Sue described what had happened.

"One thing I learned," she said. "Jackie is not The Evil One. In fact, I don't think there is an Evil One. Dr. LaCalle, I think it's just plain old anger that he calls being evil."

I wanted to concur with her, but I was not sure it was that simple. I decided to request an interview with Jackie during hypnosis.

"Jackie, there's something I've been suspecting for a while. I wanted to check it out with you," I began. "Did Christopher ever get into any trouble when he was a kid?"

"Yeah, but only when I'd get him into it. He always did what I told him."

"What did you tell him to do?"

"Lemme see . . . I told him to set a fire once in an open field."

"Why did you tell him to do that?"

"I was just mad at the old bag, so I got him to pretend he was burning her." I could hear the bravado in her voice.

"Tell me about the fire in the field."

"He set it behind a rock. Just a little fire. I wanted to see it burn. He stood back to look at it, then—" Her voice took on a vicious tone. "He put it out! He got too scared. 'Chicken!' I told him. 'Let it burn! Burn!' " She emphasized the words with fire in her eyes.

"Who were you angry at?"

"Her! I wanted to burn her!" she snarled.

"Who?" I insisted.

"Christopher's mother," she muttered, loathing written on her face. "She's so disgusting."

"Were there any other fires?"

"No. He was too afraid."

"What other things did you make him do?"

"Steal . . . lotsa things. I made him break into houses and warehouses. She never knew!" Jackie sneered as she spoke of Christopher's mother, and the mocking tone lingered in her voice. "The stupid woman! She never paid no attention. Christopher stole record albums when he was a teenager, shoplifted, took 'em home."

"His mother didn't go into his room and find them?"

Venom dripped from Jackie's voice. She seethed. "She—she didn't care, the bitch!"

"Wasn't Christopher ever caught?"

"Once. At the store. Police brought him home. He was so afraid. But I told him, 'Don't worry. She won't do nothin' to you.' " Her mouth twisted. " 'She don't care,' I told him, 'she just looks out for her own self.' "

"What did Christopher's mother do when the police arrived?"

"Nothing! She opened the door, dressed in her bathrobe. In the middle of the day! After they left, she said, 'You embarrassed me. The house is a mess. I'm not dressed.' All she cared about was herself. She didn't even think that being such a slob embarrassed Christopher."

"She didn't do anything at all about the theft?" It was hard to believe that Christopher had not even been scolded.

"Nothing. She wouldn't bother. Just like she couldn't be bothered about the bed wetting."

"Christopher wet the bed?"

"Until he was eleven years old. I felt so bad for him." Jackie's voice softened. "He'd wake up cold in the night, shivering from his wet bed. I'd be with him when he'd get up and take a shower and change his sheets in the middle of the night. He was so sad, but he didn't know it. It made me feel bad for him, and I hated her. Hated her! She never checked. Never woke him up. Never took him to a doctor. Only said, 'Don't drink anything before you go to bed.' She said that until he was eleven years old. He washed his bedclothes. Changed his pajamas. Always so sad."

I began to understand why Christopher was so moody in the mornings and why I hadn't seen Jackie's traits in Christopher before. She only came out in the early hours.

"Do you ever check the bed now, when you get up in the morning?" I ventured.

"No. Yes! Yes, I do." The new insight made Jackie smile. "I didn't think about it. I do it without thinking."

"Now we know why it's usually you who is out in the morning, Jackie." I decided to conclude my interview with her on this positive note, even though I wanted to talk more about Christopher's bed wetting, fire setting, and stealing. These were the childhood antecedents of possible sociopathic behavior in Christopher the adult.

Later, having talked briefly with Christopher after he came out of the trance, I sought out Sue. Although I was including other staff members as part of the team, Sue had become my confidante, and I needed to unwind from the session.

I told her that I was convinced that Jackie was not an Evil One, even though she was incorrigible.

"The problem is," Sue said, "that Christopher keeps insisting that there is a violent, evil part of him. If it's not Jackie, then who is it?"

"There may not be a 'who.' Not every emotion that Christopher has is necessarily encapsulated in a separate personality."

I believed what I was telling Sue, but I was also aware of the possibility of a psychopathic personality. If Christopher had been severely abused as a child, he could well have learned violent behavior. Without caring or compassion from either parent, it was conceivable that he had learned to relate to others in a cold-hearted way. For the moment, however, I did not want to raise Sue's anxiety.

We had, thus far, accomplished much more during this second hospitalization than we had in the first, when I didn't know of Christopher's other personalities. But Christopher was feeling spent from having been confronted with a reality he had tried to deny for many years. He looked tired, and I noticed that he'd stopped shaving. But he now knew that the headaches, the loss of minutes or days, the voices in the night, all pointed toward a severe disorder. He understood the diagnosis, but he had to have time to let the idea sink in. I, too, needed time to assimilate and piece together the information.

Now that Christopher was able to discern the personality behind each voice, he was also able, at times, to carry on internal dialogues with these other parts of himself. I encouraged him to communicate with the other personalities and to attempt to get them all to work in harmony and mutual support, one of the techniques I had learned from the Watkins and Watkins paper.

"They don't want to cooperate with each other," he told me. "They all have their own way of doing things and they each think their way is right."

The next day, as soon as Christopher was in a deep trance, I could see that something was wrong. He shook with a fury even greater than that day in the music room. His face was strained. He was flushed, panting, striving for control. Sweat dotted his brow.

Whatever is behind this, I thought, I don't want it to come out. If it's another personality, I don't want to see it.

Whatever was the source of the torment I was witnessing, I could not tell. Christopher could not describe it to me or let that part of himself speak to me directly.

"I . . . can't . . . get away." Christopher squeezed the words from his mouth.

I instructed him to close the door to his "safe room" and to lock it with dead bolts. I told him to close the shutters on the window and bolt them, too. He said he felt unstable, that there was a terrible force right outside and he could not escape it.

"The floor is shaking."

I instructed him to fortify the room. He built a stone wall around it and filled the basement with cement. The floor stopped shaking, he reported, but still he did not feel completely safe. He could hear the voice outside. He said it was about to speak.

Sue and I leaned forward.

"I am the essence of Christopher," the voice said. "I have no conscience. I am destructive. I am Evil."

WHO CAN TELL THE SECRETS?

Could this personality actually be so terrible?

"What is your purpose?" I asked.

"I have no purpose." He spoke slowly. "No strengths. I have no control."

"It doesn't matter," I said confidently. "Christopher is in charge. Did you know that?"

"Yes," he said. I thought he sounded almost reluctant. "It's supposed to be that way."

"Did you hear that, Christopher?"

Silence. Then Christopher drew close enough to answer. "Yes. The Evil wants me to be in control . . . but I don't feel in control."

"Well, then, come out now, Evil One," I commanded. "I want to see you."

"No. You can't make me come out." The voice was firm.

"That's true. I won't even try. But I *want* you to come out—now."

"No. I'm going to stay inside. I . . . don't . . . like . . . this!"

Once again Christopher had begun to shake all over.

"All right," I said. "Don't come out now. Instead, go all the way back inside. You can leave now, and go far back inside so that Christopher cannot hear you anymore. All the way. Far back inside."

Christopher was still shaking. Sue's eyes were glued on me

as she waited to see what I'd do next.

"You can relax completely now, Christopher. The voice is so far away that you can no longer hear it. You are completely safe in your room. Soon you will be able to come out of your room because the voice is gone."

I had abandoned this attempt. I was getting nowhere, and I worried I had taken a wrong turn. Slowly, I brought Christopher out of the trance.

"You can open your eyes now," I said. "You are awake, alert, and relaxed."

Christopher blinked his eyes and shook his head. He frowned. "Something's not right," he said.

"What's not right?"

"I don't know."

Something important might come out easily now, in this twilight period that followed a trance.

"I'll never forget one time."

"When was that?"

"When my father locked my puppy in the refrigerator. He used to hate my little dog. He'd kick him and be mean to him. It was just a poor puppy. It would yelp and cry and then he'd get more angry and he'd say he was going to kill it for crying. He said I didn't need a dog anyway. But I did need it."

I could hear the protest in Christopher's voice, almost as if he were still protesting to his father.

"It was my only friend, the only thing that made me feel good. One day he got angry with me when I tried to pick up the puppy and run away with it. I didn't want my father to torture it anymore. But he grabbed me and the dog and dragged us into the kitchen. Then he shoved the puppy into the refrigerator and stood in front of the door so I couldn't open the door and let it out."

As he continued with his story, Christopher's expression went flat. The hurt and angry feelings that the memory had provoked in him had vanished. His countenance became blank and his voice mechanical, his eyes fixed on one spot.

"He told me I could go and play. He said to come back in about half an hour and I could take my dog out of the refrigerator— dead. I thought of my puppy in there, using up all the air and then

70

slowly suffocating. My poor puppy . . . suffering. I thought of picking up my dead puppy and burying it in the backyard."

"What did you do?"

"Nothing. There was nothing I could do," he said, maintaining his riveted expression. "I wanted to kill him. I wanted to kill my father," he repeated without emotion. His eyes were cold as steel. "I thought he wanted to kill me, too, along with the puppy. But I didn't budge. I just stood there in front of him, looked him in the eye, and he looked back at me."

I shivered as I became lost in Christopher's eyes, which seemed to reflect the scene held in his memory. His eyes held the psychopathic look that must have been in his father's eyes—cruel and tormenting—as he stood in front of the refrigerator.

"Well, what happened?" I asked.

Christopher snapped out of his reverie and shrugged his shoulders. He looked at me dully, as if wondering why I was sitting on pins and needles waiting for his next words.

"After a few minutes he just walked away and I let my puppy out. The dog was okay. That happened when I was ten, and I said to myself I would get even with him someday."

His father's corrosive influence had taken its toll. Christopher had kept these homicidal revenge feelings inside of him all these years. So this was the source of the "evil" within him! I wondered if Christopher ever did get even with his father.

Sue and I sat quietly with Christopher for a while. Then I instructed her to stay with him for as long as necessary after I left and to record any pertinent information in her nursing notes. By this time, Christopher had gotten up, moved around the room, and lit a cigarette. But he said nothing more, and still appeared disoriented and not himself.

I went back to my office, faced again with the prospect of trying to concentrate on routine patients. A little more than an hour later, Sue called.

"We weren't talking to Christopher," she said nervously. "What was wrong is that we weren't talking to Christopher. He's in the safe room, afraid to come out. James came out. It was James who told the story about the puppy. I've been talking to James, but he doesn't want me to tell anyone on the staff that Christopher is no longer here."

"Thanks, Sue. Now try and get some rest. You've put in more than your share today."

Three hours later, I called the hospital and asked to speak with the second-shift nurse, Polly. I knew she'd been transferred to the unit only the day before. She wasn't assigned to Christopher and didn't know anything about the other personalities as yet.

"Polly, what have you observed about Christopher since you came on the shift?"

"I don't know Christopher very well, but from what I saw of him yesterday I thought he was on the shy side. He said he was depressed, but he'd laugh a little and smile around the nurses. Now—he's acting strangely. I don't know what it is. What's wrong with him? It's as if I'm talking to another person."

Precisely, I said to myself. I wished I could have gone back to the hospital to see James, but the day had grown too long. I had to get home.

The next morning, Saturday, I checked by phone with Sue.

"He's much better," she reported. "He slept a little. And I stuck around past my shift just in case Jackie came out or something, but he woke up as Christopher again, still disoriented."

I began to feel frustrated that I was often not available when Christopher was providing voluntary information or spontaneously dissociated. Sue, on the other hand, had interacted with two personalities without the benefit of hypnosis. But would this reinforce and encourage further dissociation? She'd stopped referring to the other parts of Christopher as ego states and was relating to each as a separate person. Had she become overly zealous, or had her experience with the personalities made her relate to them this way? I would not know until I, too, had witnessed a spontaneous dissociation. I'd seen one before in the other hospital, of course, but didn't know what I was seeing.

I had my chance in less than forty-eight hours. Ben, the psychiatric technician who had been outside the room during our sessions, called early Sunday evening to say that Christopher had been deeply depressed since Saturday afternoon. By late Sunday afternoon, Christopher was missing and James was out.

"He's causing a lot of commotion among the staff and the other patients," Ben said, "mostly because nobody knows what to do or how to talk to him. He doesn't want us to call him Christopher."

Aside from Sue's confrontation with Jackie and her talk with James, this was Christopher's only other spontaneous dissociation. All the other personalities had come out and gone back in during a hypnotherapy session with me.

Ben said James was behaving appropriately without any bizarre actions, yet the people around him were in a state of confusion, realizing the sensitivity and timidity were gone and a cold callousness was there instead.

"I'm sorry to bother you at home, but I thought you should know," Ben offered, "in case you want to talk with James—er, Christopher—before tomorrow morning."

My gosh! I thought. Now Ben is doing the same thing as Sue, relating to them as distinct persons rather than as parts of Christopher. Will the whole staff start thinking of these personalities as separate individuals?

Two hours passed, and I was unable to brush aside the idea of going to the hospital to meet James. I had to see one of the spontaneous dissociations myself. Perhaps it was even more real than when he was in a trance, I thought to myself. I told myself I would be crazy to run up to the hospital on Sunday night. But once I had made up my mind, I did not take time to do more than brush off my blue jeans, tie my hair back in a bow, and leap into my car, leaving my astounded husband caring for the children.

"Where are you going?" he shouted after me.

"To the hospital to see Christopher. I'll be home soon," I shouted back. I was glad I was already out the door so I did not have to face his reaction.

I wanted to make the best use of my time with Christopher that evening. An idea struck me, and to carry it out, I impulsively pulled into the parking lot of the local pharmacy, just as it was about to close.

Dashing to the back of the store, I scouted for the stationery section. I was looking for something James could use to write in. It had to be a notebook that looked just right. I found a nice rendition of a record book. Yes, the book exuded a sense of importance.

Arriving at the hospital, I suddenly became conscious of my appearance. I was not wearing a suit, the official "uniform" that was appropriate for Dr. LaCalle. Ah, well, I thought. We all have different parts of ourselves.

I walked up to Christopher unannounced.

My patient responded nervously and eyed me head to toe, something Christopher would never do. "What are you doing up here on a Sunday night?" he asked, half curious and half perplexed.

"Ben called me earlier to report that you have been telling everyone that you are James."

He looked away. "I should have known you wouldn't make it easy. I thought you might call—if anything. Then I could have conned you into thinking I was Christopher. You'd think everything was okay."

"Why would you want to do that?"

"Because it makes me anxious being out. I told a few people. I tried to fool you by acting like Christopher, but you knew. I came out to see how it would feel to use my real name instead of faking—letting everyone call me by his name. But it started to bug me. I'm not used to people knowing what's going on. It's like being caught . . . exposed." He looked over his shoulder as if checking to see if anyone was watching him. "I want to get out of this hallway."

I took him into a conference room, and right away James was more at ease, his behavior less constrained.

I recognized the character of James. His manner was calculated. I noticed I had spontaneously made an adaptation in my emotional frame of reference, as if I were relating to a different person. It was not quite the same feeling I had had when James was out during the trance or the one time shortly after the trance. James had become more real. He was moving about at his own command.

"Jackie is really mad at Christopher for taking off like that and leaving me in charge," he continued.

"Where is Christopher?" I asked, wondering what James meant.

"He went to the secret playroom with Timmy. He got scared and hid himself there," he said with contempt in his voice. "No one knows where it is."

"Yes, I know about the secret playroom. They can come out whenever they like. When Christopher has had a chance to rest from all of this, I'm sure he'll be back," I said, trying to plead

74

Christopher's case to James. "Is Christopher listening in right now?"

"I don't know, but I doubt it. I don't think he wants any part of what's going on."

He looked at me as if trying to integrate my appearance with what he already knew about me. "You look really different tonight. Anyway, Doc, I wanted to tell you that I've been having the strangest dreams lately. Things are starting to come back to me—things from long ago that I thought were forgotten."

This visit to the hospital was not going to be a disappointment, I thought. Then James said he remembered how he and Jackie had performed a voodoo ceremony to destroy Christopher's father.

James had shut the door to Christopher's room and barred it with a dresser. Moving the furniture back to the corners, he made space for Jackie to draw a circle on the linoleum floor. She then took a doll she had fashioned to represent Christopher's father and placed it inside a bowl. She set the doll aflame, and as they watched it burn, Jackie chanted black magic syllables while James repeatedly wished that Christopher's father would be destroyed.

I understood why he had turned away from his mother's Pentecostal teaching, but I felt sorrow that he had turned to the occult and black magic instead. James said that the voodoo worked because it was shortly thereafter that Christopher's mother returned with a boyfriend, took charge of the children, and told Christopher to order his father away. Revenge on his father was most important to him. I hated to hear that Christopher had turned to idol worship when he could have prayed to a good and loving God.

"Christopher didn't tell the old man to leave. He didn't have the guts. So I told him—and it didn't bother me," James said. "More stuff like that is coming back. I think I've been around for a lot longer than I thought. I can remember Christopher when he was only about six or seven years old."

"I'm glad the memories are returning. That's one of the things I wanted to talk to you about, and one of the reasons I came up here tonight to meet with you. I brought you a book—a book for memories—a record book for all the things you can remember from Christopher's past, all the things that come up in dreams, and all the things the others tell you. I want you to be the recorder. In a way, you'll be my co-therapist and work with me to help Christopher." James looked surprised. I wasn't backing off from him. I wasn't afraid. I was, instead, asking him to be a partner, to align with me. And I was pleased. I could see I was getting to him. "You tell me that Christopher is too sensitive. Perhaps you will be strong enough to record all the memories."

"That will be easy. Absolutely nothing bothers me." His voice was notably softer, although his words remained tough. "I don't care enough about anything to let it get to me."

"Well, in some ways that can be an asset. We can't all go around being open wounds all of the time. Sometimes, we need to keep a perspective, a sense of objectivity. When it comes to painful, frightening memories, your way of handling things may be necessary for a while until Christopher gets used to them."

"How will I keep the others from writing in the book?" There was nothing in his voice that showed a reluctance to help.

"I'm not sure. Do the best you can." It was working! James was joining up with me. "If they want to contribute something, you can let them dictate it through you. Just make sure you put a note as to who told you what. You'll be the one in charge, the one who can cope with the memories."

"You know," he said thoughtfully, "I hardly ever feel what Christopher feels. I used to be even harder on him for being so hurt all the time. Then I just started taking over for him—getting rid of people who hurt him or hurt anyone else, manipulating people until I could get them to do what I want. I don't feel guilty or embarrassed about things the way Christopher does."

I had been looking for an opening to change the subject, and this was it.

"That sort of brings me around to something I wanted to talk to you about." I paused, remembering how uncomfortable Christopher had been with the subject I was about to investigate. "Can you tell me about your sexual activity?"

James settled back in his chair and looked me straight in the eye. He grinned slyly, as if pleased that I had brought up the subject.

I had an even more distinct feeling that I was talking with someone other than Christopher. I knew that with James I would not have to mince words. My interview technique could become blunt and direct. He would give me the unvarnished truth about sexual problems.

"It's a subject that Christopher is unable to discuss with me. He becomes very embarrassed. It also seems to hurt him if I bring it up, and I don't want to upset him, so I thought I'd ask you."

"What do you want to know?" he asked.

"When Christopher goes cruising," I began, "who is usually in charge?"

"I don't know, but it isn't me," he answered flatly. "I don't have any talent at that kind of shit. Let me think. Now that I know Sissy, it's my guess it's probably her."

"Has Christopher had many bad sexual encounters?"

"Yes."

"Exactly what happens?"

"He always ends up with someone who looks all right at the start but turns out to be a real creep. If he bothers to get to know him better, it gets even worse as he finds out more about the guy. Most gays are like that anyway."

"Has Christopher ever done any dangerous sexual things?"

"Are you kidding? Him? No, he hasn't, but I have—just out of curiosity. But I've made Christopher do a couple of things that made him feel really uncomfortable."

"Like what?"

"Like bondage. I like to be tied down once in a while. But Christopher gets real upset. He starts fidgeting around and whimpering and ruins it. He doesn't know how to relax and go with it."

"Why do you think that is?"

"It reminds him of that time he was raped as a kid, I guess. That old man just wanted a blow job, and he held Christopher down real hard by the arms. Christopher doesn't remember being held down, but I do. I also remember the time the babysitter did it to him."

"A girl?"

"No. It was a teenage boy. Actually, it felt really good when he held Christopher down and dry-humped him, but Christopher didn't like it. I'm the one who's always been real sexual."

"What are Christopher's sexual tastes?"

"He likes to receive, but he doesn't like to be active. I'm the one who likes to top," he said without emotion. "I don't care if the other guy likes it or not. I just want to let him have it. Christopher? He can't even get it up when I want him to jump on someone."

"Is that when you turn on him and tell him he's a failure because he can't perform?"

"I used to, but in the last few months, I just do it myself. I just come out and take over when Christopher can't handle it."

"What kind of men does Christopher go for?"

"It's always older men—not really old, but older—who just want to get a younger guy. I like the younger ones, but I don't always have it my way."

James looked away for a second. Then he came back to me with a coy grin on his face. "I hate to tell you this, Doc, but you aren't done with us yet. There's one more of us getting ready to come out. I get the feeling he hasn't been around a long time. I haven't seen him. Sissy saw him and she told me his name is Jeremy. She said he is tall, handsome, has dark hair, and a beard."

Dark hair? Christopher is blond. And wears a beard?

I looked directly at his chin with that comment. Christopher had not shaved for nearly two weeks and was close to having a nicely tailored beard. James did not seem to notice that his face, too, was sporting a beard.

"Is Jeremy gay or straight?" I asked.

"I don't know. Sissy probably hopes he's straight. Wouldn't it be our luck—mine and Christopher's—for this good-looking, tall, dark guy to be straight?"

I looked down at my watch and was startled to find that it was after 10 P.M. I had told my husband I would be right back, and well over an hour had passed. I was courting disaster on the home front. I quickly brought our session to a close and headed toward the dark parking lot. I braced myself for the glum look on my husband's face that I was sure to find when I got home.

I had predicted correctly. His jaw was set, and he did not look up at me at first when I came in.

"Where have you been? It's almost eleven o'clock."

"I told you when I left that I was going to the hospital."

"You've been there this late? There's no need for it. You didn't *have* to go."

"No, but I *wanted* to."

"Exactly," he said with sullen anger, "without even considering your family."

I felt the blood rush to my face. I was tired, and he had pushed me too far.

"You're not back in Spain, you know, where I wouldn't be able to go out after dark without your consent!"

He sat stone-faced, without flinching. Then his words came, coldly measured. "That's not the point and you know it."

"Isn't it?" I worked to squelch the hysterical scream inside of me. "Lately I've been feeling like I have to be a rebellious child with you in order to do what I think is important. If you wouldn't act like a critical parent, maybe I wouldn't have to be fearful of what I'll find when I come home."

"Brilliant analysis, Dr. LaCalle." His voice dripped with sarcasm. "Why don't you just admit you're acting irrationally over this case. You know I don't approve of getting overly involved with your patients."

"See! There it is! That word 'approve.' Who asked you for your approval anyway?"

"Certainly you didn't. You don't seem to care at all about what I think. You're going to do what you damn well please anyway, aren't you? Well, aren't you?"

"Yes. I am. So you may as well save your breath."

I stomped my foot to punctuate the end of my sentence. Then I turned and stormed off to the bedroom. I was too hurt and angry to want to understand José's point of view. Approval. Approval. If only I *didn't* need his approval. Why did I need it?

I looked at myself in the mirrored closet doors. How pathetic! How childish I looked, sitting on the bed cross-legged with tears rolling down my cheeks. A little girl. Daddy's little girl. That's it. That's where the hurt is coming from. I always had my father's approval, no matter what I did. Now I felt empty, forsaken, without the approval of José, who always had been my biggest fan. For heaven's sake! Maybe it's not only José's approval I need. Do I really have the courage to go against all those male psychiatrists in the hospital who don't "believe in" multiple personalities either?

I fell back into my pillow. The whole thing was too much to be resolved at midnight. The following morning, I dragged myself to work, still exhausted, but determined to run my own case my own way.

James was still out. He came up to me and handed me the record book.

"I was busy last night," he said. "I didn't get much sleep."

I didn't sleep much, either, I thought to myself. How I hated going through the day feeling drowsy and irritable because of a late-night argument!

I opened the book and found five pages of writing. Several paragraphs were grouped together with two or three empty lines separating the groupings. The handwriting was different for each. Four personalities had made entries. Evidently, James was unable to prevent them from writing in the book. Each wrote a short character sketch, a sort of autobiography in brief. The content made it clear who wrote the entry. I scanned the page. No memories were listed for Ernest, Sissy, or Jackie.

I found James's entry, and I felt my stomach tighten as I read: "I remember gagging, choking. I couldn't breathe. I couldn't shout. I wanted to call my mother, but the stuff from his cock was already in my mouth."

I felt weak-kneed and sick to my stomach. Not even cold, dispassionate James could tell me that memory out loud. What a horrible way for a seven-year-old boy to be introduced to sexual behavior! I thought of something like that happening to my son, and I felt repulsion, grief, and rage well up within me.

Hadn't I been working with child sexual abuse cases for years? I told myself I must try to become less emotional about these subjects. Nonetheless, I looked at my patient with sadness in my eyes.

"James, can you tell me anything more about what you have written here?"

"I don't even remember what I wrote, or who wrote in it." He looked away from me. "I didn't seem to be able to control anything that was happening last night."

He had dissociated from the memory. He did not want to make it a part of his conscious mind. I could understand why. He would probably not open the book to read it again. I asked him only to continue to write in it and show it to me whenever he could.

I glanced again and noticed another brief entry: "I fully accept being homosexual but I cannot go along with any flaunting of affection in public." The handwriting was different.

"Who wrote this?" I asked, pointing to the lone sentence dangling unattached on the page. "Did you?"

I was still studying the differences in handwriting.

"Yes, I wrote it, but James wouldn't let me write any more. He kept tryin' to tell me it was his book."

I looked up, startled. This voice was gentle, quite unlike James's abrupt speech, and held traces of a drawl. A Southern accent? This new personality smiled at me in a friendly and amiable fashion, as if to put me at ease.

I was taken aback.

"Wait a minute! I was just talking to James. I thought I was asking James for help."

I noticed his stance had straightened. James's macho posturing had disappeared. And despite the softness of his speech, this personality held himself decisively erect. His manner was the embodiment of pride.

"I wrote it, and I thought I better own up to it. Besides, I've been wantin' to come out for a while," he said in an affable manner. "It just sort of happened."

He rubbed the neat, dark-blond beard that recently had been developing on Christopher's face. His questioning eyes gleamed as he looked down at me.

"Are you Jeremy, the one James told me about?"

"Yes, I'm Jeremy. I won't be able to stay out for long. I'm pretty new to this."

He put out the cigarette James had been smoking.

"Dirty habit he has," he said as an aside. "I've been tryin' to get Christopher to clean up his act, stop smokin'. It's not hard being gay the way he thinks it is. He really doesn't have to be antisocial, but I think a little discretion in public goes a long way. People have a bad enough impression of homosexuals to begin with."

He lifted his chin, almost as if to show off the fine, attractive beard. "He needs to get involved in gay political activities and maybe a gay church. I walked through a Gay Pride parade in San Diego just to show him how important political movements are. He has a lot to learn, and I'm tryin' to set him a good example of how to be a gay." He spoke with a sparkle in his eye.

"How long have you been around, Jeremy?"

"About four years, but I've never felt as strong as I have these last couple of months. I was around a lot over at the other hospital. Thanks to me, Christopher got to go home. At this hospital, I feel even better because one of the staff members is gay and he's really a nice, respectable guy. Then a couple other nurses have been tellin' Christopher about the local gay community groups. I really appreciate all the help I've been gettin' with Christopher."

I was about to ask Jeremy another question when he looked away. The face took on the characteristic look of someone who was pensively listening. His eyes darted back and forth and did not focus on any particular place. This expression was becoming familiar to me, a signal that a switch was about to occur.

"What's going on? What are you listening to?" I asked.

"Nothing. Nothing." His eyes narrowed. I'd seen James do that. "It's just Sissy—mad at how much attention Jeremy has been getting around here. She doesn't think staff members should encourage homosexuality."

James was back.

"Sissy's mad because everyone seems to like him so much. Jackie's mad, too. I had to come out again and not let her have control." He looked at me. Cold, controlling James again. "You know what Jackie would do right now if she had a chance?"

"No." To Jackie, I thought, Jeremy might seem like just one more authority figure. How would that rebellious teenager react? "What do you think she would do?"

"She'd probably start carving in her arms. She seems to enjoy pain—likes to see the rest of us suffer. She thinks we are the reason Christopher is screwed up. Once she slashed her wrists just to watch the blood flow. She knew she was alive when she saw the blood." He stopped to light a cigarette while he thought. "But it was also like we all wanted to feel it, feel ourselves hurt. That I don't understand. I can't let her have much control because it could really get out of hand."

James stayed out.

In some ways, it was easy to talk with James. His conversation was simple and direct. He never beat around the bush about anything. Yet I felt little empathy for him and had to work at accepting him. I began to feel the loss of Christopher, the patient I had come to know and like. There was something very likable about Christopher. I noticed that other people shared my affection for him, too.

One day went by, then another. And another. Still no Christopher. I yearned to see the warm, sheepish grin that made him seem so much like an adult version of Timmy.

5

CHRISTOPHER, WHERE ARE YOU?

On the fourth day since the appearance of James, Christopher ambled up to me wearing a flowing black plush robe with a white tuxedo collar. He looked elegant. He had shaved and showered, and was still rosy from the hot water. At first sight, I thought it might be Sissy, but when I saw the sensitive grin that looked like a grown-up Timmy, I knew that Christopher had come back.

I welcomed him happily. "Good morning, Christopher."

"Hi!" His voice was lively and chipper. I felt myself respond to his gentleness. An old friend had returned.

"You were gone quite a while. We missed you," I said sincerely, but diluted the intensity of my feelings by saying "we" instead of "I." I thought of how José would have said I was getting too emotionally involved—and letting it show. Well, I thought to myself, that's who I am, and I might as well accept it.

Christopher and I talked for a while. I enjoyed the relaxed conversation, but soon felt obliged to be more businesslike. It was my responsibility to keep the therapy focused on the issues at hand, but this responsibility, I realized, often compelled me to change the subject quickly, if not abruptly, and move on. This was one of those times when I felt pressed. An immediate issue had to do with managing his hospital stay. At the moment, I was particularly concerned about his relationship with other patients.

Christopher was acutely aware that he was different from the rest of the patients. As he got to know them, he took a few into his confidence and told them about the other personalities. But he soon discovered he wanted to down play the uniqueness of his illness. With most of them, he would reveal only that he had been feeling suicidal and depressed and had been hospitalized for that reason.

As time went by, he minimized his illness to himself, too. When he was able to get through several days without dissociating, he would begin to wonder if he was truly a multiple personality. He did not want it to be true. His self-doubts and self-recriminations would return. He'd pull me aside and say, "This doesn't seem like it can be real. Maybe I made the whole thing up."

Then, later, under stress, he was only too aware of the "others."

"Sometimes I feel as if I could con the world," he told me. "I give people exactly what they want to see and hear."

What Christopher said of himself was partially true. He did have a dramatic nature. He was overly sensitive to others and attempted to please them as a means of gaining acceptance, and, ultimately, obtaining his own ends.

By being helpless, he structured his relationships to capture attention and motivate people to please him or rescue him. Like the coy and provocative hysteric female, Christopher had a quality that said, "I am a frail and fragile person and I am at your mercy."

Christopher was in a constant search for gratification of his needs for affection and attention. Each new romance in his life filled those needs and held out the possibility of giving him the strength he lacked in himself. He was constantly disappointed in his lovers, however, and like the true hysteric, became doubtful that any man of his choice could be strong enough for him. When he got involved with a man, he was looking for the idealized man to save him, but no lover was ever capable of giving him the self-worth he needed.

I kept this in mind as I mulled over Christopher's case. I spent hours trying to think of every angle.

After a few weeks of hospitalization, The Watcher was still an unnamed, and not fully defined, ego state. I was content to think that The Watcher was not a true personality but simply served one specific ego function—recording memories.

I remained exceedingly puzzled about how to approach Christopher's treatment. For certain, I had only scratched the surface of what had happened to him during his childhood that could have caused this most unusual disorder. From the clues Christopher had already given me, I guessed that more trauma was buried deep in his subconscious and that the missing years between ages four and ten undoubtedly contained the important information. Something more terrible than being molested by his father's friend must have forced him to split into so many personalities.

In my continuing search of the professional literature, I was disappointed by not being able to find the answers I needed. Most of what had been written was merely documentation that multiple personality existed and specific case descriptions explaining how the personality splits came about. Practically nothing had been written on how to work therapeutically with the patient, and no one treatment had proven better than any other. I was stumped. I needed something that would help me know how to interact with each of the personalities and how to get them to interact with each other.

In my training, I had been taught to deal with only one conscious mind and one subconscious mind within an individual. Nowhere was I taught to treat co-conscious minds within the same patient.

Most importantly, I had to know how to manage my patient, how to keep him from harming himself or someone else. Nothing I read told me what I could do, for example, to contain Jackie when she became destructive, or to keep James from persuading Christopher to kill himself. Nothing told me what kind of relationship I should have with Timmy—or any of them, for that matter.

I became terribly confused about what to do with Timmy. Maternal instincts and child psychology texts had helped me raise my son Eddie, but with Timmy—a child within a man—I had to find something more. I finally found one article that provided some guidelines on actual psychotherapy with the different personalities. The authors emphasized not treating each personality as an autonomous entity, but only as a dissociated side of the total person. But with Timmy, this was especially hard, maybe impossible, to do. And how could I gain trust if I remained clinically distant with Timmy? The articles I read caused me to feel I had already made the wrong move with him. I could not undo what I had done, so I decided to take a chance and stick with what I had begun.

I was chagrined to realize how accustomed I had been to going to José for help on other cases. Now I was at a loss because my husband—my best resource—could not and would not help me. With a more ordinary case, I might have had plenty of opportunities to seek help from other professionals. Instead, I was left with articles that couldn't speak to me about my questions.

The psychiatrists who had patients on the same unit knew all about Christopher. They couldn't help but know because of the talk. Their patients reported experiences with Christopher. The nurses talked about him at staff meetings. Because of the psychiatrists' awareness of the case, I *might* have had lots of opportunities to request a consultation and receive helpful advice. I got none.

One afternoon, Dr. Valentine sat down across from me at the lunch table. The doctors' dining room was almost empty, making it easy to carry on a quiet conversation away from others. He is such a nice man, I thought, as he smiled at me pleasantly. As far as I was concerned, far too many psychiatrists knew about the trouble I was having with Christopher, but I didn't mind that Dr. Valentine knew. He was a nonjudgmental person, very supportive in nature.

"I hear you have your hands full, Trula." He was giving me an opening.

"I certainly do!" I started in enthusiastically, fully expecting to have a sympathetic ear. But as I talked, he became incredulously silent. No helpful ideas were offered. There was never even an empathetic "I know how it feels." He sat helplessly in front of me while I struggled with my intense need to talk, to find answers. I noticed that my voice had reached a crescendo; I could sense he was dubious and uncomfortable. Dr. Valentine had retreated.

Then he changed the subject. "Have you gone sailing lately?"

"No, I haven't had the time." My voice trailed off.

At least he wasn't condescending, I thought. Not like Dr. Hoffman.

"How do you know you didn't create those personalities?" Dr. Hoffman asked me when we were writing in the charts at the nurses' station.

I was taken aback. Doubts flooded me as I searched for a way to explain that this was not something I could have induced in Christopher.

"I saw marked shifts in his personality during his first hospitalization," I answered. "But I could not account for them. I saw them as extreme changes in mood and manner, but I could not find an appropriate diagnosis for him."

"Maybe he's manic-depressive and those were mood swings you saw."

I felt insulted. I wasn't going to explain how foolishly simplistic I thought his comment was.

"He reported hearing a voice," I went on, ignoring his statement, "yet he was clearly not schizophrenic or psychotic."

"Manic psychosis, probably."

He wasn't listening, but I continued hopefully. "Paula Reynolds went through a diagnostic checklist and verified all the symptomology. Hypnosis was used after all signs pointed toward multiple personality." I wondered if Paula would have had a better come-back for him. I'd have to ask her.

He was quiet. Then he smiled patronizingly and turned back to writing in the chart. I would have preferred an adversary instead of the silence I received. Please, I thought, not more silence to shut me out.

After that conversation, I went back to my library search to see if multiple personalities had ever been hypnotically induced. A couple of researchers had claimed to have produced multiple personalities through hypnotic suggestion. I rejected their conclusions, though, because I knew that Christopher's personalities had more aspects to them than did the "personalities" reported to have been created through hypnosis. I found the researchers' definition of a personality extremely one-dimensional and artificial in comparison. I smugly made a copy of the research articles and kept them in my arsenal of rebuttals.

Another friend and colleague, Dr. Smith, was curious enough to ask, "What created all the personalities?"

"I don't know," I had to tell him. "Everything I know about my patient so far does not add up to enough trauma to cause it. The only thing I can assume is that he has no memory of something that happened to him when he was very young."

He looked at me skeptically, without saying a word. Why don't I give up? I asked myself. I was wasting my time and effort explaining to people who weren't really trying to understand.

As the days with Christopher passed, my life lost its routine. Preoccupied with this case, my mind was deluged with jumbled thoughts and feelings. My thoughts were so confused by him that I often paid no attention to what was going on around me. I began to forget the everyday tasks and details of life. So I started making lists for everything from groceries to phone calls, to make up for my absent-mindedness.

Each time I spoke with James or Jackie or one of the others, I felt fragmented. Each mental shift, each instantaneous emotional adjustment, disjointed my own sense of reality. There were sessions with Christopher in which I spoke to four different personalities within ten minutes. In some instances, the shifts were so confusing I was not sure who I was addressing.

I took up reading Thigpen and Cleckley's *Three Faces of Eve*. I had put off reading it for three weeks, hoping to get my own unadulterated impressions of Christopher before reading any detailed case studies. When I came to the passage in *Eve* wherein the authors claim they had postponed reading other doctors' impressions, I smiled with the recognition that their motives were the same as my own. Unfortunately, I also felt cheated that they had not divulged more of their own personal responses. I was looking for more that would help me comprehend what was happening to me personally in this therapeutic relationship. I felt alone with Christopher. Except for Paula Reynolds, I had nowhere to turn for suggestions or understanding. But as good a friend as Paula had been to me, I couldn't take advantage of her by calling too frequently. I didn't want to become a burden to her.

I knew someday it would all be different. I would have more answers. I would be able to look back on all this without the topsy-turvy feeling I was now experiencing. But meanwhile, I had to cope with the turmoil of my uncertainty.

Part of me was always with Christopher. Christopher was not "another man" in my life, but he may as well have been for all the thought-time he occupied. I was captive. And I became defensive, fearing I was not behaving professionally.

Christopher's name became well known in our office. He had created so much turmoil at the hospital that calls were always coming in from either Christopher himself or hospital staff members. As soon as Christopher's name was mentioned, I could see my husband bristle.

"Your patient kept calling you at the office this morning while you were out," José said one night at dinner. "The secretary told me that my 'competition' was calling you. What do you think about that? Even she notices how overly involved you've become."

"I think," I said sarcastically, "I would like to have a secretary who used more discretion about her flippant remarks."

José pursed his lips, and pushed away from the table. "See? You've become so defensive, I can't even say anything about that case anymore," he pointed out emphatically. "You can talk about your other cases in your customary way, but with this one you jump as soon as I mention his name."

"I jump?" I countered with annoyance. "I thought I was the one who wasn't supposed to mention this case because you didn't want to hear about it. You didn't want me to bring my work home with me."

"You've had other difficult cases before, and we've sat down and discussed them," he reminded me. "I ask you for consultations, too, don't I?"

"I can't talk about this one with you." I was stymied.

"Isn't that because you don't want to hear what I have to say?" His voice held a challenge in it.

"Partly. I know what it's like to go through this and you don't. All you have to say about this case makes me feel like I'm being played for a fool, like I don't know what's real and what's not real." I could feel myself getting more defensive. "I get enough of that kind of response elsewhere. I don't need it when I come home, too."

"Then you don't really want to discuss it." He slapped his

hand on his knee. "You want me to agree with everything you say about it."

Now he is being unreasonable, I thought. "No. I don't want you to agree with everything I have to say about it." I worked to control the tone of my voice. "But I want you to support the basic premise that what is happening is real, and then our discussion could help me find ways to manage this case." My words had come out stiff and formal.

"I'm best at being a devil's advocate. You know that," he said patronizingly, "but you can't seem to listen to any other point of view."

I contained my anger as best I could. "Your point of view is that Christopher's disorder doesn't exist."

"I didn't say that. There's just something about this that seems pretty theatrical."

"It's no hoax!" I shouted, losing control.

"Then," he said, maintaining his customary cool manner during an argument, "how come you didn't notice it sooner? It sounds fishy to me."

"I did notice it, sort of," I faltered. "But I misdiagnosed it. Multiple personality is often misdiagnosed—schizophrenia, borderline personality, manic-depression—you name it," I said, trying to defend myself.

"And the personalities only come out under hypnosis?" he asked dubiously.

"No. They also come out spontaneously, and my patient is unaware of it. He has memory lapses, or 'blackouts,' that he's simply grown accustomed to over the years. He ignores the fact that he loses track of minutes, hours, or even days."

He wanted a simple, persuasive statement, but it was not that easy to explain.

"I'm not convinced." His skepticism grew. "He's sure getting a lot of attention for this, isn't he? Wouldn't that by itself encourage him to make up these personalities, especially if he's got an hysterical nature to him?"

"I've thought of that." Maybe now was my chance to convince him. "Even Christopher has thought of that. He's said to me that he thinks he could con the world because he always knows how to give people what they want. He's said that he thinks he has a very manipulative side to him. He's also said that the whole thing seems so unreal that he feels he must be making it up." My words came out rapid fire.

"Sounds to me like he's telling you he's making it up and that you're a fool for believing him."

He was hitting below the belt. I felt doubly wounded—for what he said, and because he was using such a tactic.

"I know it sounds that way," I said, biting my tongue to keep from escalating the argument further. "But you have to know him to understand what I am seeing. No one could be that good an actor. No one could portray the terror I have seen in his eyes. I've seen him writhe in pain and shake with fear. No one could be so consistent with the story. Each personality is complete and unique and consistent in personality traits in every way. The more I get to know about him, the more I know this is true."

I'd spoken my piece, stated my case in the best way I knew how.

"Now this is what really bothers me," José responded. "Look how intense you are! Doesn't that tell you something is wrong here? You never get that intense about your other patients."

I threw my hands up in the air and sighed with total frustration. "I'm intense because this case is intense." I was disappointed at how shrill my voice had become. "And because I'm struggling so hard to try to explain to you what I have been experiencing."

"No. It's more than that." His mouth twisted wryly—that damned familiar expression! "You've had Christopher on your mind every waking moment. You're constantly preoccupied with him."

My stomach tightened with this new side to José's argument. This was another blow below the belt. I felt accused of having some sort of love affair. Was he jealous? "He's my patient," I said firmly. "My *gay* patient." I emphasized the word, pausing to give him time to catch my implication. "I think about him so much because it takes every bit of my energy to understand what is happening to him. It's so new to me that I have to process all the information over and over again to try to digest it and plan my next move."

"Don't tell me," he said, spacing out each of the three words emphatically, "that it's an intellectual exercise. You've become passionate about it. I say there's a lot of countertransference

92

going on here . . . treating him as if he were a significant person in your life. You know that's not professional—or therapeutic. You're not handling it well."

He squared himself off in a broad stance, arms crossed tightly over his chest.

"I'll agree that there's a lot of countertransference," I said. "I have been treating him differently, getting emotional about it." I knew I had to control my frustration and anger, and I reluctantly acknowledged José's reasoning. "You're right about that, and I have to be on top of my feelings." I had to bring this conversation back entirely to a level of reason. "But I'm not sure I agree with your statement that the way I'm handling the countertransference is neither professional nor therapeutic. For me, that's still an open issue. Certainly, Christopher didn't have an adequate rapport with me the last time he tried to kill himself," I said, unable to keep the pleading out of my voice. "And yet, I had conducted myself very objectively and coolly with him, and he respected my clinical skills. I know that I will be criticized for the intense relationship I have with Christopher. Maybe the next time I have a multiple personality patient—if ever—I won't feel so intensely."

He tried to interrupt, but I pushed on. "I also know that any therapist who has had a successful therapeutic relationship with a multiple personality patient has been criticized for personal involvement with the patient."

I jumped up from the dinner table and went to my desk. "Here, listen to this. It's a criticism of Sybil's psychiatrist, Cornelia Wilbur, that was published in an Australian medical journal the year after the film *Sybil* came out. It says, 'The psychiatrist tended to behave as if she were a good mother. Despite being warned about this by a colleague early in the film, the warning seemed to go unheeded.' " I paused for effect. "And that was written about the most respected psychiatrist in this field!"

José folded his arms over his chest in a stubborn confirmation of his stance. "I've had a long day at the office," he said. "The last thing I want to do is to come home and fight about a patient."

"I didn't realize we were fighting." I was denying it. "I thought we were just disagreeing."

He seemed ready to calm down. "Well, your voice has been pretty high pitched."

"You're right." I was only too ready to smooth this over. "I do feel defensive and agitated. I've got to settle down about this case." I tried to lighten things up a little. "Be glad we aren't two trial attorneys married to each other," I quipped.

Nevertheless, inside I was still hurt, wounded. It was hard for me to realize that José did not have the same interest in something that was so important to me. This was so unlike all our married years together up until now.

Riddled with so many uncertainties, I was more pleased than ever that I had tape recorded the sessions with Christopher. And I kept on with it in anticipation of the meetings with Bob Slater and Paula Reynolds that would start within a week. Playing the tapes back to myself, I made notes on interventions with Christopher—things I might say or do the next session. I took copious notes, too, after each session, and soon began to keep a log of my own feelings and reactions as well. Since I had no one to turn to regularly, the writing in my log helped me cope with the emotions. And I gained some objectivity by seeing my feelings on paper.

The day of the meeting I had been so anxiously anticipating finally arrived, and I walked into Bob's office full of excitement and apprehension. He stood up and came over to greet me with a warm grin and an embracing handshake. For me, Bob represented one of those silver-haired psychiatric sages that, earlier, I had been looking to rescue me. From his confident look, I knew he would be able to help me. He inquired about José, how we were both doing. He wanted to know if this case was putting any strain on our relationship. I confessed that we were having problems. "I've always like José," Bob said, "but I thought he might have trouble accepting a phenomenon that doesn't readily lend itself to reason."

Thankful that he understood, I filled him in briefly on the time since he and my husband had worked together. I turned to greet Paula, who had been watching Bob and me renew our old friendship. She pressed my hand warmly in response to my greeting.

"Before we start," I said, "Christopher said to say hello to you, Paula. He knows I'll be consulting in depth with you." I was feeling protective of Christopher's right to confidentiality even though I had his permission to speak freely and to tell Bob and Paula the details of his history.

I related how I had been struggling on my own for the past month. Now that I had found my sanctuary, it seemed to me that the tension eased from my body for the first time in weeks. Bob and Paula clearly understood what I had been feeling.

As Paula began to discuss her own case with Bob and me, we compared notes on the similar dilemmas of each of them. Mostly, I wanted to know how to work toward the integration of the personalities. With the enthusiasm of a novice, I didn't realize I was asking the most difficult question of all. Paula and Bob were not sure exactly what occurred at the time of integration or how it worked. Yet over a period of two and one-half years, Paula's patient went from twenty-two personalities to three.

"How did that happen?" I asked Paula.

"Usually, my patient would announce a fusion after the fact that one of them had merged into another and was no longer distinguishable as a separate entity, although that personality had not really 'died,' so to speak."

"From what I've read so far," I said, "there seem to be four or five ways to get them down to one personality. One way is to try to get the main personality or original personality to take over. Then there was the outcome that was supposed to have worked for Eve and her three personalities. A fourth personality, Evelyn, who represented a fusion, was the one who supposedly took over the body. Apparently, that didn't work either because Eve later wrote a book claiming she had thereafter developed more than twenty personalities. And I'm still not sure how the final integration occurred with Sybil. Then, there's the idea that a doctor can force integration or fusion through hypnotically suggesting that the personalities simply are no longer needed and may disappear. But I can just see how that would work with Christopher. I can hear Jackie or James yelling at me, 'Oh, no, you don't, you're not going to get rid of me that easily!' "

Bob had been sitting listening to me, with his head bent. He looked up at me with a devilish grin and added, "You forgot Dr. Allison's approach—exorcism. He vanquishes the evil spirit that has possessed the body."

"Are you kidding?" I asked, dumbfounded. "I haven't read about that one yet."

"I'll loan you his book, *Minds in Many Pieces*. Actually, he makes several good points in the book, and he probably under-stands as much about multiple personality as anyone, but his religious background put him onto the idea of spirit possession. He's taken a lot of flack about it since the book came out."

"I can see why. I'm a religious person myself, but I could never buy that concept."

As our discussion went on, I could see that neither Paula nor Bob had the hoped-for answers.

"You know, Bob," I said, "the treatment approach I find most difficult is that of getting all of the personalities to work together cooperatively. How do I keep Jackie from recklessly running the car off the road? How do I keep James from trying to get Chris-topher to kill himself? How do I keep Christopher in the hospital when Sissy says she's going to flee in her car—at ninety miles per hour—because she is bored in that place?"

"It's hard enough to keep a regular patient from doing any one of those things, isn't it?" he remarked sympathetically.

"You can say that again! What if I can't get any of them to cooperate?"

"Remind them that one of them would end up killing all of them, including Timmy, whom they all protect."

"When Jackie is out," I said thoughtfully, "she sometimes says that she is more powerful than any of them. No, that's not true. James came out to keep Jackie in control. James seems to be the strongest one."

"You might consider getting one of the others to call you on the telephone when James or any other personality is in a life-threatening situation."

"I could probably get Timmy to call me for help, but he's so small and powerless that I don't know if he could get out if the others were ganging up against him."

"Tell him to turn to either Jackie or James for help in making the call, depending on which of them is in a cooperative mood at that point in time."

"This is all so complicated. Why is it I still feel that I'm pio-neering in some dangerous and unknown territory, even though the first multiple personality case was documented a century and a half ago?"

"There are lots of us therapists who need help with these cases," Bob said. "I've been getting a few calls here at the university. What would you two think of expanding our consultation into a study group for therapists of multiples?"

I realized that Paula and Bob had spent hundreds of hours in the study of multiple personality. Between the two of them, they had personally come to know almost all of the people in the country who had had experience in the treatment of this disorder. Because of their continuous study and their nationwide network of colleagues, they knew as much about multiple personality as anyone in the country.

"In my opinion," Paula suggested, "the intensity of the therapeutic relationship requires that every therapist treating a multiple have a way to keep from overstepping the boundaries of the therapist-patient relationship."

"We can help each other maintain objectivity and support each other in coping with the many problems treating these patients," I added.

"Then we'll begin next month," Bob concluded. "At least with some definite plans for starting up."

It turned out to be just what I needed. In the weeks to come, the harmonious atmosphere of the monthly study group turned out to be in direct contrast to the everyday reality I faced at the hospital.

The tension among the psychiatric staff at the hospital was mounting—Christopher's illness was so out of the ordinary that patients and staff alike did not know how to react to it. Each time a new personality came out, albeit infrequently, a crisis occurred on the psychiatric unit. I was distressed at having to resolve staff conflicts, and I was growing resentful that even more of my time was required at the hospital to take care of these problems—valuable time that I could have been spending with Christopher. But I could see that he wasn't to blame. Even though Christopher avoided situations that would put him or one of the personalities on display, it was inevitable that some dissociation would take place in front of other people.

The initial response to Christopher was one of fear. Other patients began to ask, "Is he dangerous?" They did not understand why the heavy tranquilizers that they were taking would not benefit Christopher. When they saw what was happening to him, they classified it as "real craziness." They began to avoid him as if his sickness were contagious.

The staff did nothing to alleviate the fear among the patients because they were having trouble coping with their own anxieties. During one group therapy session, James came out in his usual forceful and cold manner, nearly throwing for a loop several members of the therapy group, including the therapist, Sam, who was leading the session.

Afterward, Sam—shaken and slightly hostile—came to me. "How am I supposed to manage this?" he asked. "I already have eight members in that group. Now with Christoper there, I have the other seven plus his six! It's more than I can handle."

Christopher was not to blame. He did what he could to keep calm and reduce the risk of dissociating. He interacted in the group as little as possible to prevent discomforting feelings from coming up. But he knew he would stir up more conflicts if he refused to go to the group.

I knew Sam was stunned by seeing such a clear-cut splitting of the personalities, but he did not want to admit how unsettling it was to observe the switch from one personality to another. Sam distrusted his own sense of reality for a moment, and he found this to be emotionally alarming. Every staff member who had been able to witness the transition from one personality to the next was shocked by it. When they communicated the experience to other staff members, they often did so in a superficial way so as to mask their own sense of surprise and inadequacy. However, since the information about Christopher was passed around in this fashion, those who had never witnessed the switching could not begin to comprehend its impact or nature. The staff members who were not directly involved with Christopher teased and joked about Christopher's personalities, rather than admit their discomfort.

The staff inevitably became divided between believers and nonbelievers. The believers wanted to talk with me at every opportunity. They were interested in learning and often expressed appreciation for an opportunity to witness such a rare mental disorder. Some nonbelievers thought I had misdiagnosed Christopher and that he was, in fact, suffering from something else. Other nonbelievers thought he was attention-seeking, malingering, and theatrical, or that Christopher had read enough books to feign the illness. Nonbelievers were gravely afraid of being manipulated or of having this patient play an elaborate joke on them.

The believers grew defensive with the nonbelievers and soon tired of constantly having to counter the skepticism. The nonbelievers withdrew, not wanting to be part of such nonsense. They were sure that Christopher's behavior was a conscious manipulation over which he had complete control—a way to avoid taking responsibility for his own behavior.

I tried, sometimes in vain, to explain that the dissociation was a psychic defense, outside Christoper's conscious control. I explained how uncomfortable Christopher felt when he lost track of time or found himself in situations or places without knowing how he got there. I was convinced that Christopher—or any other multiple—would never knowingly choose such a chaotic, dangerous, frightening way of life. Why would someone choose to suffer this way? I made an analogy to the typical emotional defenses we all have such as avoidance, rationalization, and denial. I told them that if any of them were under stress or under attack, they would begin to use their most familiar defenses as a means of self-protection. Yet, they would not consciously have to say to themselves, "Okay, now I'm going to rationalize, and then I'm going to deny." They would automatically put blame on others, deny their own faults, or try to escape from unpleasantness whenever they could not immediately cope with a situation.

I went on to explain that over a hundred cases of multiple personality had been documented in the professional literature. Yet despite this documentation most clinicians were taught that the disorder is exceedingly rare. Therefore, fewer cases were found because no one was prepared for them. Physicians and psychologists who "believe in" the disorder tend to find it more often. But that does not mean that certain doctors are creating the disorder.

At the same time I was trying to gain cooperation from the nonbelievers, I was advising the believers to use caution with Christopher. I told this faction that the names of the other personalities were to be used only as labels and that no personality was to be accepted as having autonomy. They were not to take sides with one personality over another. I solicited their support in helping me to teach Christopher slowly that each personality was really a part of him, and not separate from him.

Resentment grew among those who did not want to allow Christopher the extra time or help he needed. The feeling among the older, more staid nurses was that therapy was to be meted out in more or less equal quantities. Christopher, they asserted, was demanding too many special favors. Sue, they said, was getting too involved because she insisted on maintaining the one-to-one relationship she had developed with Christopher.

As more and more psychiatrists and psychologists on the staff began to get wind of what was happening on the sixth-floor unit, it soon became clear to me that I would have to address the doctors' concerns directly. As I had anticipated, Dr. Bernstein, who had been overseeing the staff's work with Christopher, made an official appointment to talk with me.

He sat behind his massive desk, drumming his pencil on a table as I entered his office. "There seems to be some concern about your patient," he said in a tone that implied he was understating the situation

"Yes," I said. "I'm aware that the unit is in turmoil over Christopher." I was suddenly feeling like I had just been called into the school principal's office for being disruptive in class. "I'm doing the best I can to manage the situation."

I hated the way I had to bolster myself and try not to be intimidated by him.

"Have you had a meeting with the nursing staff to work out the problems?" He peered up at me over the top of his bifocals. I nervously shifted my weight from one foot to the other as I stood before his scrutinizing look.

"We've had the regular staff meetings, plus other more informal get-togethers to discuss specific issues. Unfortunately, I don't have the answers for all of the questions. I'm trying to keep the staff from becoming divided and to encourage more cooperation," I said. I knew I sounded apologetic. I didn't want to take that tone, but I couldn't altogether avoid fulfilling the expectations dictated by Bernstein's manner. "The problem seems to be one of mounting anxiety, almost hysteria, on the unit."

"So I've heard. It's also taking up too much of the staff time and distracting from the needs of the other patients," he said—predictably, I thought. "The other doctors are complaining."

Since I knew he would say what he did, I was prepared with a solution. I had no intention of being caught off guard. "The other doctors have been left in the dark, and I think it would alleviate the situation if we could have a meeting among ourselves."

"Someone on the medical staff did ask if Dr. Reynolds would be willing to come to one of our psychiatric committee meetings and do a presentation on multiple personality." He left off with a questioning tone, a hint that he wanted me to take action.

"That would be very helpful. Thank you for suggesting it," I said, pretending I had not already thought of the idea. He expected deference. Working in a man's world, I was walking the line between determination and defiance. The latter only caused trouble.

"A few of the nurses could attend also," I continued, pushing the limits for the sake of the staff. I paused and waited for him to comment. He was silent as if nothing more needed to be said. "I'll get in touch with Dr. Reynolds and see what I can arrange."

I came away from my encounter with Dr. Bernstein feeling extremely burdened. Not only was I supposed to treat a rare mental disorder that I was only beginning to understand, but I was also supposed to be the mediator of a discordant psychiatric team. Now I had to take on this new assignment: help educate and inform the other doctors.

I knew I would have to put up an even better front to mask my insecurities and behave as if I felt confident about what I was doing. I knew that if I failed, I stood the chance of being ostracized among my colleagues or asked to have my patient transferred elsewhere. And I longed to be able to go home to a husband who was on my side. Like the divisiveness at the hospital, there was a divisiveness in my home. I had no place to rest.

In spite of all the turmoil, Christopher continued to make progress. This was my sole consolation. The suicidal feelings were no longer present and, increasingly, he had periods free of depression. Soon he was allowed the same privileges as the other patients, and he went to the group outings and was able to leave the unit for short periods to take a walk or go to a nearby store for a pack of cigarettes.

As Christopher began to feel better and was no longer a suicidal risk, he would soon be given a pass to go home for a few hours or even the weekend. Since he would eventually have to be discharged from the hospital, Dr. Swenson and I knew we would have to give him increased privileges in order to help him readjust to his life outside the hospital. I had some vague apprehensions but nothing I could put my finger on. Christopher seemed to be doing well enough.

When Christopher's friends Diane and Sylvia invited him to a Saturday night dinner at their home, I thought it would be a good opportunity for him to try a six-hour pass. He could leave the hospital at three o'clock and be in by nine. He wanted to stop by his apartment to check on his mail and then go to join his friends, with whom he was likely to feel at ease and secure. Jerry Swenson agreed this was a good opportunity for Christopher and wrote the order for the pass without hesitation. Christopher left on Saturday at three o'clock.

I'd gone to bed early Saturday night, feeling guilty for leaving José and the kids in front of the television, but I was completely exhausted from the previous week. I was getting hopelessly behind on household chores. Maybe I could tackle a closet or clothing repairs on Sunday afternoon, I thought as I fell asleep.

A call from the hospital woke me up at 10:00 P.M. after the rest of the household had gone to sleep.

"I'm sorry to disturb you, Dr. LaCalle," said the nurse, "but we thought you should know that Christopher never signed in after his pass."

What! Fear clutched me. Just like a mother, my first thought was that Christopher had been hurt—or had hurt himself. I hurriedly searched through the telephone list that I kept at home, but I did not have the number for Christopher's friends Diane and Sylvia.

Then the phone rang again. It was Christopher's roommate Luke, calling through my exchange.

"Dr. LaCalle," Luke began, "I just called the hospital and they said I should call you." His usually officious tone was anxious. "I kept waiting and waiting for Christopher at the apartment. He never showed up. Finally I got worried and called the hospital to see if he was there." Luke's words were rushed, frenzied. "I've kept in touch with Diane and Sylvia. He hasn't been there either."

Be logical, I told myself. "I haven't heard anything from him,

Luke." I tried to keep my voice calm, hoping to mitigate his anxiety. "It's too early to do anything but wait."

"Well, if you hear from him, will you give me a call?"

"Sure. I have your number."

I hung up and went back to bed, but, of course, I couldn't sleep. I listened to the sounds of José's breathing. He was awake. Damn! He needed his rest, too. I got out of bed again after half an hour and went to the phone to call Luke. I had decided to ask him if he would take a drive around the small beach city where they lived to see if Christopher's car was at any of the local hangouts. I let the phone ring several times, but there was no answer. Then I realized that I had forgotten to get Diane and Sylvia's phone number from him.

Now I was stuck.

Angry that I had placed myself in such a powerless position, I could not go back to sleep. I went into the kitchen and turned on the light. A glance at the clock told me it was 10:45. The night was still young. I poured some water into a cup and put it in the microwave to heat up for tea.

I stood in the kitchen and tried to figure out what could have happened to Christopher. Then I remembered that he had mentioned a birthday party that was being held by one of his acquaintances on the same night. He'd said he was glad he had an excuse not to attend. Harvey, the man who was holding the party, was a rich but shady character who was heavily into drugs. Christopher was wise enough to know that it was better that he not attend the party. Instead, he was looking forward to a quiet dinner with his closest and most supportive friends, Diane and Sylvia.

Then I also remembered that Sissy had been restless earlier in the week, saying that she could not stand that boring hospital much longer. Could Sissy have taken over and gone to the party? No. That did not make sense. The party did not start until later, and Christopher would have already been at Diane and Sylvia's house. Conceivably, he could have decided not to stop off at home to check the mail and, perhaps, did not realize that Luke was expecting to see him. But all of the personalities liked Diane and Sylvia. Timmy, Ernest, and Jackie were especially eager to see them. Where could Christopher have gone at three o'clock in the afternoon?

I began to get fidgety and restless from straining to put the clues together. I propped my feet up on the sofa and sipped the chamomile tea I had just made, hoping it would settle my stomach.

The phone rang and I jumped. I could hear José grumble and roll over as I got up to catch the phone in the studio next to our bedroom. It was my exchange.

"Dr. LaCalle, a girl named Diane just called. She said to tell you that they went out with Luke to look for Christopher."

"Did she leave her number?"

"No, she seemed to be in a hurry."

Damn! I'm stuck again, I thought. At least the three of them had thought about checking the local hangouts. Keeping my fingers crossed that they would find him, I settled back on the sofa and turned on the television to distract myself.

The next time the phone rang, I dove for the receiver, hoping to hear that the threesome had picked up Christopher.

"Dr. LaCalle," said the answering-service voice, "I have Christopher Kincaid on the line." Pause. "He says he has to speak to you."

Christopher. Yes! Please!

"Put him through," I ordered breathlessly.

The voice on the other end of the line was weak and shaky. "I don't know how I got here," he said tremulously. "I know where I am, but I don't know how I got here."

I listened intently. I could barely hear him.

"I don't know where my car is. The last I remember, it was three-thirty."

It was now 11:15.

"Where are you now, Christopher?"

"I'm on the coast highway next to the Safeway store," he answered with great effort.

"What's the phone number? What's the number on the phone where you are calling?" I asked slowly and distinctly.

"It's not on the phone. It doesn't have one."

He sounded as if he were shivering.

"Do you have your jacket?"

"No. I'm cold. I don't know what happened to my jacket."

"Diane just called me. Luke was very upset that you didn't come by the apartment this afternoon. He called the hospital,

104

and he called me. He and Diane and Sylvia went out looking for you." I found myself keeping my language slow and simple. Christopher was having a hard time concentrating. "I'm going to call Diane, Christopher, and if she is back at home I will tell her to come and get you and take you back to the hospital."

"Okay," he replied feebly.

"What is Diane's number? Do you remember?"

"9 . . . 9 . . . 3 . . . 14 . . . 92," he recited, his voice fading into the distance.

"993-1492," I repeated. "Is that right?" I could hear a barely audible confirmation. "How many dimes do you have?"

"Enough for two calls."

"Save enough to call me again if you have to," I instructed. "Use the rest to call Diane to explain to her where you are. Wait two minutes and then call Diane. Stay where you are, Christopher. Don't go anywhere. Don't wander off. Diane will come and pick you up. Call Diane in two minutes. Got that?"

"Stay here. Call Diane," he repeated.

"Fine. Hang up now."

I dialed the number Christopher gave me, hoping he had given it correctly. The phone rang several times without answer. I was about to hang up when Diane answered, sounding winded.

"Oh, Dr. LaCalle! The phone was ringing as we were coming in the door," Diane explained. "We didn't find Christopher."

"I know. Christopher just called me from a pay phone. He's at the Safeway store on the coast highway."

"Which one?"

"There are two?" It had not occurred to me that such a beach town could have two Safeway stores on the same highway. "Oh, dear," I said, feeling foolish. "Well, he said he recognized it so it must be one he passes frequently," I offered.

"Then it must be the one near Coral Bay," Diane concluded.

"I told him to call you in two minutes. You can get a further description when he does," I proposed. "Please go and pick him up. He must get back to the hospital. If he's lost his car, he is probably in no condition to drive. I'd appreciate it if you could take him back to the hospital." I hoped she'd consent. "If you can't find him, I'll have to call the police."

"Okay. I'll hang up and wait five minutes for his call. If he hasn't called by then, I'll go and look for him at the Safeway where I think he is."

I immediately called the hospital to make sure that they would receive him when he came in. I rushed to finish the call, knowing that Diane or Christopher might be trying to get through to me again.

My husband moaned loudly from the bedroom. The ringing of the phone was keeping him awake. "What's all this about?" he called to me. I was afraid to tell him the whole story.

"It's about Christopher," I said, half apologetically and half defensively. I could hear him swearing into his pillow. I wished José could be more patient with all of this, but I reminded myself that he had a right to his sleep and his privacy. I closed the bedroom door tightly, hoping he would fall asleep, but I knew the phone would probably keep him awake. I waited for it to ring again.

And it did—instantly.

"Dr. LaCalle, I have Christopher Kincaid on the line again."

"Christopher?"

"Yesss."

"Did you call Diane?"

"No . . . I forgot."

My stomach sank. He was completely disoriented. I might have to call the police, although I didn't want to because he would be frightened if the police came to pick him up.

"Christopher, are you across the street from Coral Bay?"

"Yes. I just can't remember. I can't remember what happened," he stammered. "This has never happened before."

I was thinking to myself that it *had* happened before, but he was never so aware of it. Nor did he ever have so much at stake. He had to get back to the hospital, and he knew it.

"I'm out later than my pass," he said fearfully. "They've gotten me into trouble. I might be discharged. Those are the rules. They've really done it now. They've gotten me into trouble."

I wondered if Christopher's ability to communicate with the others was still intact, or if the amnesia barrier had returned. "Who did it, Christopher?" I asked, trying to test the limits of his awareness. "Was it Sissy?"

"I don't know. But I had a feeling they would do this." The fear in his voice was an indicator that he was not trying to shirk responsibility for being out late. Nor was he able to communicate with the others.

"I thought of that, too," I said. I was kicking myself for not putting two and two together ahead of time. "We certainly had enough clues."

I surely would not have let him out on a pass if I had been smarter. Now, I was almost certain that wild, irresponsible Sissy had started all this.

"Well, let's just talk awhile as you wait for Diane to come and get you." I knew there was nothing else to do. "She is on her way, Christopher. Just be patient."

"Uh, huh . . . I just can't remember."

"You will remember later." I tried to reassure him. "Didn't you tell me that Harvey had a party tonight?" I asked, changing the subject.

"Oh . . . yeah . . . that's where I came from. But . . . I don't remember how I got here." That's where he came from? I had triggered a memory by referring to Harvey's party. Suddenly I was suspicious.

Christopher had a history of alcohol abuse. Alcoholic "blackouts" are often fragmentary memory losses, and the alcoholic can begin to recall events when memories are triggered. If Christopher was able to remember a little, he may have been able to remember more.

First I had to establish how much he had been drinking. His speech was not slurred, so he did not sound drunk.

"Have you been drinking?" I asked cautiously, attempting not to sound too confrontive.

"I don't know."

His answer puzzled me. Could I believe that he did not know? "Can you smell alcohol on yourself?"

"No. I smell cigarette smoke."

"How does your stomach feel?" I asked. Christopher's ulcer would probably act up if he had been drinking.

"I can't tell. I'm so cold."

"Did you go to the Clam Cooker?" I asked, hoping to trigger another memory.

"Maybe, but I don't remember."

He was responding more promptly, and his voice sounded calmer. We talked for a few more minutes until Christopher had pulled himself together and was responding almost normally. I began to wonder why Diane had not arrived.

Thinking that Christopher was stable enough to follow instructions, I told him to hang up the phone and stay by the phone booth. I wanted to get off my line so that Diane would be able to reach me. Sure enough, as soon as the line was free, she rang through.

"I couldn't find him," Diane told me. "I looked all around Coral Bay. I'm calling from home now."

"Diane, he was so disoriented when he first called that I'm not sure if he is where he thinks he is. He may have wandered off for a moment and then come back."

Diane laughed. "Disoriented?" she said. "Dr. LaCalle, we found his car."

"Was it near the Clam Cooker?"

"Did he finally remember where he left it?" she asked irritably.

"No. But he said it was possible he might have been there."

"Was he ever!" she remarked nastily. "Joe, the bartender, told us that Christopher came in and downed four glasses of wine immediately. People around him kept telling him all afternoon to call you, but he wouldn't. He never listens to anyone, and we are all getting fed up."

I could hear Luke in the background shouting his agreement with Diane.

"Are you going to look for him anymore?"

"No. We've had it!" she said angrily. "He's probably just drunk and that's why he doesn't remember anything."

"I don't blame you for being angry and wanting to quit," I said sympathetically. "I can send the sheriff over there." I hated to do it. I stood up and looked at the clock. It was 12:45, an hour and a half since Christopher first called. There was no telling what had happened to him or what danger he was in. I was fairly certain of one thing. He was not inebriated—at least, not now. If the police found him, they would take him to the hospital and not to the drunk tank. I called the sheriff and local police and gave them a description of Christopher. I asked them to return him to the hospital if found.

The phone rang again. It was Christopher, using the last of his phone money. I could tell he had become frightened and needed to hear the sound of my voice again.

"Where are you now?" I asked.

"I'm still here, but I just needed to talk to you." His voice was more strong and stable. "But I'm getting awfully cold."

"Diane couldn't find you. They found out you went to the Clam Cooker and that made them angry so they went home. I had to call the police to come and look for you. Is the phone booth out where you can be seen from the street?"

"No. It's kind of behind some trees."

"Then stand out toward the street. If you stand there, the sheriff's patrol may stop. If they do, tell them who you are and ask them to take you back to the hospital."

"I'm afraid, and it bothers me that I can't remember where I left my car or my jacket, and I can't figure out how I got here."

"Your car is parked near the Clam Cooker. You were there, and you were drinking up a storm."

I was still too worried to get angry about the drinking.

"The last thing I remember it was between three-fifteen and three-thirty and I was driving down the coast highway and I could see the Clam Cooker up ahead. You know, the Clam Cooker is about a mile from here. I'm feeling okay to drive now. I'm going to walk down there and pick up my car."

"Do you have your keys?"

Christopher stopped for a moment to check. "Yeah. They're here in my pocket."

"Do you want me to call a cab for you so the police won't see you walking and pick you up?"

"No, that's okay. Either way I'll be fine. I'm just glad to know where my car is."

It was 1:15 when we finished. I went back to bed thinking that I would be awakened again when Christopher arrived at the hospital. I could hear José softly snoring. It didn't bother me this time. I was thankful he was asleep. Then I awoke, startled to realize it was 6:30. I checked with my exchange. The hospital had called to say Christopher had arrived at 2:30 A.M., and the nurse had asked that the message be held until morning. I fell back asleep, relieved.

When I awoke again, I felt exhausted. I had not yet been able to rest from the previous week's work. I dragged myself to the telephone to check in at the hospital. A different nurse was in charge of Christopher for the weekend. I had never met her, so I introduced myself in a tired and gravelly voice.

"Dr. LaCalle, Christopher is still asleep," the nurse reported to me. "I read the chart. No wonder your voice is hoarse this morning," she said sympathetically. "It appears from the notes you were up half the night."

"It seems that way, but it was actually only until about one-thirty."

"He's lucky to have such a caring doctor."

Or such a gullible one, I thought. Now that I knew Christopher was safely in the hospital, I could experience my anger and let it swell and recede like the tide. I felt resentful, used. I must be insane to put up with three hours of phone calls and intrigue.

I chastised myself. What was happening to me? Was José right about over-involvement? Was I losing my clinical judgment? My resentment set in like drying cement. Christopher was probably lying to me. He could easily have stopped at the Clam Cooker, gotten drunk, and had a blackout from too much booze. Someone else could have picked him up and taken him to Harvey's party after he was already three sheets to the wind. He was just a plain old garden variety alcoholic, I thought with sarcastic bitterness. He was probably just starting to sober up when he called me. And there I was, ready to fall for it, helping him get off the hook with this multiple personality excuse!

I had now joined the league of the nonbelievers. Come Monday, I was prepared to confront Christopher.

6

THE RISKS OF CARING

I was bristling when I stepped off the elevator onto the sixth-floor psychiatric unit that Monday morning. My irritation had fermented the rest of the weekend. Christopher was going to be made accountable for his behavior. Out five hours after check-in time! No patient of mine was going to keep me awake with non-sensical phone calls, all because he had been drinking. José was right. I had been a pushover, but I was drawing the line—here and now.

Christopher was curled up in the corner chair by the pool table. He looked as if he had had a rough weekend and did not want to socialize with any of the patients. I had no sympathy for him. I took him to task right where he sat.

"Okay, Christopher," I said sternly. "let's talk about how much you had to drink Saturday."

"I don't remember."

"Let me help you then. Joe, the bartender at the Clam Cooker, said you downed four glasses of wine right off, when you first came in."

"I don't remember being there. The last thing I remember is driving down the coast highway and seeing the Clam Cooker up ahead."

"All right. Then let's talk about how disoriented you were when you called me the first time. You said you *forgot* to call Diane. How could you *forget* something from one minute to the next if you weren't drunk or hadn't been taking some drugs?"

"I don't know. I was at the phone booth, and then I was about fifty feet away from the phone booth and I had to walk back to it." Christopher began looking frightened of me, and he cowered in his chair.

"Christopher, don't play games with me. If you can remember that much, you could have remembered to call Diane."

Christopher flinched. He looked bedraggled, unshaven, and tired, yet I felt myself becoming increasingly suspicious of his apparent suffering.

"You might want to talk this over with Diane and Luke," I challenged. "They might give you more information."

"No. I don't want to talk to anyone," he said, his voice beginning to tremble. "I already called Luke. He kicked me out of the apartment . . . told me to never come back . . . said he'd hold my stuff for me and that was all. He said that Diane and Sylvia are mad at me, too . . . this always happens."

"What always happens?" I asked without backing off.

"I do things that I don't want to do, get myself in trouble, and people don't want me around anymore. They get mad at me—especially my mother." His voice lingered over the word "mother." I knew he felt the anger in me, and it had triggered memories of his mother's wrath.

As I shifted my weight in the chair, Christopher startled. His instant reflex of lifting his arms to protect himself let me know that he had been hit as a child.

His pitiful look disarmed me. "How do you feel right now, Christopher?" I asked.

"Uncomfortable," he responded miserably.

"I saw you stiffen just now. What did you think was going to happen?"

He laughed nervously. "You'd slap me," he said in garbled tones.

"Did I hear you say you thought I'd slap you?"

"Yeah, in the face," he mumbled. "Like my mother did. Hard. Real hard."

"When did she slap you?"

"I don't know."

"Yes, you do."

Christopher jumped up and looked as if he was about to spring at me. "Damn it! Will you lay off him? Can't you see that he don't feel good today?"

Jackie had come out—fighting mad—to protect Christopher from his "Mom."

"Anyway," she continued, "Christopher don't remember what happened that night. Why don't you ask Sissy? That piss-ass is the one who got us all into trouble." She glared at me, hands on hips. "Go into one of those rooms," she commanded, "and I'll make sure she comes out to talk with you. Ernest wants her out, too."

Jackie disappeared as quickly as she'd come.

I led Christopher into a conference room and I helped him to relax and put himself in a light trance so that Sissy could come out more easily.

Within a few seconds, Sissy looked out at me.

"It's okay. I can come out today without much hypnosis. Christopher doesn't have any control today. He's falling apart."

"Were you out Saturday night, Sissy?"

"Yes." She sounded contrite.

"Were any of the others with you?"

"No."

"What do you remember? Were you drinking?"

"Yes, but it wasn't *that* much. I just wanted to stop off for a little wine. I had a couple or three glasses pretty fast, but I wasn't drunk. The guys around me were drinking a lot more than I was. Harvey had come into the bar with his friend. They started to party early. It was Harvey's birthday, and he was going to have a party at his house."

"Do you remember Harvey's friend?"

"Yes, he was putting his hands all over me," she said with disgust. "I just wanted to loosen up a little and have some fun before Christopher went over to Diane and Sylvia's, but this guy was putting his hands all over me. They wanted a three-way. I felt really weird and creepy about it."

"Did you leave with them?"

"No. I just use men that way. I get them to treat me to some wine, and I use them. I didn't have any money on me." Sissy became wistful and melancholy. "All I remember was the sun setting, watching it go down slowly. I began withdrawing and feeling more distant. Harvey's friend made me remember something from when I was a little girl and I started feeling really weird and I didn't want to be around anyone."

My anger was forgotten. Sissy was clearly disturbed by memories from a distant past.

"What did it make you remember?"

Sissy squirmed and writhed in her chair the way each of the personalities would always do when any uncomfortable memories came to mind. "I don't remember anything," she said evasively.

"Yes, you do. You just told me you remembered. What is it?"

"She was always yelling and screaming at him. So mean. She knew everything but she just let it happen." I knew by now that the "she" was Christopher's mother. "What did she let happen, Sissy?" I pressed.

"The showers."

"What showers?"

"Me and Dad."

"What happened in the showers?"

"I don't remember."

"Yes, you do."

Sissy's face showed her anguish, but I continued to push for the memories.

"She knew we were in the shower together."

"Yes, children sometimes shower with their parents, especially when they are really young," I said matter-of-factly, suggesting that nothing unusual had occurred. "How old were you when you were showering with your dad?"

"Three or four."

She pulled her knees closer together and crossed her hands in front of her, one on each knee, a gesture of self-protection.

"Did your father scrub you down?"

"Yes, he rubbed me all over. He touched me all over with his hands."

"Did you scrub him?" I pursued.

Silence.

"Did you scrub him?" I repeated.

"I touched him."

"Where did you touch him?"

"She slapped me."

"She slapped you in the shower?"

"No, not there. In bed. They were in bed, and I crawled in to lie down with them. I touched him the way he always wanted, and she slapped me when I touched him. She said I was bad."

"Where did you touch him?"

Silence.

"Did you touch his penis?"

"Yes . . . I have a headache." She closed her eyes as if trying to block out the distasteful memory.

"In the shower, too?"

"Yes, she knew about it. She knew about it! I have a headache . . . I can't do this anymore." She truly looked as if she could not go on. I did not want to be like Christopher's punitive mother, so I stopped in order to protect Christopher from any further distress.

"All right, Sissy, that will be enough about that for now. Let's go back to finding out what happened Saturday night. It seems that you don't remember anything after about five-thirty."

"No. I think somebody else took over. I just couldn't take being out anymore. Things at the bar weren't turning out the way I wanted."

"Okay, then I want to talk with whoever took over the body at around five-thirty. You can go back in now to rest, Sissy."

Christopher's body relaxed, and his eyes remained closed.

"Can I please speak to any part of Christopher that knows what happened after five-thirty?" I still had my doubts that any memories were there because I was thoroughly convinced that in two hours Christopher had become intoxicated.

"Sure, I remember." The eyes opened. "Sissy doesn't know a good thing when she sees it." Right away I knew I was talking to James. "I took off with Harvey and his friend. There was plenty of time to have a little party of our own before the other guests started arriving."

"Were you drinking?"

"Not me. They were. I didn't want to drink and not be able to perform. It's not easy to be able to satisfy two guys at once, you know."

"Then what happened?"

"The other people started arriving, and I didn't really feel like partying. I was pretty worn out. So I let Sissy come out again. But she didn't seem to enjoy it much either. She just wandered off from the party and started walking down the road."

"Then may I speak with Sissy again so I can hear the end of this story?"

"Sure."

He closed his eyes, and after a few moments Sissy returned.

"I didn't really want to leave the party," she said, "but Christopher came out for a minute and looked at his watch and realized he was late getting back to the hospital. Since he didn't know where he was, I came out again and walked down the road to a pay phone. The phone at Harvey's house was in the kitchen, and there was too much noise. I let him out just long enough to call you so you wouldn't be worried about him, and then I decided I'd walk back up to the party for a while. I couldn't seem to stay out though. I only got out of the parking lot before Christopher took over again. I was getting tired of being out anyway. It was too cold."

"Could it be that you didn't let Christopher call from Harvey's house because you knew I would be able to tell he was at a party and he'd get in trouble then?"

"Who cares?" she snipped defensively. "I don't want to be in this dumb hospital anyway."

"And what about Christopher's friends being angry with him?" I reminded her.

"Same thing," she scoffed. "They aren't my friends. Diane and Sylvia act like a couple of old ladies. And Luke has no room to talk—he parties all the time."

"Nevertheless, you, Christopher, and the others will all have to suffer as a result of your need to have fun," I pointed out.

"How?"

"Even if you think they are old ladies, Diane and Sylvia are the only real friends you've had, and it will be your loss if they give up on you. Now that Luke has kicked Christopher out, where do you plan to live?"

No answer.

"So, you see?" I said with satisfaction now that I had made my point. "You've got to learn to cooperate more with Christopher and Ernest if you want to watch out for your own skin."

"I guess so," she said reluctantly.

"I've found out everything I wanted to know for now. You can go back in and let Christopher come out."

"I can go back in, but it's going to be hard to get Christopher to come back out. He thinks you're really mad at him."

"Okay, I'll talk to him about it. Just go back in, and he'll be able to hear me."

Sissy did not close her eyes, but instead took on the dazed look that Christopher always had when in transition from one personality to another. "You can come out now, Christopher," I said. "I'm not angry. I understand now."

Christopher came out with a dog-faced expression. The amnesia barriers were down, and he did not like what he had just been able to hear from the others.

"That's really awful what happened. I would never have done that. I wanted to go and see Diane and Sylvia. They had a nice, quiet evening prepared for me. I'm really sorry about what happened. I almost wish I didn't know about it."

"I hope the part of you that is Sissy will be more cooperative now that she realizes that she cooks her own goose with her compulsive need to party. There was really no excuse for stopping off at the Clam Cooker to begin with—even if you didn't have too much to drink."

"I know. I'm really sorry about what happened."

The anger I had held at the outset of that day was dispelled by the knowledge of what happened to Christopher during that lost evening. If it had been a true alcoholic blackout, Christopher would not have been able to remember all that had happened even when hypnotized. He had been drinking just enough to let another part of him take over to perform a sexual act that he found abhorrent. He had not been drinking at the time he parked his car, so it was logical that he remembered where he left it. And why, I asked myself, would anyone want to stand in the shivering cold for three hours making telephone calls if all he had to do was walk back up to his friends' house or take himself back to the hospital immediately?

I had to believe Christopher's story.

And now I was more concerned with what he had told me about his mother and father. He had reported abnormal behavior on the part of his parents, and I had to find out more. I had been suspicious of both his parents from the outset; I knew that some-

117

thing extremely traumatic had to have happened to him. Aside from that, Christopher had now provided a hint of an incest triangle.

Customarily, incest occurs with a passive, often alcoholic father who becomes aggressively seductive and sexually abuses his daughter. The mother sometimes knows it is happening but tries to ignore it. Most often, she denies it to herself, even though all the clues are there. In this case, the dynamics were the same, except that the daughter was Sissy, who had been created in Christopher's mind. I used to be very naive about incest. I would have passed by Sissy's description thinking that the showers were innocent fun, or thought that Christopher's mother had over-reacted to physical teasing. That was before I had treated dozens of incest victims and their parents. I no longer thought of such reports as a child's distortion of the truth.

Now I had to find out more about these two parents. I started out boldly with Christopher the next day.

"Christopher, you can tell me anything you wish about what happened between you and your parents. Anything which may seem shocking to you will probably not surprise me."

"Nothing unusual ever happened to me when I was growing up."

"You don't consider what you told me yesterday unusual? That your mother slapped you for fondling your father's penis?"

"Not really. Maybe it's because it didn't happen to me. At least I didn't think it did, until now."

"Well, then, it certainly bothered Sissy."

"Then you'll have to talk to Sissy about it."

Using hypnosis, I regressed Sissy, going backward in time from age nineteen. She stopped me at age six to tell me about an incident with her mother that both confused and disturbed her.

"It made Christopher feel funny . . . strange," she started out.

"What did, Sissy?"

"That she, Christopher's mother, used to walk around in that nightgown without any clothes on underneath. I could see through it. She did that until I was a lot older, but I don't remember how old."

"When would she wear the nightgown?"

"Always. She always had a nightgown like that. If anybody else came in, she'd put on a robe. I don't remember how old I was when she started, either."

"Then it was all the time you were growing up?"

"Uh, huh. Christopher didn't like it. It made him feel strange, kinda anxious, so I'd come out. Girls can look, you know."

Apparently, Christopher had been made to feel uncomfortable by both parents' sexually seductive behavior.

"Then what happened?" I asked, wondering if Christopher's mother had carried out any outright incestuous acts.

"Then she left us with Dad and ran off with another man. I woke up in the morning, and I knew something was wrong. The house was very quiet. The ironing board was up. There was a note—I think—yes, a note, she left it on the ironing board. It was so very quiet without her there to yell at us . . . so strange. Dad said, 'Your mother is gone.' " Sissy's voice was flat as she imitated her father's announcement. "Christopher failed school that year. I was worried. I didn't know who would take care of us. At least my mother always took care of us . . . my little brother and me. I sat in the back of the car when Father took us to that family's house. I was glad to go. He had been drinking all the time and there was no food, no clean clothes, and our house smelled of garbage and cigarettes. Those people were nice. Dad dropped us off and I remember he said, 'Your dog died. Now I won't have to find a home for it.' I don't know what happened to Christopher's dog. It just wasn't there anymore. He was drunk. 'Your dog died,' he said in a mean voice."

"Why did Christopher's father leave the children with those people?"

"He wanted to go back to the base. He couldn't take care of us."

"Did you miss your mother and your father?"

"I didn't miss her, I just missed being taken care of, and I wanted her to come back and take care of us. Dad? I didn't miss him and I didn't *not* miss him, either. I didn't feel anything."

The more I came to know of Christopher's past, the more I realized how impoverished he was as a child, both emotionally and economically. Timmy was Christopher the child, lonely and abandoned. It was his pain that continued to linger on inside of Christopher.

As the days went by, I turned more and more to Timmy. Through the guided imagery of the playroom, we played together and I spun the big red top with him. Taking the place of the missing mother in his mind, I soothed him, and nurtured him, and spent time listening—the kind of quality time I knew I should have been spending with Eddie.

Timmy visualized me holding him in my arms. Since Timmy was inside a grown-up man's body, I could not, in actuality, hold him and be tender with him and re-parent him the way he needed. Through hypnosis and guided imagery, however, I could do all of those things. I could help him conjure up images of us playing together, with normal mother/son affection being shared between us. Timmy could be a little boy being taken care of by a loving mother surrogate. In this way, he and I grew to care for each other in a very special, unprecedented way. I became more fully appreciative that the mind is a wonderful and powerful instrument that can make almost any fantasy seem real.

I looked for a way to make a link between our "playing together" and the *reality* of our relationship, which, in fact, was a nurturing and caring relationship for Timmy, as well as the others. At last I recalled the object-relations therapy that Paula had discussed with me earlier, and I decided to give it a try.

The gift shop at the hospital provided just the object I was looking for—a small teddy bear, small enough for Christopher's cupped hands to hide from view. If I was going to give a stuffed toy to an adult man, I could not select one that would be conspicuous. Christopher would have to be able to hide the teddy bear easily from the other patients, yet it had to be soft and cuddly to bring forth in him the feelings of safety and protection that small children experience with a favorite blanket or stuffed animal. I put the cute, furry teddy in a paper bag and took it to Christopher.

"Timmy, come out," I summoned. "I have a nice surprise for you."

Timmy was nearby but kept his eyes closed. He was not in the mood for surprises.

"Do you want to know what it is before you open your eyes and come out?" I proposed.

His timid, wee voice responded. "Yes." He nodded.

"It's a teddy bear," I said cheerfully. "It's just for you."

Timmy cautiously opened his eyes and peeped at me, as if not trusting that I could really have brought him such a thing.

"I know you really like the teddy bear that's in the secret play-room. So I thought I'd bring you one that you can keep always, one for your very own that you won't have to share with any-one."

Timmy took the teddy bear into his hands and incredulously stared at it. Then he turned it over slowly and examined it from all sides. His too-large, grown-up hands repetitively petted, stroked, and rubbed the tiny toy, as if trying to convince the new owner that it really existed and was actually for him alone. Awe and adulation filled his face. It was the look that four-year-olds get when mom and dad turn on the Christmas lights of a freshly decorated tree. I felt exuberant watching him, but at the same time deeply saddened. How could such a small thing mean so much to Timmy? I struggled to blink back the tears that rimmed my eyes. My own children never reacted with such emotion over a gift. They were accustomed to receiving; Timmy was not. This was the right gift for Timmy, and I had seldom felt so right about giving.

After many moments of watching Timmy's silent adoration, I interrupted him.

"The teddy bear can mean anything you want it to mean, Tim-my, just so it means something good, something that will always make you feel safe and warm when you hold it."

"It will be my friend," Timmy announced. "Now I have a friend, a friend like you. He will stay with me all the time, and I'm no more alone."

"Yes, Timmy, a friend," I repeated.

I knew that Timmy's "friend" was a little part of me that he could keep with him to comfort him when I was not around, but I wished I had more ways to help lessen his deep sadness.

"You can go back in now, Timmy. You will be able to play with the teddy bear later."

Timmy closed his eyes and left. The teddy bear dropped to the floor. To insure that Timmy would indeed be able to play with it later, I called upon one of the adult personalities to assist him. Since James had become increasingly accepting of Timmy and, yet, was at times at odds with Christopher's weakness and child-like qualities, I thought I had better have a talk with James.

"James, were you listening?" I asked.

"Yes," he said as he took charge of the body.

"Will you and Christopher let Timmy take out the teddy bear and play with it any time he wants?"

"Yeah. Sure."

"Then why don't you pick up the teddy bear and put it in the bedstand in your room?"

James looked at the teddy bear nervously and handled it awkwardly. I noticed that now the teddy bear was not fondled in his hands. James hurriedly slipped it into the paper bag. He showed no interest in or feeling for the stuffed animal. I had some concern that the teddy bear might embarrass James or Christopher and, therefore, Timmy would not be allowed to have the toy.

The next day when I came back to see Christopher again, the nurse reported that the night shift had walked in for bed check and found him asleep in his bed with the teddy nestled under his chin and grasped firmly in his hand. In my mind's eye, I could see Timmy curled up in his bed, looking peaceful and secure. Just like Eddie, when I'd check him at night before turning out the lights. I'd run my fingers through my son's hair and kiss his forehead. How sad that Timmy never had anyone do this for him—and never would.

Later, when I approached James, he silently handed me the record book—he had something to tell me that he was not comfortable saying aloud. Inside the book James had written: "Timmy loves his Teddy Bear. I'm beginning to like Timmy. I think I'll take good care of him and make sure he can play. I'll be his friend, too." I breathed a sigh of relief, then allowed my elation to take over. A grin filled my face. No need to convince James further. Cooperation among the personalities was taking place, and Christopher was beginning to heal.

In spite of such successes, however, I continued to have times when I felt pangs of guilt over my relationship with Christopher. I had become an ally to each of the personalities, allowing them to demand my time and energy in ways most beneficial to their unique needs. I had become a very special person to Christopher, better than any family member had been to him. My guilt stemmed from the fact that I had not been equally accessible to my own family, in particular to my own children.

This feeling of being torn between family and career was not new to me; I had grown accustomed to the more commonplace guilts and conflicts of the working mother. What disturbed me the most about the situation with Christopher was that I was directly giving of myself to Timmy in a way that I needed to be giving to my son, since they were both about the same age.

In particular, my sessions with Timmy were rich with patience, attentiveness, and creativity. I thought often of Eddie, and realized how few hours had been recently devoted to him with the same richness. At least, I told myself to soften the guilt, the Timmy part of Christopher was teaching me more about the special relationship between a little boy and his mother. The other personalities freely commented upon my successes with Timmy, or, sometimes, the lack of them. My parenting effectiveness was held under scrutiny by the others, especially Jackie. And I found it to be a definite advantage to be working with the child in Christopher while utilizing the perspective and retrospective wisdom of the other personalities. As a result, I found myself more finely tuned, more acutely sensitive, to my son's needs.

Timmy and Eddie each needed me, but I was going to have to tear myself away from them both. José and I had planned our yearly, just-for-two December vacation. While most of our patients were busy with holiday preparations, we always spent a romantic week at a tropical resort. This year, it was to be Cancùn, Mexico.

José and I were still at a stand-off. I had exhausted my resources. Instead of giving to my husband, loving him the way I could and wanted to love him, I expected him not to need my attention but to give to me instead. I knew I was expecting a lot, but I wasn't being adult about it. Maybe the upcoming vacation would be a chance to set things straight between us.

Three months before, I had been excited about the trip, but now the time arrived too quickly. The day for our departure came before I was ready for it.

My husband and I were prepared to take an 8:00 P.M. flight. I wanted to make sure that I had time that day to get to the hospital to see Christopher before I left. The morning was a blur of activity. The evening before, I had left the children with their grandparents, and I'd felt a rush of separation anxiety as I left them. They were so little and needed me so very much, even if they did have grandparents to care for them. I had little time to get my own things ready for the trip. I spent an hour in the morning hastily packing our suitcases before I rushed to the office. Several hours were spent in the last-minute phone calls, appointment-setting, and dictation that had to be finished. Whenever I planned to go out of town, it seemed as if everyone knew it and decided to get in a last-minute comment or request. It soon was five o'clock, and I still had not had time to get over to the hospital. I dropped everything and went.

When I arrived, the nurses told me that Christopher had been despondent the whole day and that they had called my office to be sure that I was coming. Jerry Swenson was just finishing up with Christopher when I came up to the nursing station. I knew I could rely on Swenson to take good care of Christopher while I was gone. He greeted me with a wry grin, obviously relieved that I had finally arrived.

"Christopher is really bummed out," he said, ambling over to me.

Bummed out? I laughed to myself. Leave it to Jerry to drop his Harvard terminology when it was not as expressive as the colloquial.

"Bummed out?" I repeated.

"Yes, he's really been having a tough time facing the fact that you are leaving. Leave instructions to put him on suicidal precautions, if you think it is necessary to have him checked every fifteen minutes or so."

I walked into Christopher's room. The four-bed dormitory was empty except for Christopher and a nurse who was talking with him. He sat in a high-back chair facing the window. The only light left of the day encompassed him, and the sunset warmed his blond hair to shimmering golden tones. His profile was ablaze in the shadowy rays of the darkening room. The nurse, Marie, sat on the corner of the bed next to him, her own image silhouetted against the evening sky.

She talked in hushed, reassuring tones, telling Christopher that I was on my way up to see him and that he would have a chance to say goodbye. I paused to listen a moment, to remind myself that I was leaving Christopher in the hands of this warm, gentle woman, the competent Dr. Swenson, and, of course, Sue.

There was no reason for this anxiety over our separation that I was beginning to feel.

The two looked up, surprised to find me. Christopher hid his face in his hands. He had been crying and was embarrassed to let me see that he had been in tears over my impending absence.

Marie motioned for me to step aside with her for a moment.

"Timmy has been around for most of the day and has been quite tearful. Christopher has been depressed but tries to deny that it is because you are leaving."

I went back to Christopher.

"Do you want to stay here," I asked him softly, "or shall we go to a conference room?"

Somewhat to my surprise, he chose the privacy. We got up and moved into the conference room.

As soon as I closed the door, I could see that he didn't want to look at me. When he did, the tears began to flow, and he hid his face in his hands again.

"Marie told me you've been having a hard time today," I said. I wanted to convey to him there was no reason to hide his feeling from me.

He did not look up, but sat, head in his hands, embarrassed. I looked for a way to change the subject so I'd help him save face— and also keep myself from getting caught up in the emotion.

"I understand that yesterday the hospital cashier's office told you that your private insurance will not pay much longer. The sixty days your employer's group plan allowed will soon be used up. And, now, you're being asked to sign up for public assistance in order to stay in the hospital." I was finding a ready subject to latch onto, even if it wasn't a pleasant one.

"I never thought I would have to stoop to taking welfare," he said, almost choking.

"Yes, I can see that must be very hard for you to accept, especially when you've prided yourself in your work and have always been self-sustaining."

Although we had shifted to a worrisome subject, his mood lightened. He talked of the dilemmas of finding work and shelter when he left the hospital. But then he turned away and stared vacantly at the wall.

"That's just the top of it," he mumbled.

I knew he was trying to tell me that his sadness was not about his having to accept public assistance. I knew we would have to talk about the separation, and I searched for a way to broach the subject with him. In all of Christopher's lifetime, he had never formed a close, long-lasting relationship with anyone. He was distant from both parents. His brothers were strangers to him. His baby sister was the one he loved the most, yet that relationship had not developed fully because she was so much younger than Christopher and just a small child when he left his mother's home to go into the military. As for his friends, he had none, other than Diane and Sylvia, and he could not call them intimate friends. Lovers were only pawns to him.

I knew that what he was feeling in that moment was a first-time experience for him. I was hoping he would continue to let himself experience the feelings as Christopher—instead of as Timmy.

"Christopher," I addressed him tenderly, "have you ever felt really attached to anyone?" I knew that he would have trouble with the answer. Tears filled his eyes, and he attempted to speak, but couldn't.

"I know how very scary it is to be so attached to someone, to feel dependent on the good feelings you have when you're with that person." I watched for his reaction. He nodded his head up and down in agreement, and the tears streamed down his cheeks. "It's an awfully big risk," I went on, "to allow yourself to be vulnerable, to need someone. What if that person should not care about you in return? What if that person should not want you anymore? What if something bad were to happen to that person?" I paused again. I was about to make my point. "What if that person should go away?"

I touched a chord in him, and he lifted his head. His look let me know his deep comprehension of what I was saying. His innocent blue eyes opened wide, and he blinked at me through wet lashes. For that one moment, his delicate aspect was so pure and pale that I thought Michelangelo would have been inspired. Angelic in the openness of his expression, he confessed his feelings to me. "I've never felt so vulnerable." His trust in me was complete, and I knew I would do everything in my power never to betray it.

"It's so much easier," I went on, "to never allow yourself to feel what you are feeling right now. This is painful, I know, Christopher. I have had those same vulnerable feelings in my life before. I, too, have been afraid to need someone so much. But if you never have those feelings, you will never fully know what it means to live." I suddenly thought of José and wished I wasn't feeling so estranged from him. "It is only through taking that risk that you can eventually learn to experience the joy of love and intimacy."

"I had it all together before," he sighed.

"Did you?" I asked. "But weren't you lonely, adrift, detached?"

He looked at me silently, knowing that I was repeating the description that he had given me of himself only a few weeks before. He could not speak.

"It's hard, Christopher. I understand. It's hard." My time was running short, and I knew I had to prepare to leave. "Listen, Christopher," I said, all the while thinking of Timmy. "I've brought something I want you to keep for me while I'm gone. You might think of it as sort of an insurance policy that I will be coming back soon."

I reached into my purse and pulled out one of two items I had stashed there that morning.

"This is an old coin that my father gave to me," I said while turning it over to him. "Dad had it for a long time, and I think his father gave it to him. I know that it is somewhat rare, but it may not have great value other than the sentimental value it holds for me. I've always loved my father greatly, and it reminds me of him. He has collected coins all his life."

I knew that Christopher had never received anything that was passed down from his own father. There was no history, no tradition, no heritage, no cohesion from one generation to the other in the Kincaid family. When his father died, Christopher had inherited no money—only a few worthless items that he threw away.

"You keep it for me, Christopher, until I get back. I will definitely want it back, so you can rest assured that I will be here to get it."

He smiled with understanding and studied the coin with wistful reverence. Then he nodded his acceptance and carefully put the coin in his shirt pocket. His composure indicated that my gesture had assuaged his childlike fear that I would not return. I was gratified that I had chosen the right "insurance policy."

Then I reached into my purse and pulled out a seashell. "I've had this seashell since I was a child, Christopher. This might seem to be a silly thing for a child to treasure, but when you grow up in Arizona, as I did, the beach is nothing more than a fanciful dream. See this pearly pink part, right here?" I asked, putting my finger on the spot. "I used to sit outside under a tree and study that shell and rub this soft, smooth place. I found it soothing. It was a good way to daydream, and if I was disturbed about something, the worries would soon be gone."

"It's better than smoking," he said, laughing out loud. He gladly took the seashell and rubbed it in the manner I had shown him.

"Keep it, Christopher, and let it mean something soothing and peaceful to you while I'm gone."

He nodded his head several times, confirming his acceptance. The strain had slipped away from his face altogether as the understanding of what I was saying became more complete. He finally spoke.

"James has been hanging around all day, telling me he's going to take over pretty soon. He says I've been acting like a big baby."

"The part of you that is James wants to block what you've been feeling today because it is all new to you and because it carries a certain amount of discomfort with it. But, Christopher, it is terribly important that you let yourself feel what you are feeling now," I emphasized. "It's part of being a whole human being."

I groped for a way to let Christopher know that I understood and could share in such human feelings. I knew it was time for me to be more honest about my own feelings with him. Self-disclosure is not a part of what conservative clinicians usually do. Sigmund Freud would turn over in his grave, I thought, if he could hear what I was about to say.

"I want you to know that this is hard for me, too," I began haltingly. "I took my children to their grandparents' house last night, and it was hard for me to say goodbye. It's hard for me to say goodbye to you, too, Christopher."

Christopher looked down at the floor.

"It's perfectly all right," I went on, "that you should need me now, because you won't need me forever. But while you do need me, I will be here for you."

Christopher looked at me intently.

"You know," I continued, "I made a decision when I realized the nature of your illness. I knew that helping you would require a heavy investment of my time and energy and a commitment to stay with you for several months or even years, if necessary. I knew that I would have to learn to relate to you in ways that I customarily don't relate to my patients."

His head bowed and he nodded in agreement.

"So you see, I made a decision, and I've taken a risk, the same as you have. We've begun on this very special journey together." I paused. "What if you should decide you want a different doctor? Don't forget, you're not the only one who takes the chance of having hurt feelings." I paused again. "One of these days, you will have become a complete and integrated person, living out the potential for happiness that is within you. When you reach your goal, we will feel a touch of sadness, because we will have finished our journey together."

Christopher looked deeply into my eyes as if to search for the truth of what I was saying.

"Separations—even good and necessary ones—can be hard," I added. His piercing gaze, I thought, was reaching into the heart of me and pulling out as complete an understanding as two people can find.

I could feel his strength renewed as I shared myself with him. He got up and confidently walked me to the door, knowing that it was time for me to leave. Then, as he was about to reach for the doorknob, he hesitated and looked at me again. Between friends, this would have been the time for a parting embrace, but we were not friends. I was his doctor, and he was my patient. We had never touched except for the time I had taken Timmy's hand when I first met him. Some of my patients—men and women alike—readily offered pats, handshakes, and hugs. I was comfortable with these gestures of affection. Christopher was not an affectionate person, but instead was rather awkward and stilted. Yet I could definitely sense in that moment of hesitation that he wanted to be near me. A handshake would not do.

"Do you want to give me a hug goodbye?" I asked cautiously.

"Yes." He spoke with a spontaneous smile and embraced me readily.

But still, the tension I felt in his body signaled his ever-present uncertainty.

"Oh, boy!" he said under his breath as he pulled away from me. He heaved a painful sigh. "So much to learn."

For once, words escaped me. I departed and left the hospital, swallowing hard, consciously aware of the lump in my throat.

Waiting at the airport with José for the flight to Cancùn, I was still entrenched in an emotional tug of war. I'm going away for only ten days, I kept telling myself. Gracious! Why did I feel such pain?

I had bonded so closely with Christopher that it was like leaving part of myself behind. I felt foolish about my maternal feelings toward him, even though the journal articles I read reported that countertransference was a commonplace problem among therapists of multiples. Then I remembered something Bob Slater had pointed out. "It seems to me," he had said, "that certain therapeutic rules we all learned in school must be broken. Most of these patients have been severely deprived of mothering. Is it possible to treat them any other way? The countertransference and bonding are therapeutic to the patient. But it's so very draining to the therapist."

How right Bob had been, I thought. I could sense that José was becoming annoyed with my emotional distance, so as we sat down on the plane I reached over and took his hand.

"Oh! You know I'm alive!" he said sarcastically.

I refused to take the bait. Why can't this be easier? I thought. Why must every move provoke conflict?

"We *are* going to have a nice, relaxed week together," he went on in the same way. "Aren't we?"

I stiffened. "I think that's better left unsaid, or we're going to start quarreling again."

"No, we're not," he said. "I have no plans to ruin our vacation. Do you?"

This wasn't going to be easy.

"Not me. But . . ." I dreaded getting off on the wrong foot with him. "Let's be smart and not get into any serious discussions until after we've had a couple of days' rest."

Would he recognize that we'd been under too much stress to handle this without being defensive?

"Agreed," he said.

I took my hand away and thankfully put on my stereo headset, slipped out a paperback book, and curled up with a blanket around me. After a while, José reached over to turn the cover of the paperback toward him so he could read the title.

"*Sybil*! You're not going to read *that* on our trip, are you?"

I pulled off my headset with indignation. "It will mean something different to me than it did five years ago. Besides, what does it matter to you what I read? A book is a book."

"Yeah, well, I'll see you at the end of the week," he said bluntly, and turned away. I felt as if cold water had been thrown in my face.

"Just what is that supposed to mean?" I asked before thinking twice.

"It means, I don't know where you'll be, but you won't be with me—like you haven't been for two months."

"You're exaggerating. I haven't been neglecting my wifely duties." Instantly I regretted my choice of words.

"Duties? Not exactly a word I'd associate with you. I can think of one wifely duty you do with a lot less frequency."

Damn! He would have to bring that up at the start of a vacation! I hadn't been as interested in the bedroom, but I was tired from conflict and overwork and irritated with him—and he wasn't seeing what he had done to help create the situation.

He went on after a pregnant pause. "But that's not my point right now. I'm saying you have no idea what I'm doing from day to day. Liz told me she had to put the newspaper under your nose at the office so you'd see the *Times* article about the case I'm working on."

"Okay. I admit she had to point it out to me." I was relieved he'd dropped the subject of sex. "I don't have time to read the newspaper these days. Headlines about court trials and murderers don't appeal to me, anyhow. Besides, your cases get too much press for me to follow each story entirely." I turned to look at him more closely. I faced him fully, squaring off my shoulders. I was on the offensive now. "You know, José, I find it interesting that you feel neglected." I wasn't feeling sympathetic. "Does my attention to your work really matter that much to you?"

"Of course, it does."

"But you get so much attention from everyone. I'm always hearing 'You're Dr. LaCalle's wife? He was outstanding on the witness stand last week—our best expert testimony.' "

"The public attention is nice, but it doesn't matter to me as much as knowing you're by my side."

I sat quietly for a moment trying to empathize with his feeling. I knew he was right, but I couldn't drive away my own hurt. "Then why is it when I need your support, you don't seem to understand?"

"Are we back to that Christopher case again?" he said angrily.

"Yes. I'm hoping you'll see *my* point."

"I *am* supporting you, Trula. I just don't agree with your thinking. You don't seem to know the difference."

"You're right. I don't. And we'd better stop here. It's a long flight, and I thought we'd just agreed on no serious discussions for a couple of days."

Cancùn was spectacular, and neither of us wanted to say anything that would further spoil the beauty of that week. We made every effort to be light and relaxed. I could see he was trying, and I felt gratefully warm toward him. We lounged on the beaches, danced until midnight, and made love through the early morning hours. I was determined to make it up to him—and to myself. Two days went by, then three and four, until the week had passed without anything serious said between us.

Christopher was not mentioned, but he was never far from my mind.

José could read me, and whenever he caught that distracted look in my eyes, he sulked silently. No matter how I tried, I couldn't conceal my worry about how Christopher had fared in my absence.

Chapter
7

I'M HIDING IN THE BASEMENT

Sue bubbled with spirited news of Christopher's accomplishments during the week I was on vacation. I had phoned her immediately after returning home, so I could be prepared for any bad turn of events. Thankfully, no crisis had occurred while I was gone!

"James had to come out only once, right after you left," she said. "He stayed out only a couple of days, just long enough to be sure that Christopher would be able to begin phone calls and start making financial arrangements for himself. James started it, but it was Christopher who did most of the real work himself. Oh, and Timmy slept with his teddy bear every night."

I smiled to myself, pleased that Timmy was comforted. And I was relieved to learn that Christopher had begun to make some housing arrangements and to think about employment after he left the hospital. As for Christopher's job, it was doubtful that he would be rehired, but he'd called his former employer to see if Mr. Woods would interview him.

When I arrived at the hospital in the afternoon, I found that Sue had spearheaded a surprise birthday celebration for Christopher.

"While you are with him, Dr. LaCalle, I'll go and set up a table in one of the conference rooms," Sue said on the sly. "We have a birthday cake. Every once in a while we do this for the patients who have been here for a while."

I found Christopher awkward and excited. He looked at me sheepishly and attempted to be casual.

"Happy birthday, Christopher." I smiled at him.

"Thank you. I think the staff is going to have a cake for me," he said, trying to hide his pleasure. "Will you stay and have a piece with us?"

"Of course I will." Christopher's excitement made me wonder how many birthday cakes—or how few—he had had in his lifetime. "How did you do while I was gone, Christopher?" I asked cautiously, remembering the notes I had seen in his chart. The nurses had written about his longing for my return.

"Uh . . ." He looked away and stretched his arms in his distracted and characteristically kittenish way. He could not look at me, but he grinned and murmured shyly, "I missed you."

"How did you feel about me coming back?"

"Relieved," he said, now looking me in the eye.

"Well, I thought about you, too. I even brought you a little something." I pulled out an onyx ashtray wrapped in newspaper, a tourist's trinket purchased with a few Mexican pesos.

Now, I began to feel awkward as I became fully aware I had done something out of the ordinary . . . not something that doctors do.

"That's nice! I like it," he said with genuine pleasure. "Thank you." Then he suddenly looked serious. "I wish I had some friends to come on my birthday. I haven't even had a phone call."

"Someday, Christopher . . ."

"I have your coin, right here," he said, promptly reaching into his shirt pocket. He had not forgotten and had come prepared for our visit. "Thanks for sharing it with me, Dr. LaCalle."

Then, giving in to the need to relax and enjoy the spirit of the day, I ushered Christopher to the room where preparations had been made for his celebration.

Sue had set out a paper tablecloth, cups of punch, forks and plates, and a small, unadorned birthday cake. Christopher's name was not on the cake, and there were no candles. But it made no difference to Christopher. His eyes danced as if lighted candles were reflected in them.

Sue helped him cut the pieces and pass them out to the staff. There was no singing—the hospital was still too somber a place for lively frivolity. Yet Christopher smiled cheerfully. The happier he became over such a simple gesture, the sadder I felt that Christopher's childhood had been so impoverished.

Sue stood aside from the gathering and spoke to me without restraint. "I just love Christopher. I wish I could have done more for him today."

With the party over, I watched Sue as she left, walking away from us down the long hospital corridor. I envied Sue's open affection for Christopher. I rationalized that it was easier for a nurse. She didn't have to be in charge, I told myself, while the doctor's role is different. I couldn't fool myself, though. Years of training had taken away my ability to act naturally with Christopher without analyzing my every response. I had changed in a direction I didn't like. I had lost my spontaneity and openness. The big city . . . the competition . . . sure, I had learned how to survive. But for what? To lose the gentle small-town girl in me? I wanted to regain that part of myself. But how was I going to do it and yet be tough enough to stand up for what I believed in the face of mounting criticism? Yes, Sue had it easier, I thought, as I watched her reach the end of the corridor and disappear through a door.

Time was running out. The hospital was not geared for stays much longer than two months. The luxury of being able to work with Christopher while he was hospitalized would not be permitted much longer. Hospital policies and limited insurance coverage were prohibiting the long-term treatment that Christopher needed. I would have to move quickly. I wanted him to remember as much as possible—all the trauma, I hoped—before he left the safe environment of the hospital.

The day after his birthday, I plunged into the treatment again.

"I don't want to remember everything," Christopher said. "I'm afraid. I have a strange feeling that—I feel like if I remember everything"—his voice grew tense and louder—"I won't be gay anymore," he blurted out. Then he became more anxious and perplexed as he contemplated what he had just said. "That is strange, isn't it?"

"Yes, it's strange that you should be worried about *not* being gay, when you had fought your homosexuality for so many years," I said, raising one eyebrow at the irony of it. "Are you comfortable with being homosexual now?"

"Not really."

"That's what I sensed from you."

"It is funny because I prayed so hard that I wouldn't be gay. I attended church every week and frequently went to see the chaplain when I was in the service. I hoped he would help me save myself from it."

"What happened?"

"I don't remember, but I know it didn't work out with him and I tried to kill myself afterward."

Jackie came out and was only too eager to tell me how the chaplain had failed with Christopher. I could just imagine that chaplain's face when she took over for Christopher. The chaplain had been counseling a wayward and sincere young man about sexual sins and then . . . *pow!* The chaplain was hit with a barrage of Jackie's wrath.

"What do you remember most about Christopher's appointment with the chaplain?" I asked Jackie.

"His face . . . the look on his face. He was *so* disappointed in Christopher," she said mockingly. "Christopher had been such a devout Christian. It was like Christopher had failed. He was sure that Christopher had just not had enough faith."

Jackie's face began to flush with anger as she recalled the chaplain's attitude.

"I felt violent," she continued. "I wanted to hit him or hurt him somehow. He didn't care. He didn't care about Christopher. Just himself . . . to prove he was right . . . that if only Christopher had prayed hard enough and had enough faith, he wouldn't be homosexual. But I didn't care anymore," she said bitterly. "I was going to help Christopher myself by telling everyone and getting it over with." Jackie clenched her fists.

Just when I thought that Jackie's rage might get out of hand, James came to the rescue. He, James, did not remember anything from the chaplain's office.

I redirected James's attention so that Jackie, who was listening in, could calm down about the incident in the chaplain's office.

"Let's leave the place you are in right now, James. Let your mind drift to a different memory about Christopher's homosexuality and his fear of it."

James allowed himself to go into a trance so deeply that he did not seem to have the motivation to talk. But, as we had arranged, he signaled me with a slight move of his index finger to let me know he was remembering. When Christopher opened his eyes after the trance, he tried to piece together the meaning of the memory he now had.

"I know why I don't want to be straight anymore," Christopher said fearfully. "I know why it's better that I stay a homosexual."

I sensed that we were getting to something important, something that stirred apprehension in me. "Why?" I asked.

"I might hurt someone. Kids."

"What kids?"

"My own."

"So being straight means being married and having kids, kids you would hurt."

"I already have," he said mournfully. "I mean, I don't like having kids around, and I've already hurt them."

"You would be or have been abusive to children because you have been abused?" I asked, seeking clarification.

"I don't know if I was abused, but I do know I abused some kids."

I held my breath, hoping he would not confess he had committed a crime. Yet, he had to confess whatever secret he held, for his own sake. His mental health depended on his coming to grips with his past.

"What did you do, Christopher?"

"I've never told anyone. I can't." He shook his head.

"You . . . you *can*." I nodded slowly.

"No, honest. I can't." He nervously rubbed his thumb. The tension mounted in him, and in me, too. "I can't hear myself say it. That would make it too real."

"And you've tried to make it unreal so that you could forget it. But if what you've just remembered is true, you cannot change what has already happened, whether you confess it or not." I peered at him unwaveringly. "What did you do, Christopher?"

"I pushed him around," he faltered. "My little foster brother." His voice became constricted. "I pushed him." I could tell that he was making a conscious effort to stifle the rising pitch in his voice. "I beat him. I was jealous. I wanted to hurt him bad, really bad. That's the evil in me. I wanted to do to him what had been done to me."

"What had been done to you?" I followed.

"I don't know," he said sincerely. I waited quietly for a few moments, but Christopher revealed nothing more.

"You said 'kids.' Who else did you hurt besides him?" I probed.

"Two more." His answer came reluctantly. "I feel like I did to them what was done to me. Maybe I ruined them, too."

"What did you do?"

"You know."

"You hit them?"

"No."

"You sexually molested them?"

"I didn't think of it as sexually molesting them," he said, furrowing his brow. His head dropped between his slumped shoulders. "I didn't think I really hurt them—until now."

"So what did you do?" I urged.

"To the little one, the three-year-old, I only pushed my body next to his."

"With your clothes off?" I asked relentlessly.

"Yes."

"And how old was the other little boy?"

"He was seven or maybe nine."

"What did you do to him?"

"The same thing, but I was forcing him, harder." Christopher shuddered in disgust. His face was that of a man who had just witnessed an abhorrent crime. He threw his head back as if to thrust the memories from his mind. His neck and face were strained. And, flushed with self-loathing, he involuntarily shuddered again.

"It's not real," he said of his despicable sexual behavior. "Not real." He shook his head. "I can't believe I did such a thing."

"How old were you when you molested those boys, Christopher?"

"Fourteen the first time. The second time I was sixteen. I was old enough to know better," he said with self-contempt.

"Let me remind you how your life stood at that point. You

138

were a tormented teenager whose parents had recently divorced. You were so distraught that you had made a suicide attempt. You received insufficient help from a psychologist. You had started into the drug scene." I paused to let him reflect a moment. "This does not excuse your behavior, Christopher. There can be no excuse for sexually molesting innocent little boys," I stated. "But you must understand that at a point of tremendous stress in your life, you reverted to a reenactment of what had been done to you as a child."

"I'm saying it had happened to me, but I don't *know* that it has. For some reason, I feel like it has happened, but I don't remember it. I'm probably just looking for an excuse," he said. He rocked to and fro in his chair, the kind of rocking I had seen abused children do, reflecting an unremitting negation of himself.

Perhaps Christopher was right. Maybe he needed an "out" so that he could live with himself. But it was evident that Christopher's past held a secret so sordid that his conscious mind refused to remember the trauma and instead, fragmented into other personalities in order to survive. The clues, thus far, all pointed to Christopher's father, yet I could find no more evidence. Sissy, James, and Jackie knew nothing, in spite of age-regression hypnosis.

The memories had to be stored in The Watcher.

Several painstaking hypnosis sessions had been devoted to calling out The Watcher, but to no avail. The resistance within Christopher was insurmountable. No part of him, in particular, The Watcher, who had probably seen it all, was willing to bring forth the memory of his childhood trauma. None of my urging, support, or reassurances would suffice. No part of Christopher was ready to cope with the past.

December was drawing to an end, and Christmas had arrived before I knew it. Like most people, I was caught in a flurry of pre-Christmas shopping and social obligations that made my divided loyalties even more burdensome. Christopher grew depressed as the other patients planned to spend the Christmas weekend at home with their families. Christopher's mother and brother did not call. He had no one with whom he could spend the holiday. Curious about my family, he wanted to know how I would be spending the three days with my parents in Arizona.

Christopher wanted to hear stories about my family, especially my son. He wanted happy thoughts to keep with him on Christmas Day.

On December 24, Christmas Eve, I scheduled three hours to be with Christopher before I left for Arizona. I was utilizing every bit of hospital time available. We'd be traveling at night, after work, on Christmas Eve—how foolish for both José and I to be working so hard that we had imposed this schedule on our family.

In order to prepare Christopher, I called the hospital from my office early that afternoon and told Sue of my plans for an in-depth session. She understood that I was feeling pressed for time because of the inquiries from the hospital's administrative office and the officials' concerns over the length of Christopher's hospital stay. Sue said she would make sure that Christopher was ready to take all the time necessary with me before I left.

I found Sue and Christopher together in one of the consultation rooms. A small, sparsely decorated Christmas tree—a dismal recognition of the season—was lost in the corner of the room. Sue had set out a few Christmas cookies and some coffee in an attempt to create some holiday spirit. I had brought my own Christmas cookies—store-bought, not homemade with the caring that having more time would have let me express. I added them to the assortment. Despite the effort at some degree of festivity, Christopher and I talked with anxious anticipation in our voices.

We both knew that a long session would be more likely to wear down Christopher's defenses and begin to uncover the memories. I, myself, realized that the Christmas holiday and my short leave of absence created stress and depression in Christopher, making him more fragile than usual. It may have seemed cruel to an outsider for me to intensify the probing while Christopher was at his lowest ebb and when I was just about to leave. But I knew that Christopher would be well cared for in the hospital, and I could be reached by telephone if really needed. I also knew that the breakthrough Christopher needed was most likely to occur when he was most vulnerable and least able to use his accustomed defenses.

The three of us chitchatted awhile. Christopher revealed that he was worried about the hypnotherapy scheduled for that day because he had a feeling something was going to happen. I was pleased to hear of Christopher's "intuitions." The foreboding he felt let me know he could not defend against the forbidden memories and keep them repressed much longer.

It took him more time than usual to go into the depth of the trance. Christopher went into the trance recounting many of the memories that had come forth in previous sessions. What was curious, however, was that Christopher himself was now recalling the memories that had, heretofore, been housed within the other personalities. I was intrigued that he had accepted the memories—in detail, one by one—as his own and had begun to integrate them into himself.

Then his voice changed. I could tell he had stopped being Christopher. He was Timmy.

"But I love Daddy," he said, and then the four-year-old voice became a whisper. "I feel . . . my stomach hurts," he whimpered. "And the back of my head." He moaned.

"What happened to your head, Timmy?" I asked softly.

"He threw me on the floor," he answered, his voice quaking. "Put his foot on my stomach." Timmy struggled as he appeared to be attempting to escape.

At this point, his words changed back to the present tense. He was reliving the incident as if it were actually happening to him in the moment. "I can't breathe!" he cried painfully. "No! Daddy!" His voice quivered. "Don't do that to me!" He flinched. "Not to me! Do it to him! Put it in him!"

"In where?"

"Where I go to the bathroom," he trembled. "No. No. I won't go in the bathroom with you!" He shrieked. "I'm not going. He can go."

I was about to ask who was the third party in the bathroom when the telephone in the conference room rang. I jumped in my seat. Dear Lord, not now!

Before Christopher was wakened by the second ring, I quickly gave an instruction that he would not hear anything in the room, not even the sound of my voice, and would instead go more deeply into the trance until I touched him on the forehead, signaling that he hear me again. Christopher drifted more deeply into the trance, enabling me to answer the telephone. My office had called to say I was a half-hour late for my office appointment. My next patient was sitting in my waiting room. I looked at my watch in disbelief. How could three and a half hours have passed so quickly?

I could not leave Christopher now. My other patient would have to wait, I told my exasperated secretary. I went back to Christopher, touched him on the forehead, and continued to talk to him. He remained deeply in the trance, although he could hear my instructions. He was motionless and did not speak. I knew he needed to rest, to escape into the farthest reaches of his mind, where he could feel peaceful again. I allowed him to remain in this quiet state for a while, and then attempted to bring him slowly out of the trance.

Christopher was not eager to wake up. Most of the feelings and memories were likely to remain with him, and I sensed he wanted just a last few moments of serenity.

After yawning and stretching like a cat waking up, Christopher hung his head. He began recalling the events.

"I didn't know," he said aghast. "I never suspected. It all makes sense now. It's all starting to fall into place. I was even younger than four, maybe three. Mother told me I always hung around my father when I was small, that I went everywhere with him when he was home on leave, but I didn't remember that. Now I know why Timmy always misses Dad."

But the pleasant memory of the warm and loving relationship that Timmy had always wanted with his father was juxtaposed against the memory of a brutal, terrorizing father. The opposing thoughts, the conflicts within him, tormented Christopher, and he began to sob uncontrollably.

"I always thought that my father just got too angry sometimes. But now I know he beat me. That's what happened to Timmy. His father would be affectionate, and then he would turn around and beat him violently." Christopher's face was wet with tears. "How could I have kept missing my father so?"

I searched for an explanation to give him. "Christopher, battered children usually want to return to the abusive parent. At least they feel some connection with that parent. At least that parent gives them some attention, even if it is negative. Children prefer attention—any kind of attention—to neglect or indifference. Your mother left you alone in the playpen, alone in your room, alone in the yard, alone in the fields. You got nothing from her."

"But my father," Christopher interjected, "picked me up and held me."

"So you wanted him. He also beat you violently. From today's session, it seems he probably sexually abused you as well."

"I don't remember anything sexual. Timmy was afraid of something like that, but nothing sexual really happened to him. He just had a feeling it would."

"My guess is that it happened to one of your other personalities. I don't know which one, except it has to be male. Timmy kept saying a 'he' would go into the bathroom with your father. At least that clarifies that it didn't happen to Sissy, the way I had suspected."

I immediately realized that I was explaining this more to myself than to Christopher, who was only half listening to my final sentence. He had curled up in a ball in his chair and clutched his abdomen as if someone had just dealt him a blow to the stomach. He shuddered fiercely and gripped himself more unremittingly than before. An irrepressible sobbing seized his entire body. And as Christopher struggled to quell the tears, I wished I could ease his pain. Had I pushed him too far, too fast? Had he forgotten what Timmy said in the trance, and had I mistakenly forced the memory onto Christopher? Whether or not I had, I couldn't possibly leave him alone with this suffering now. Surely my other patient had gone home by now and José was impatiently waiting, but I had to stay longer.

"Christopher, please let the tears out," I told him. "Share this with me. You're no longer alone with this memory. You must allow yourself to feel the pain and the sorrow and to cry all the tears that you never cried as a child, all the tears that you've held in for so many years. Allow yourself to share this painful feeling with me."

Christopher let himself go and released the tears he had been trying to suppress. His suffering overwhelmed me. Exhausted from the four-hour marathon, I could contain myself no longer.

I dropped the personage of the doctor and went to Christopher as a person who could not allow him to suffer alone in his imposed isolation. I sat beside him and put my arm around his shoulder as he remained in his hunched, self-protective position. The urge to hold him and comfort him was far greater than the need to retain my professional reserve.

I closed my eyes and felt the gentle heaving of his body next to mine. I held him in this manner until the sobs slowly subsided. With agonizing slowness, Christopher moved his arm away from his abdomen and curled it around my waist. We stayed poised in this embrace for what seemed an eternity, while the shuddering and sobbing came to a culmination. When I felt that he had finished, I carefully pulled away.

I stood in front of him, and he looked up at me with complete vulnerability and trust in his doelike eyes. Words seemed superfluous.

"I'll see you Monday," he said finally, in hushed, listless tones. "Merry Christmas."

I felt a heaviness in my chest as I left Christopher there alone. I had accomplished what I had hoped for in that long grueling afternoon. The repressed memories were beginning to break through. I knew the entire story would be surfacing as a result. I hated to have to leave him there, even though I knew he'd be with Sue until evening. I wished I could have brought him home with me for Christmas.

Christmas at my parent's house was indeed a merry one—the kind of Christmas that everyone dreams about, but, unfortunately, so few people have. My mother had cooked and baked for weeks ahead of time. Her house was spotlessly clean, and the Christmas tree and living room were decorated with gilt and glitter. Neighbors stopped by with friendly greetings, and the phone was busy with well-wishers and relatives. Church services for the family were a must, as was the traditional turkey dinner. The children scampered restlessly throughout the house as the excitement grew and presents were about to be opened.

In the quieter hours after the discarded wrappings had been gathered up, my mother and I talked happily while we did the dishes together. My husband and father had retired to the living room to "talk business," the two of them pleased with their comfortable, man-to-man relationship. It was a simple, conventional day we had spent together, and I wouldn't have wanted it any other way.

I was filled with a deep contentment, but later that day my happiness was tinged with a sorrow for Christopher. I tried to imagine what Christmas would have been like for Christopher while he was growing up. I imagined him in a dismally meager home, surrounded by a family filled with strife and tension. What kind of Christmas would Mrs. Kincaid have prepared for her children? She was depressed when she stayed with her offspring, so she was out of the house at every excuse.

I knew who she was firsthand. I had met Christopher's mother shortly after he was hospitalized the second time. Eager to have as much information as I could about his family, I had asked Mrs. Kincaid if she could make a trip to our city so that I could have an interview with her. After complaining that she was not feeling well and that she did not have the money for gas and that she would have to wait until she could get a day off work, she unenthusiastically conceded. I did not think she would actually come, but Christopher was sure she would be there because she had a strong need to appear to be a supportive mother.

When she arrived at the hospital, I watched her give her son an awkward, obligatory peck on the cheek. Instead of a comfortable embrace, they both stiffened at the touch and instantly repelled from each other's arms like two same-poled magnets.

I would never have guessed that she was Christopher's mother, either from their manner together or from her appearance. She was a tall, sturdy, large-boned, masculine-looking woman with an olive complexion. Her hair was unkempt, and I thought she had the overall appearance of a skid-row alcoholic.

She was the total opposite of Christopher. It was incredible to me that she could have produced such a delicate, fair-haired, and polished son. Christopher had told me that he was the physical image of his father, and after seeing Mrs. Kincaid, I knew it had to be true.

But some of Christopher's stories did not seem to fit the image she presented. She was certainly not the type of woman I could imagine strolling seductively about the house in a transparent nightgown. Nor could I see her as the type who would run off with a lover or find employment as a cocktail waitress. It was easy, however, to envision her iron-handedly manipulating her husband into cooking the meals, cleaning the house, and tending the children while she went to work.

Mrs. Kincaid was guarded about her family's history and the stories of Christopher's childhood. She more freely told me of the aches and pains that were currently plaguing her or the many illnesses she suffered through the years. She said she was only seventeen years old when she and Christopher's father married. Left alone with a baby while her young husband was away, she was unable to cope with the responsibility. Severe depression consumed her for several years while Christopher was small. As a way of coping with an intolerable marriage and an unfulfilling life, she became increasingly fanatical in her religious beliefs. Most of the time she was unaware of what Christopher was doing. Even as a baby, she left him alone while she slept or sat mesmerized by the television.

By the time Christopher was six years old, her life began to change. Because of her deepening depression, she started seeing a psychiatrist, who told her to take a job as a way of making her life better. As soon as her husband was stationed near their home, and was, therefore, able to care for the children, she took an evening job as a cocktail waitress. The work was good for her. She gained confidence, and the depression lifted. As the years went by, however, she and her husband grew steadily apart.

Mr. Kincaid began to drink more than ever. An otherwise passive man, he would become violently aggressive while drinking. She described him as being singularly unaffectionate with her. Their sex life was so unsatisfactory that she felt like nothing more than an object of his drunken convenience. Frustrated with her sexual relationship, she took a lover. This was paradoxical to her religious beliefs, but—somehow—she rationalized the conflict. When her husband learned of her affair, he picked her up at the cocktail lounge one night, brought her home, and raped her in the living room. Christopher was in the room when it happened, but Mrs. Kincaid claimed that Christopher was fast asleep on the couch and did not wake up in spite of the noise of the brutality.

On several occasions thereafter, Mr. Kincaid severely beat and kicked his wife, until she began to fear for her life. Like many battered wives, she was afraid to leave and afraid to stay. Finally, she got the opportunity to make her break. This was her reason, she said, for abandoning her children and fleeing in the middle of the night, leaving only a note that she had left the state with another man.

Christopher had been able to tell me about his mother's abandonment of her children, but he had not recalled any of the events that led up to it. If there had been brutal beatings, Christopher had probably witnessed them but did not consciously remember. I pressed Mrs. Kincaid so that I could learn more about Christopher's now deceased father.

She said that Mr. Kincaid was an illiterate man who was unable to hold down a regular job or to function outside of military service. He had been one of thirteen children, and his parents, who had never attended a day of school, raised the children to fend for themselves. He grew up in the Louisiana swamp lands, far from civilized society and without moral upbringing. She suspected that her ex-husband's childhood was fraught with problems and unusual experiences. He left the swamps at age fifteen and began to work in New Orleans. He joined the service when he turned eighteen, and by the time she met him, he had put on an outward appearance of stability and maturity, which she thought would be her own salvation.

I had asked her to describe Christopher's relationship with his father. She said that for the first three years of Christopher's life, Mr. Kincaid was gone most of the time. When he was at home, Mrs. Kincaid was less depressed, and, therefore, even as a baby, Christopher began to look forward to his father's arrival. When Christopher was three or four, he spent many hours alongside his father, wanting to be close to him.

Mrs. Kincaid thought they had had a nice relationship when Christopher was that age because his father seemed more affectionate with Christopher than she had seen him be with anyone. He was harsh in his discipline of Christopher, but she made light of that fact. She sometimes felt jealous of what she saw between them and would try to win back Christopher's attention. Then she gave up and simply decided to leave the children with their father while she went to work at night. As Christopher approached school age, Mrs. Kincaid said that there seemed to be less affection between father and son. She attributed this to the fact that Mr. Kincaid had developed friendships with several drinking buddies and always had these men over to their house, leaving less time for Christopher.

On many occasions, she would return home from work at 2:30 A.M. to see men scampering from the house like sailors jumping a sinking ship. They all knew that when she arrived she would raise hell about the drunken chaos she found. More than once, neighbors had called the police to break up brawls that frequently broke out among the "houseguests."

By the time Christopher was thirteen, she could see the open animosity between father and son, and again, she believed it was because of Christopher's dislike of his father's friends.

My interview with Mrs. Kincaid burned in my memory after the last agonizing session with Christopher. The few quiet, inactive hours I had at the Christmas holiday provided just enough time to speculate about Christopher's father. He must have had a rigid, intolerant personality that adapted well to the military but could not adjust elsewhere. He was not raised with the moral taboos that most of us know. Conceivably, he, too, could have been physically or sexually assaulted as a child. He was uneducated and unable to use words to defend himself.

Since he was passive when sober, the anger would build up in him. Then when he drank, as he did frequently, the anger became explosive violence. He could not control his wife's behavior. She was psychologically emasculating and had increasingly become independent of him. The only power he had was when he terrorized his wife and his son, Christopher, the child who loved him most.

Sexually, he must have felt terribly inadequate with his wife. He donned an apron and did the household chores while she went out to work. She also cuckolded him and channeled her sexual favors to other men.

His male friends were disreputable. They were his match when it came to unwholesome character. At least one of them was known to have sexually molested Christopher. Birds of a feather . . . I thought to myself. And Mr. Kincaid was capable of equal misdeeds. I knew there had to be much more to uncover when I returned to the hospital and saw Christopher.

I came home from the Christmas trip on Sunday in the late afternoon. Unpacking took hours because of the abundance of toys and clothes that my children had received. I hurried to the store and then fixed dinner. I watched my husband playing with the children in the family room. Arms and legs flailed everywhere amidst the giggling, tickling, screeching, and tumbling. It was not until the three of them were in their pajamas and snuggled in on the sofa that I took a break to call Christopher at the hospital.

"I've been . . . okay," he said in answer to my question, but his voice trailed off with a hollow, faraway intonation that contradicted his statement. More truthfully, he went on, "I'm feeling confused. I came out about an hour ago and I don't know why. This is James."

It didn't sound quite like James, so I was glad he told me. The personalities are beginning to blend a little, I thought.

"What went on today, James?" I asked.

"Nothing special. It's just that some of us are afraid. As for me, I'm feeling angry right now, and I don't know why." He paused for a minute, contemplating what to say next, I thought. "There's something else." He stalled again. "I don't know how this writing got on my hand."

"There's writing on your hand?" I asked blankly.

"It's not there anymore," James said mysteriously. "It was written with a ballpoint pen, but I scrubbed it off."

"What did it say?"

"It was the number twenty-four and the word 'sand.' I don't know how it got there. Neither does Christopher."

"Could one of the others have put it there?"

"Maybe. Jackie was hanging around when I was taking a shower. She's really angry, too. Wait . . . I lost my train of thought. I . . . get confused sometimes when I come out . . . especially when I don't know why I'm out. I feel sleepy, too. Things are so complex, so confusing."

As he talked, I quickly tried to piece things together. But I came up with no guesses. The writing on the hand dumbfounded me. How childish it was to write on his hand. Who could have done it? Timmy? No, he was too young to do such things. It couldn't have been Jackie. She was too old by now, and more direct in her expression. Then who? I wondered.

"Something else has been going on," James continued. "But I can't tell you here."

"Is there a staff member or patient listening?"

"Yes."

"Is it about a staff member?"

"Uh, huh. I talked about him once, do you remember?"

"I'm not sure who you are referring to."

"I don't think I should tell you anyway. It would ruin it. It's all going to get messed up."

"We'll talk tomorrow," I said reluctantly.

My mind began to sort through the information I now had. Given that I had just been separated from Christopher for three days, he would have been experiencing the abandonment feelings and would be resisting his dependency on me. This, I felt, would duplicate the experience he had had with his mother. In his original family triangle, he would then be emotionally thrown toward his father. In this case, he would seek a father surrogate. If my deductions were correct, the staff member who concerned him would be the homosexual male nurse who was several years older than Christopher. Because of the potential for physical affection, this man would be the perfect target for Christopher's transference feelings.

I changed the subject. "Did any of your friends or Christopher's family contact him on Christmas Day?" I asked.

"No, but after you left on Christmas Eve, Christopher called his mother," James reported. "He wanted to tell her what he remembered during the hypnosis and to see if she thought Christopher may have been sexually abused. His mother cried on the telephone and told him she was sorry. Then the silly woman said she thought something like that might have happened but didn't want to think about it. When those kinds of thoughts crept in, she said, she pushed them away, telling herself that it was just her dirty mind."

My hunch was becoming more clear. Christopher was realizing he had been emotionally abandoned by his mother all of his life. No wonder Jackie was angry. Like many third parties in the incest triangle, Christopher's mother had known, on some level, that her son was being abused but had looked the other way rather than protect him.

Christopher was out again the next day, and I immediately presented my suspicions to him. "You're feeling attracted to Dennis, aren't you?"

"Here we go! I knew you'd figure it out, you always do. Well, it's not an attraction, just sort of. An affection fits better. It doesn't make any sense, none of it does. James is just making a big deal about it. He's the one who's attracted. My feelings are that I just really like Dennis. He's stable, intelligent—he's got his act together. I need someone like him as a friend after I leave the hospital. He told me he was interested in pursuing some sort of relationship after I was discharged."

An alarm went off in my head. Nurses, especially psychiatric nurses, customarily do not promise friendships or more intimate relationships to patients. I would have to investigate this matter further with Dennis. For the moment, I simply listened as Christopher continued to volunteer his feelings.

"Timmy is really hurting, though. He wants Dennis to love him, and he's afraid he'll be rejected. The others are afraid that James is going to ruin it for Timmy. James is trying to convince them that Dennis should know that James has much stronger feelings for him, sexual feelings. Timmy just wants to be close to Dennis."

"This *is* getting quite confusing, isn't it?" I submitted. "The several parts of you have such conflicting needs and feelings."

"I know. Then on top of that, I still don't know who wrote on my hand. It had to have happened in less than five minutes." Christopher looked away. "Maybe something rubbed off on my hand," he mumbled.

"You told me it was written in ballpoint pen."

"Oh. Yeah. I really don't want to think that someone inside of me was able to do that without my knowing. At least, I hope not." He laughed nervously. "I don't know. I'm really tired. I just want to get out of this hospital."

"You mean you don't want to deal with it?"

"No. Or with Dennis. My first instincts were to run away, to just leave come Monday before Dennis came on his shift."

"We need to know how the writing got on your hand. I think it was a message regarding Dennis. After all, that is what has been disturbing you, hasn't it?"

"Maybe the person who wrote on my hand is really hurting and doesn't want to come out and confront it." His tone became firm. "Really, this has gone too far. It's absurd." He was resisting.

Christopher required a lot of convincing to allow me to use hypnosis to discover more about the writing. The induction was painstakingly slow. I caught the distinct impression that a part of him was hiding itself from me.

Carefully, I questioned each of the personalities, as if I were a sleuth stalking down a culprit in a crime. Having exhausted the possibilities, I solicited the help of *any* part of Christopher that knew about how the writing got on Christopher's hand and knew what it meant. I thought, perhaps, The Watcher might volunteer.

"Let the resistance go, Christopher," I instructed. "Let it go. You do want to know. The knowledge is there, and it will help you to have it. We're going to find out about the number twenty-four," I continued hypnotically. "Some part of you is feeling strongly about it. Some part of you has those feelings." Christopher's eyelids began to flutter, as he held them closed. His face was more animated, in the characteristic look that let me know a personality was about to emerge.

"There you are!" I exclaimed. "I see you coming closer. You are the part of Christopher that knows. You're almost there. Yes, you are. You're going to come out and talk to me." The eyes would not open but I knew that someone was listening to me. The face bore the animated countenance of another personality.

"You scared me," this new presence said with irritation. The eyes were still closed.

"I'm sorry. How did I scare you?"

"You startled me. 'There you are!' " he mimicked.

"It's just that I could tell you were getting close and I didn't want you to go away. You do want to tell me who wrote on Christopher's hand, don't you?"

"I did."

"What does the number twenty-four mean?"

"I don't know."

"You're hiding it from me. You don't want to do that."

"It means nothing."

"Yes, it does. It's an important number, so important that you wrote it on Christopher's hand and scared him."

"It was supposed to scare him, and the rest of them, too."

"Well, it certainly did that," I agreed.

"Everybody else is so big. I had to scare them to get them to stop."

"Who are you? Have I talked with you before?" I wondered.

"Maybe." The answers continued to be evasive.

"But you are smaller than the others," I said. "How old are you?"

"I'm six. Two years too late."

"What does that mean?"

"Two plus four is six. Two years too late," he said, with an inflection that made me think of the Mad Hatter's tea party.

"So that is the number twenty-four. It's really two plus four?"

"Yes."

"Timmy is four years old. Will it be two years too late for Timmy?"

"Timmy is growing up, but he doesn't know me. Nobody knows me."

"Why not?"

"I'm hiding. Under the floor."

"Why are you hiding under the floor?"

"They're all on top of me. I'm in the basement. I got out for a minute though, to scare them. They didn't know I was here."

DADDY CALLS IT PLAYING, BUT PLAYING DOESN'T HURT

"You want to be able to come all the way out," I suggested hypnotically. This personality's tactic of hiding and watching and listening was beginning to sound awfully familiar to me. "You want to be able to open your eyes and come out to talk with me." I thought of The Watcher, who wouldn't give me his name. "All the rest of you who are listening, move over and let this young person out of the basement. Move over James, Sissy, Ernest, Jackie, Jeremy. You, too, Timmy. Okay, little one, you can come all the way out now."

"No," he answered boldly. "You can't make me. Besides, I'm dirty, so I'm going to stay right where I am."

He squirmed.

"Okay, just stay there halfway out, and talk to me," I said, giving in. "What's your name?"

"Alfred."

"You're six and you can write?" I asked suspiciously.

"I'm very smart," he replied with mischievous pride.

"Alfred, what else did you write on Christopher's hand?"

"Sand. The word 'sand.' "

"What sand do you mean?"

"Beach sand, where Dennis said it would be fun to go."

I was right. It had to do with Dennis. "Dennis said he would be going to the beach with Christopher?"

"Yes, he said he's going to the beach to play. Christopher

doesn't know how to play. I thought Dennis might try to play with me." He spoke anxiously. I could see his eyes darting back and forth under his eyelids, as if even with his eyes closed, he was vigilantly watching. What did "play" mean to him? "I want to get out of here," he said nervously. "I'm going away."

Instantly, he was gone.

The mysterious voice that had never before been identified had left. I could not bring him back. My hope rested on Christopher's ability to tell me more about Alfred after the trance ended. And when I brought Christopher out of the trance with the instruction to remember, the hypnotic state—a twilight period—was still hovering about him.

"It wasn't Alfred," Christopher stated immediately. "It was Richard. He just used that name to fool you. He always tries to fool people, then he runs off and hides like that. It's funny, that's the first time I've seen him, but I sort of know about him."

Was Richard, then, The Watcher? Richard? Of course! I had forgotten about Richard.

"Is this the Richard that Timmy told me about a long time ago, the Richard he was afraid of?"

"Yes, but there's something I don't get. Why is Richard only six? If he's supposed to be a part of my past, then he should be older—maybe ten or even twelve. I remember being that old when I'd hide under the house, in closets, in the attic, and places like that. I heard and saw all kinds of things I wasn't supposed to. I seemed to like those dark places, where no one could find me."

"What else can you tell me about the beach sand, Christopher?"

"Once I—you know—got it on with a guy at the beach. I felt really dirty and guilty about doing it there. I'm not sure why it made me feel so bad. It sort of reminded me of a feeling from a long time ago."

Christopher was unable to be more specific. Richard himself would have to be the one to reveal this part of Christopher's past.

"So it was Richard who wrote on my hand," Christopher mused to himself. "What does he want?" he questioned. "Why is he here now?"

"I'm not sure. It does seem to be a warning not to get involved with Dennis—which might be a sensible idea. What I really wonder is what Richard remembers that the others don't. Whatever it is, it has to be the most critical of the memories. Let's try to find out soon."

"You want to know a secret that nobody knows?" Christopher asked.

"Something you remembered?"

"Yes. It came back to me after a hypnosis session we had. I remember listening in on a phone conversation my mother was having with her boyfriend." A cloud came over his face, and his tone darkened. "She said my sister was his baby. I used to read her letters, too. I was really sneaky."

I wondered how much Christopher remembered and how much was shielded from him by the amnesia barrier and therefore known only to Richard.

"When my mother was caught by my father," he went on, "he brought her back to the house and raped her. He forced her to say that she loved him and not the boyfriend. It happened in the living room, and I think I was beside the couch on the floor. I was pretending to be asleep. I wanted to know what she would let him do to her. I was really angry at her for not fighting back. I think he was drunk. I remember his odor."

"Why didn't you let them know you were awake?"

"He might have turned on me. Besides, I wanted to know how she was going to . . . she just let him . . . just let him. I wanted her to hit him or scream or try to get away, but she wouldn't. I was so disappointed in her. She was almost as big as him, but she let him beat her and rape her. I feel disgusted now remembering it."

"Your mother told me about this incident, Christopher. I would never have mentioned it if you had not brought it up, but I think you should know that she remembers the brutality of that night."

"What made her think of telling you that?" he asked, dumbfounded.

"I was asking her about the difficult years she had when you were growing up."

"She doesn't know I was awake?"

"No."

"She should have known," he said bitterly. "My father was probably so drunk he didn't even notice I was there. But she knew it. And she had to know his screaming and shouting foul names at her would wake me up."

"It does seem strange to me also. I think your mother has a way of denying realities to herself. Christopher, are you ready to know what Richard remembers?"

"Probably nothing," he answered evasively.

"It's always nothing, nothing important, isn't it Christopher?" I reminded him.

"I'm willing to find out whatever there is," he said, "but I don't know what he could tell you. These days I usually have some hint of it. But I just don't feel like there is anything there."

"Uncomfortable?" I asked.

"Paralyzed, actually," he said, his head still bent. "Lately I've been feeling really frightened right before and right after the hypnosis. I keep telling myself that there is nothing there, nothing to remember. That's the only way I seem to be able to make myself go through with the session."

"Perhaps there is nothing there, Christopher," I said, trying to allay some of his resistance. "It's also possible that if you uncover something your conscious mind truly cannot accept, you will simply not remember it after the hypnosis. And I promise I will not tell you about anything that you cannot spontaneously recall after the trance. I promise to wait until you let me know you can cope with the memory—whatever it is."

Christopher raised his head and looked at me trustingly. "You really wouldn't tell me a secret I didn't want to hear, would you?"

"No, I wouldn't. I've told you that before, and I don't think I've broken that promise yet, have I?"

Christopher shook his head.

"I would use the information, Christopher, to give me a direction that I needed to work with you on a conscious level, to prepare all your parts to accept the repressed material that Richard probably remembers. As soon as enough of your co-conscious minds were ready, you would probably remember all by yourself, without hypnosis."

Christopher seemed to comprehend fully and to trust what I was telling him. Less frightened now, he was ready.

As soon as Christopher was in a trance, I called to Richard. "Richard," I beckoned, "I believe you are close by today. Where are you?"

"Just behind the corner," he answered, to my relief. At least he was going to talk, even if he wouldn't let me look into his eyes.

Richard was hiding, immobile.

"Richard, I need to know what you remember, what you've seen and heard that nobody else has seen or heard. Tell me, what memories do you have?"

"Only unimportant ones," he said with characteristic evasiveness and understatement.

"Tell me about Christopher's father, Richard. Was he your father, too?"

"Yes."

"What do you remember about your father?"

"I don't want to be like him."

"Why not?"

With a tormented look on his face, Richard began to twist his body in the chair. He seemed to want to get away, to run. He shook his head at some unnamed threat.

"Richard, you keep shaking your head. Why are you saying 'no'?"

"Afraid . . . afraid to hear."

"Nothing will harm you today because you are listening. You can tell me what you are hearing. There is no need to be afraid."

I watched his body relax.

"I don't remember nothing," he said adamantly. "I don't . . . remember . . . any nights. No nights. I just remember the parties. I just remember when Mom was home."

"Yes, Richard, you remember the parties and you remember the nights when your mother was home. You remember the nights when your mother was not at home. You remember the nights when there were no parties."

"I don't remember."

"Yes, it's all there. You don't need to be afraid anymore. You can tell me about the nights when your mother wasn't home and there were no parties."

"My head hurts," he protested. His fingers pressed his temples as he grimaced in pain. But his eyes remained closed.

"I know." My voice softened. "You get a headache when you try to keep the memories locked away. The memories are trying to come out."

He shook his head.

"Let the memories out and the headache will go away."

Richard had calmed down but still appeared frightened.

"You are inside Christopher's body," I said, "and Christopher is all grown up. He is no longer helpless, and he is getting stronger every day. You can help him get stronger. You can help him by letting the memories out."

Richard pouted. "But I'm not grown up! I'm still little, and I can't be strong enough."

"I understand. But now you have two grown-ups, me and Christopher, to help you. You are no longer alone. Ernest and Jeremy are there to help you, too. You don't need to be afraid. Just relax. Let's go back to those nights. Where is your brother?" I asked this deliberately, aware that I was changing to the present tense.

"He's in Mom and Dad's room . . . asleep."

"Why is he in there?"

"Because he's a little baby."

"What's your father doing?"

"I don't remember." But his face contorted, and tears rimmed under his closed lashes.

"You remember," I urged. "It is right there in front of you. What is happening?"

He squirmed and wiggled in his chair, his face and body twisted.

"Why are you wiggling like that, Richard?"

" 'Cause I hurt!" he sniveled tremulously.

"Where do you hurt?"

"My back."

"What's wrong with your back?"

"I fell off my bed," he cried. Then he shouted in anguish, "I hate him!"

"Why do you hate him?"

"He's always mean. He hurts me."

"What happens on the nights when your mother is at work and there are no parties?"

"He takes me in my room . . . always . . . on the bed."

"What is he doing now? Your brother is asleep in the other room and your mother is gone."

"Daddy calls it playing," he said as he restlessly twisted in his chair.

"Do you like this playing?"

"Sometimes."

"What is it you like?"

"Just being with Daddy. First he holds me," he said, his voice breaking.

"Do you hold each other?"

"No, he always holds me."

"How is he holding you?"

"Down!" he said sharply, with an angry resistance in his voice.

"Where?"

"He is pushing my shoulders on the bed, just biting me on the neck, biting me on the . . ." Richard let out a piercing shriek. "Oh, no! Please, Daddy, don't poke it in me. Please! Please!" he cried pathetically. His voice fell to a hollow whimper. "Ohhh." He moaned in pain. "It hurts, Daddy." He swallowed his tears. "Playing doesn't hurt, Daddy."

I felt sick at my stomach. His voice drifted away as he mumbled something inaudibly, and his body lay limp and spent. Richard was exhausted. The scene had ended. He could not reveal any more of the long-held secrets. There was no energy left to find the words.

I gave a hypnotic suggestion to Christopher to remember as much as he was ready to accept. I hoped that whatever Richard was not able to tell, Christopher would be able to tell for him.

Christopher came out of the trance looking as if he had been a thousand miles away. He appeared sleepy and spent. "Hmmm," he said to himself, "hmmm . . ." He sat silently and stared into space. Minutes went by. I sat in anticipation. Would Christopher be able to describe what had happened to Richard?

"Tell me what Richard remembered, Christopher."

"Just being held down." He paused for a moment to think. "I was never there. I don't remember anything."

"But you remember what was happening to Richard?"

"Yes. But that can't be real. It was always dark. And . . ."

"And what?"

Christopher laughed, nervous with embarrassment, as if he were being asked to tell a dirty joke in polite company. "Just that—no, no, my father *couldn't* have been that bad," he said with disbelief.

"It's important that I know what Richard was experiencing," I said.

"Just that Dad had him down on the bed and he couldn't move." He sat frozen. "It was scary . . . just hurt all over . . . couldn't move."

"You said your father couldn't be as bad as that. As bad as what?"

Christopher's voice suddenly crescendoed out of control, and he said loudly. "What he was doing!" He jumped up from his chair. Then, calming himself, he sat limp again and mumbled something under his breath. He was talking to himself and had forgotten that I was in the room. After a couple of minutes, he looked up at me with a startled expression, as if I had just called his name. "Huh?" he asked, breaking his reverie.

"Saying what you are thinking makes it real, Christopher."

"It's just not possible . . . not easy to say."

"Please continue with what you were telling me. Richard was being held down on the bed."

"My father was biting him someplace. Not hard, though."

"Where did he put his mouth?"

Christopher's back stiffened, and he sat rigidly upright in his chair. He braced himself. "It's hard to say." He took a deep breath. "Uh—basically—he was going down on him, that's all."

"That's what he did."

"Yeah. It doesn't work, though. It's not the same."

"What do you mean?"

"It's just too small, and I don't think it excited him enough because he then got more rough and angry."

Torturous silent moments passed before Christopher could

161

continue. "He must have been masturbating—on Richard—rubbing his body up and down against him to get excited."

The images nauseated me. I began to feel lightheaded, but I had to press on. I had to finish this once and for all. Christopher had fallen silent again and had closed his eyes, trying to block out the picture in his mind. It was useless. Now that the memory had come back, it would not go away. "Oh, this is awful!" he lamented painfully. "He got hard and . . . then . . . he—he . . . it hurt so bad when he—he . . ."

I knew Christopher could not get the words out.

"Penetrated Richard." I finished the sentence.

"Yes!" he shouted shrilly. "Oh," he moaned again. "I'm going to be sick."

He wailed, grabbing his abdomen. He leaned over in his chair. I waited with the certainty that the contents of his stomach would spill on the floor, but he retched dryly, heaving empty spasms of air and saliva. My own stomach turned over. Nausea nearly got the best of me. This is excruciating, I thought to myself, more than I can bear!

I wanted to flee. Any refuge would do. I considered running to the restroom, if not to relieve the contents of my stomach, at least to be alone. But I could not abandon Christopher at a time like this.

The memory had been frozen in time. Now, brought to light, it was as fresh and real as if it had just happened in front of my eyes, just as vivid and intense as when the sexual abuse had first occurred. He had relived it, and I had experienced it with him.

Christopher and I did not speak further as we tried to regain our composure. I was able to quell my nausea, spurred by the desire to help Christopher.

"It all adds up." Christopher began to talk at last. "The same traits, the same traits I've picked up. Wanting to be held down. Having some guy go down on me . . . or the masturbation. Wanting it when somebody does it on me."

"Yes, Christopher," I said in hushed tones. "It all makes sense."

We looked at each other in full recognition of the truth. Then I had to look away, to shield myself from the overwhelming pain I saw in his eyes.

"But it would have to come from somewhere," he persisted

courageously. "All these confused feelings I have about sex have to come from somewhere, don't they?"

"Yes, Christopher. The pieces will begin to fall in place now over the next few days. You can begin to make sense of it slowly."

I knew his mind was flooded with ideas, I knew, as he stood up and began to pace the floor, trying desperately to sort through the internal chaos. He could not wait until later to put together the shambles of his life.

"My first sexual experiences were like that," he said. He turned his back to me and faced the wall. "Once when I was thirteen, I was thrown into juvenile hall. There was a guy there, a few years older than me. He wanted to rub it against me and I wanted him to." I could see the back of Christopher's neck flush red. "I was afraid of something, but it wasn't like I was *aware* I was afraid he'd put it in me. He never did, but somehow I knew he could. Why would I even have considered that when I was thirteen?"

"Why do you think?"

"It had to have happened to me before. I didn't know any homosexuals or know anything about being gay or what gays do. I didn't *want* him to put it in me. I was *afraid* he would do it."

"It seems that from what you remembered today, it was done to you before—by your father."

"But I don't remember anything with my father," he protested. "I seem to remember all the other horrible sexual things, but I don't remember doing it with my father."

"Richard remembers your father doing it to him, and Richard is a part of you." I studied his face to see if he was going to accept this reality fully. "You are Richard and Richard is you," I repeated, hoping the words would sink in.

Christopher flinched. "I know," he said reluctantly. "It must be true, but I still don't want to accept it. It makes me feel strange because I don't remember it myself. I can see it happening to Richard, when I think about it. I don't see it happening to me."

"It's easier to think of Richard being the victim of incest and not you."

"Incest? Is that what it is—incest?" Christopher looked

shocked. "I always thought I was abused. I was pushed around, and my parents didn't care about me. After talking to my mother on the phone, I thought I may have been sexually abused. But I never thought of it as *incest*." He frowned. "I guess it was incest."

"Christopher, don't you remember telling me about those little boys you sexually molested when you were a teenager?"

"Yes. I said I felt like I was doing to them what had been done to me. But I couldn't figure out where I was getting that feeling. I didn't remember anything—ever being sexually abused. Now I find out it really had been done," Christopher said incredulously. "Richard is me. It had been done to . . . to . . . to *me*." He choked. "By my *father*," he added in horror.

I could not find words. It was impossible. How could I ever fully comprehend?

"I suppose I'll start figuring out the rest of my traits pretty soon," he said without enthusiasm.

"I think you will."

"If I'm just repeating what was done to me, is there any chance I can stop repeating it?" he asked hopefully.

"A good chance," I answered reassuringly. "Consider that you haven't sexually molested any little boys since you were not much more than a boy yourself. With new insights, very likely some of your feelings about sex will change."

"I always thought I was born homosexual, that it was in my genes," he said pensively. "I remember wanting men from the time I was very little. One time I remember feeling really close to a man who was Dad's friend. He took me bike riding. I sat on the back with my arms around him. It felt special."

"Lots of boys want to be close to adult men—physically close and affectionate. That doesn't mean the boy is developing homosexual feelings."

"I loved that man."

"It's too bad you weren't raised in a healthy way so that you would have known those feelings were normal. Of course, you loved that man. He was being good to you."

"Homosexuality isn't in my genes?"

"No one knows if homosexuality is biological or if it is a learned or adaptive behavior."

"If it's something I learned, not something I was born with, then maybe it could be changed. If I'm repeating what was done to me, maybe I'm not gay."

"That's a possibility. You once told me you didn't want to remember everything because if you did, you wouldn't be gay anymore."

"I did say that, didn't I," he said with amazement. "But do you understand why I said it? It's because I can't imagine myself any other way. Being gay is all I've ever known," he said with anguish. "It scares me to think about being straight."

"That would be a major change in your life. You don't have to think about such a monumental change right at this moment. Take one day at a time. Most important for you now, Christopher, is to absorb what you have learned about your past today."

Christopher nodded in agreement. "One day at a time, one idea at a time," he concurred.

I left the session with Christopher totally depleted. The prolonged tension took its toll on my body. I felt as if I had been hit in the stomach, wrestled to the ground, and in the process had wrenched every muscle. My stomach hadn't settled down much. My head pounded, yet I could not turn my mind off. An image of the incest scene replayed in my imagination. I kept thinking, struggling with the unresolved issues that Christopher had presented. What was the origin of his homosexuality? Could it be reversed? If he worked through the trauma of the incest, would he no longer want men as sexual partners? Would he be happy as a straight person when he had been repulsed by a seductive and paradoxically rejecting mother? Worse yet, could he end up in a sexual never-never land, neither gay nor straight—nor even bisexual?

I looked at my watch and was glad to see it was just noon. I had a two-hour lunch break that I badly needed.

I took the elevator downstairs and started heading for the cafeteria, but soon realized I had no appetite and could not eat. I quickly turned around and headed for the quietest spot in the hospital—and the only getaway I could think of—the basement. The basement, I said to myself, ironically, the very place that Richard had used to hide in his house.

165

I had to walk and release the tension and let the trembling subside, but outside the January weather was too windy and chilly to comfort me. So I wandered through the bowels of the building, hoping no one would notice my aimlessness. I paced the darkened hallways that dead-ended in closets and furnaces, turned around on my heels, and retraced my steps. Like a rat in a maze, I randomly went from hallway to hallway. It did not matter. I was not thinking about any destination. I did not care. My thoughts were filled with Christopher and all that we had been through together. I was still shaking inside. I had to walk.

I knew my experience with Christopher's trauma was unique, a first for me. It wasn't that incest was new. I had heard too many heart-rending accounts of fathers and daughters. I had sat through too many tearful stories of little girls and teenagers and grown women as they told me their ego-shattering secrets. Their faces flashed before me. There was Sandy, who became promiscuous. Beth, who hated men. Theresa, who had lost all sexual desire. Betty, Sarah, and others who had turned to other women as lovers. Heather, who felt guilty about normal sexual relations. And Lorraine, who felt nothing but a pervasive numbness. Too many hated themselves. Too many names for me to remember. I thought of the fortunate ones who were able to go on with their lives, love, marry, and behave as if it had never happened, even though—if they hadn't worked through the trauma—they weren't strong on the inside.

But the truth of Christopher's past tore me in two. I had never treated a male who had been sexually abused by the same-sex parent, which was even more sexually disorienting. A father like Christopher's could be extremely sexually sadistic. Nothing could have been more difficult for me than to be there with Christopher as he relived it. This was no ordinary memory. Richard felt every blow, every thrust to his body, as if he were being retraumatized.

When Christopher was a little boy, he didn't want it to happen to him, so he made up Richard and let Richard be the victim. "It's not happening to me. It's happening to someone else," he said to himself. And every time something bad would happen, it happened to someone else—to Timmy or Sissy or James or Jackie—not to him. Christopher had defended himself against human brutality. He had fragmented, split apart to survive. It was perfectly clear to me. His multiple mind was a reality.

You must have created this illness with hypnosis. The words rang in my ears. *He's manipulating to gain attention,* a voice resounded in my head. *He does not merit any special treatment,* the argument persisted. *Don't encourage his pathology.* The admonishments echoed in my memory. The words were accompanied by the angry clicking of my heels reverberating in the empty halls. They don't know! No one has been there with me!

My hands went to my temples to stop the pounding in my head. I was alone, just as Christopher had been alone. I thought about Christopher's trauma. It was easy to understand why he had escaped into insanity. I thought of a photograph I had seen of six-year-old Christopher, and the eyes that knew too much. I felt as if I was going to cry. And I did. I let go of the pain, let go of the hurt I felt for Christopher. Oh, God! Please don't let anyone see me! The shrink is acting crazy, wandering around in semi-darkness, eyes full of tears.

Pulling myself together finally, I looked up at the bare pipes hanging from the ceiling. Staring at the barren, isolated structures suspended with no visible support, the symbolism struck me. I smiled. Then I told myself that even cold mindless pipes have somewhere to go. And so do I.

I went back up to the first floor and ducked into a vacant restroom. Confronting myself in the mirror, I told myself aloud, "It's time to get on with business, Dr. LaCalle." Cold water felt soothing to my mascara-smeared eyes. I stalled for a few moments, combing my hair more than needed. My appearance did not betray me. No one would have ever known that I had shattered under the stress.

The cafeteria was still open. I found a seat in the doctor's dining room and ate what lunch I could as if nothing had happened. I looked across the table at the unknowing faces, and felt even more alone.

ALONE IN THE DARK

A month had passed since I had met with Dr. Bernstein. Arranging the educational program we'd agreed upon was no easy task, but finally the long-awaited day of Paula's presentation at the hospital arrived. Bureaucratic slowness had kept this from being a more timely event. An announcement of Paula's lecture had been sent out—and the nurses were included. Now that all was ready, I worried about how Paula would be received by doctors and staff.

I prepared to leave a little early for the noon meeting so I could help Paula set up. On my way out of the office, I took a minute to remind José of the lecture.

"You *are* coming to the psychiatric committee meeting today, aren't you?"

"I doubt it. I've a tight schedule."

"Oh, José!" I said with disappointment—then immediately became irritated. "How silly of me to ask." I couldn't hold back a little jab. "Of course, you wouldn't have blocked out time to hear a talk on multiple personality."

"I hear all I want to hear about it—and more—in my own home. Say hello to Paula for me."

I had no time for this. I shut the door firmly behind me, muttering to myself, "Ignorance is bliss."

When I arrived at the hospital meeting room, I was astounded to find it nearly full. Paula stood up in front writing on the chalkboard, a microphone already looped around her neck. I walked up to the lectern next to her, found the switch to the reading light, flicked it on, and waited a moment while she finished.

"Hi, friend," I said, and gave her a hug. "I really appreciate your doing this for me."

"Looks like a good group." She smiled confidently, surveying the audience seated at tables in a U-shaped arrangement. "They're very impressive."

I looked over the audience and had to agree. This was the gray gabardine crowd. Dr. Bernstein was sitting at the head table, flanked by the members of the psychiatric old guard.

"Can I get you some water, Paula? I don't know about you, but my mouth is dry."

"No, I'm fine. I heard Christopher has caused a furor on the psychiatric unit since he's been here."

"Yes, he has. I've got a lot at stake in your being able to settle the controversy here today."

"I think they're ready," she said as she looked over my shoulder. "Switch on my mike and I'll give this my best shot."

Just as I was sitting down, José came in and took a seat by the door. Noticing my anxious reaction, he gave me a devilish grin. "A lot at stake." I repeated my words to myself.

José leaned back in his chair as Paula began. He pulled open the jacket to his three-piece suit, folded his hands over his vest, and twiddled his thumbs. His gestures were like telegraph messages to me. I knew what attitude he was taking. His forehead furrowed as he raised his eyebrows in that characteristic way of his, lifted at the center. This meant only one thing. He was going to believe half of what he heard and be skeptical of the rest. Paula's lecture wasn't going to change his thinking.

But it didn't matter. He had come. He was with me. And there was still hope that I could get him to support the legitimacy of my efforts, even if he couldn't agree with my thinking.

He sensed that I was looking at him and smiled at me knowingly. In moments like these, he looked strikingly handsome. His face was his best feature. I loved the large, dark brown eyes that radiated his intelligence, the neatly coiffed graying hair at the temples, the salt-and-pepper mustache, and the character lines of a distinguished middle-aged man. Yet, I could see on that picturesque face that he was not going to be more agreeable after the lecture.

169

As Paula talked, I scanned the room and noticed how intensely some of the members were listening. Others whispered to each other following her more surprising statements.

I could see that Paula's talk would help to unify the staff by explaining why the diagnosis of multiple personality was controversial. She went over the diagnostic criteria that were not listed in the *Diagnostic and Statistical Manual* and shared some of her research and experience. Best of all, she used Christopher as an illustrative case.

Afterward, José broke away from a couple of his friends and came over to greet me. He started in with his predictable criticisms. "It was too basic," he said with dissatisfaction. I felt smug. After living through this with me, now he had become an expert, too. "She should have gone into treatment techniques," he continued. "That's what would have been more appropriate for this audience."

"It may surprise you," I told him, "but this audience needed to hear the basics. It's one thing to read about multiple personality in the textbooks and quite another to have your first exposure to one. Christopher has been stirring up their patients and creating confusion and dissension among the staff. I wanted Paula to help me gain understanding and support from them. From the attendance and the applause, I think she may have just done it!"

"I see your point," he conceded. "I'll see you back at the office," he added, squeezing my arm in an affectionate farewell. I smiled warmly in response, feeling a familiar love toward him.

I turned to Paula, who stood nearby. No one had come up to either of us afterward to discuss issues further. This troubled me. They seemed interested, but why weren't they staying to ask questions? Had they been convinced, or only entertained? "I'm anxious to see if your talk will yield any positive benefits," I told her. "I wish we could have brought you in sooner," I added with dismay. "Christopher has been in the hospital over two months, and I'm now preparing for his discharge."

"Let me know what happens," she replied as she put away her notes.

"I'll call you tomorrow."

I left the meeting room and went back up to the psychiatric unit. Christopher was talking with a few of the nurses who had attended the meeting. The staff's response to Paula's presentation had been positive, and Christopher was already enjoying the fruits of Paula's success. He beamed with contentment and relief.

Within a short time, the staff's increased support made a difference in Christopher's progress. Discharge plans went into full swing as Christopher's depression waned and his ability to concentrate on daily responsibilities grew. The social worker, Sheila Fox, began looking for places where Christopher could live when he left the hospital. In spite of his personal gains, he would not be secure enough to live alone. Nor would he have enough money for rent. Sheila was able to locate a halfway house where he could temporarily live with a small group of men who were managed by a house "mother." Most of the occupants of the halfway house were recovering alcoholics, although mental-health patients were occasionally placed there.

When we met together to talk it over, Christopher balked at the idea of his becoming a resident. "I'm not an alcoholic," he protested.

"Where else are you going to go until you have a job and some money?" Sheila reminded him. "You have only two hundred dollars in the bank. Besides, you must admit that you have had drinking binges." Sheila was not one to mince words. She had worked hard to find this placement for Christopher, and she was not about to let him lose it.

"But what if I can't stand this place and I get really depressed just being there?" Christopher asked anxiously.

Sheila was frustrated. She had exhausted all of the placement alternatives. "Don't pass judgment on it so soon," she answered him firmly. "You haven't even seen it yet." Christopher cowered, as he usually did when a woman became forceful with him. Although she was unrelenting in her manner, she simultaneously continued to offer him her help.

"You are going to have to make some compromises when you leave here," Sheila admonished him. "Not everything will go as smoothly as you'd like." She reflected a moment, and I could see her expression soften. "I'll tell you what," she suggested. "Let's get in my car this afternoon, and I'll take you over to the house to meet Mrs. Green, the director. *Then* we'll talk about whether you could survive a few weeks there."

Christopher's instantaneous impression of the halfway house was negative. He told me that worn-out sofas carried the scars of dropped cigarettes and spilled coffee. Tables and chairs were scratched and nicked and never repainted. Instead of carpet, a yellowing linoleum covered the floors, except in the places where it had been torn, exposing the decaying wooden floor. The shabby conditions Christopher saw created an immediate reflexive reaction. This place reminded him of his childhood and the conditions in which he was forced to live. The men were reminiscent of his alcoholic father. Without any effort to know them further, he categorized them as rootless, lazy, and not to be trusted.

He was certain he would not live there—until he met Mrs. Green. He found her to be a kindly lady who was genuine in her warmth and concern. Timmy haunted Christopher with his fears, but Christopher had good feelings about Mrs. Green, and he could see that she was there to help him. Mrs. Green assured him that he would have a room to share with one of the more tidy boarders. The two of them could keep their personal quarters as immaculate as he would like. Mrs. Green pointed out to him that she was not able to keep up the exterior of the house, but the kitchen was free of grime and the bathrooms were okay. "That's good," Christopher told her. "I hate feeling dirty."

The days following that visit were harmonious. Christopher was readying himself to leave the hospital. The other patients had accepted his uniqueness. The staff was closing the rift between the factions. And there was harmony among Christopher's personalities as well.

The personalities were cooperating with one another as if they were all part of a family, and I had become a sort of family therapist. The Watkins and Watkins approach had begun to work. Christopher prepared himself to go to his job interview with his former employer. Sissy would be careful of the dress. Ernest would think through the issues of salary and duties. James would be aiding the others in being more outspoken. Jeremy was going to be the best influence of all—he could help Christopher display confidence and sociability. Timmy and Jackie agreed to "stay home" since they had nothing to contribute. Richard was again in hiding and was not about to come out for any reason.

On one of his better mornings at the hospital, Christopher dressed in a crisp outfit and left on a pass for his interview. I knew it took every ounce of courage he had to be put under the interviewers' scrutiny—and he told me he could hear Jeremy's voice prompting him.

His former employers were surprised at his display of self-assuredness. He looked healthier than ever, they said. When would he be ready to go back to his old job? Christopher hesitated, listening to Ernest. "Don't jump in with both feet," Ernest cautioned. Christopher asked to be put in a nonmanagerial position for two or three weeks before returning to his supervisory position. "I want to break in slowly," he mouthed Ernest's words.

Christopher returned to the hospital triumphant. Staff and patients alike congratulated him on his success. Somehow Christopher felt he should share the credit with the "others," but he kept this to himself.

I could sense his sadness at the realization he would have to be leaving the hospital. "Goodbye" was hard to say. The feeling was new to him. Nonetheless, the depression was gone and so was the underlying loneliness that plagued him. He had not thought of suicide in weeks. There was no reason for him to stay, but it was hard to leave the friends he had made. And Diane and Sylvia came by the hospital again, willing to give him another chance. They had too many years invested in the friendship to give up without giving it one more try.

This hospital discharge was different from the first one. Christopher now knew about himself, and I knew about him, too. It had seemed longer than two and a half months. So much had happened. We had created a special bond between us.

"It's good to know you'll be there for me," Christopher said.

"Only a phone call away," I replied. This time I knew he would call if he was in trouble.

We agreed that he would continue with intensive psychotherapy—two extended sessions per week. Christopher was discharged from the hospital in mid-January. He scheduled his first two-hour appointment for the day after he left the hospital.

He reported that his days passed uneventfully. His work was

easy. At the lower-level position, he did not have to be responsible for anyone but himself, and taking care of himself was enough responsibility.

But the halfway house was stressful for him, and the blackouts continued. He was preoccupied with what was happening "behind his back." The "others" would not always tell him. My office was a safe place for him to discover what the other personalities were shielding from him.

As James was talking in one of the sessions, he heard someone calling his name. He stopped to listen to the voice inside his head.

"Who is it, James?" I asked.

"It's Richard."

I was surprised at the answer. Richard had not been mentioned in weeks. "He's been hanging around a lot lately. He hates the halfway house where we live."

"Is there anything else bothering him?"

"He's tired of being in those cold, dark, and dirty places. He doesn't want to be there anymore."

"Let's get him out of hiding then."

I beckoned to Richard to come forth. To my amazement, he came out easily. For the first time, he opened his eyes and was out fully. Now I had the full sense of Richard. He slouched in his chair and sat on his hands. One foot rested on top of the other. His head tilted downward, and when he looked up, he gave a sideways glance. But he would not look at me; he gazed at the floor. His tense expression and lack of eye contact made him look like a guilty child who had just been caught in the act of some dirty deed. He was out, but still hiding.

"Richard, where have you been that it is so dirty?"

"Everywhere, everywhere I go, it is dirty," he said without feeling. "I am dirty. Dark places are dirty."

"And the things that happen to you in dark places are dirty?" I asked, challenging his self-assessment. "You don't seem dirty to me."

"I'm just a creepy kid."

"A dirty, creepy kid who must hide himself in shame?"

"Yes," he said sadly. "I am bad. I am a bad seed."

Richard's self-condemnation reminded me of a conversation I had had with another incest victim only a few days before. This victim was only thirteen years old, a Polynesian beauty with long hair tucked behind one ear with a comb. Her shining agate-brown eyes penetrated mine as she spoke. "My parents will send me away, so just put me in a foster home right now." I tried to reassure her that her mother and her new stepfather loved her and had no intention of sending her away. "Oh, yes, they will," she said, "because I've been too much trouble. I'm no good." As I talked with her, I let my eyes wander out the window to the gray February sky, hoping that the sunbeams breaking through the rain clouds would be like rays of hope to her or would, at least, give me the strength to cope with the pain I felt for her.

"You seem to feel you don't deserve their love."

Her large goddesslike eyes continued to pierce mine. "I don't deserve it. I don't. I was born with something evil in me. Don't you know? It's like the devil possesses me."

How innocent her face! Only thirteen. How much evil could she have had in her, at age three, the first time she was molested? How much evil would it take to deserve to be molested by her father, her mother's second husband, and an uncle?

"I have to be evil," she proclaimed, "or else why would all those things have happened to me? And why didn't they happen to my sister? Why did my father treat my sister right?"

No one deserved what had happened to her. No one could be born with enough original sin to be subjected to the sordid sexual deviations of the adult men closest to her. Yet what kind of reason could I have given her for why those terrible things happened to her?

She had the reason. "God is punishing me for being evil," she said. "My mother always said that God punishes you when you do something wrong, even if no one else knows you've done something sinful."

The "bad seed," just like Richard. Richard's mother, too, would have spoken of God's wrath and the idea that suffering is always well-deserved. The anguish in her voice haunted me, as well as her absolute conviction that she was sinful and deserving of punishment.

My words to this young girl were choked with tears I felt but stifled. They sounded so feeble, so inadequate, so unable to take away the pain or the tormenting self-punishment. "You're not bad," I had said to her. "You're not bad because those bad things happened to you." And I heard those same feeble words ring in my ears as I spoke to Richard.

"Richard, *you* are not dirty, creepy, and bad," I said to him vehemently. "What was done *to you* by your father was dirty, creepy, and bad."

Richard frowned. "No." He shook his head. "Nobody likes me. I'm always by myself."

"If you let people see more of you, you won't always be by yourself."

"Nobody wants to be around somebody who does bad things."

"Did you want to do bad things?"

"Sometimes."

"Did you sometimes like what was done to you?"

"Yes. Sometimes."

"That must really confuse you, Richard. Sometimes it was dirty and creepy. Sometimes it felt good. Sometimes it hurt. Sometimes you wanted it to happen. That's very confusing, isn't it?"

"Yes. But sometimes I liked it, so I must be bad."

"Oh, no, Richard," I replied strongly. "A lot of victims of incest feel that way. Certain parts of our bodies are meant to give us pleasure. When those parts are stroked or caressed without pain, it is supposed to feel good," I tried to explain. "It only felt bad to you because you knew your father was not supposed to be doing that to you and because he often did it in a way that was painful. It's okay to feel that kind of pleasure in your body when you are grown up and doing it with another grown-up person, especially a person you love. But children are not meant to do those things with grown-ups, and that's why your mind said, 'Oh, this is terrible.' "

"But sometimes I didn't hide. Sometimes I knew he was coming, and I just waited."

"If he didn't find you that time, Richard, he would have found you another. You were helpless. There was no way for you to make it stop happening. You were not to blame. You are only a child. An adult, your father, had the power. Your father was grown up, and he made the wrong decision."

"I'm not always so small, like now. Sometimes I'm more grown up. Sometimes I'm eight. Sometimes I'm ten. I know better when I am ten. I know it is wrong. I know I'm not supposed to do that."

There they were—the missing years!

Christopher had blocked out the years from ages six through ten. He had no conscious memory of those years when I first began to work with him. Those were the years when the incest was at its peak. It must have stopped when Christopher was put in the foster home before his parents divorced. From what I could determine, the mild sex play started when he was only three, the showers and touching and fondling. Somewhere around age five it became more serious, until at age six the occasional sexual assaults were so brutal that Christopher had to block the whole thing from his mind. Evidently, Richard's age spanned all those years.

"Even if you are sometimes ten, Richard, you are still a child. Your father was the one who decided to have sex with you. You have felt dirty and guilty, but, Richard, you must believe it wasn't your fault."

Richard still would not look at me, but his face seemed to brighten. The tension around his mouth relaxed. His shoulders were a little straighter. He sat a little taller. It was as if an enormous burden had just been lightened. But then he slumped back in his chair and scowled.

"No! I don't believe it!" he exclaimed. "I am dirty. I watch Christopher do dirty things with other men. I watch them, and I know they aren't supposed to do that. I watch them anyway."

"You are a part of Christopher, so you can hardly escape from watching."

I felt frustrated. I knew I could tell him a hundred times that he was not dirty or bad, and he would not believe me. Somehow he had to *experience* that he was not dirty. Richard had to do something that would help him discover this for himself. Only then would he be able to accept what I was saying.

"Look, Richard. I'm going to show you that you're not dirty."

I reached out and touched Richard on the shoulder, but he disappeared as quickly as if he had gone up in a puff of magician's smoke.

Christopher came out with a startled look on his face. "What happened?" he asked.

"I touched Richard, and then you came back out. Why did Richard disappear so abruptly?"

"He didn't want to get you dirty, too."

What should I have expected? I should have known he would resist contact. But even in his resistance, I felt a kind of caring, a protectiveness of me. Somewhere inside of Christopher there was a seed—not a bad seed, but a seed of hope, a potential to go beyond learning to receive love, but to learn to give love, too.

How to share love: It was a basic point of the human experience that I wanted to teach Christopher. It seemed so simple to me, so natural, so much a part of my life . . . or had been, until the conflicts between José and me began. Things remained strained between us, but, at least, I didn't need to be defensive all the time. I was more relaxed now that José and I had stabilized our relationship. I felt stronger, more able to give. And Christopher continued to need my strength intensely.

Nonetheless, as time went by, Christopher's dependence on me was making me uncomfortable. I was not accustomed—even now—to being needed in quite this way. Yet for a while, Christopher could not stand on his own.

Bob Slater was the only other person who knew enough about Christopher to be able to help him. Fortunately, Christopher had come with me to meet Dr. Slater at the university. He was glad that Bob was informed about his case and pleased that Bob's study group was helping me. If Christopher got himself in trouble, Bob was a second person who would know what to do. But it was not the same. Although Bob had become a sort of distant father figure, there was no bond between them. And a bond was important. Christopher's trust in me was what made him feel safe when he was not able to understand the chaos within him.

But I would have to be absent from him again, this time for several weeks. I had put off my surgery for months. "Elective surgery" is what they call a hysterectomy. But it wasn't elective to me. I felt I had no choice. I couldn't walk more than a hundred yards. I couldn't stand at the kitchen sink to peel potatoes. And I was, predictably, exhausted, irritable, and full of pain each month.

But the surgery would mean that I could have no more children. Carmen was already two—and growing so fast. As I thought about this, I remembered that Timmy had begun to mature and had recently announced that he had turned six. Small children were so precious, but even if I had more babies they would of course begin to grow up, too. I knew I wouldn't be able to keep a little one home with me forever. Even so, I felt depressed when I thought about *never* being able to have any more. José wanted another child—I was certain of it—although he would never come out and say so, and I was grateful that he put no pressure on me. I agonized over making the decision, especially with my mind so filled with Christopher and all my other responsibilities. I knew I had to do it. I just had trouble getting used to the idea.

My impending absence was not timely for Christopher. His life was becoming more and more stressful. He had found a roommate and moved into an apartment only a few days before. The move brought him some relief from the emotional discomfort he was feeling at the halfway house, but it did not compensate for the pressure he was under at work. The company had moved him into the management level again, but this time they transferred him to a different store—one that had been having problems with the employees and was not producing enough income. It was as if the company wanted to give Christopher the most difficult assignment possible to see if he would be able to cope.

To test him further, he would have to get by for a while without me. I braced myself for making the announcement.

"I have to go into the hospital for some surgery," I told him unenthusiastically. "I won't be back in the office for six weeks. It's nothing serious, but I mustn't put it off any longer. I'll feel much healthier when it's over."

Christopher made no attempt to appear brave. "What will I do without you?" he asked worriedly.

The constant threat of suicide was something I had to learn to live with. I had to come to grips with the fact that I might not be able to save him. The limits to what I could do were all too real to me now.

"Dr. Slater will be available if you need him. Don't forget that I'm not the only one who can help you. After the first few days following surgery, I'll be able to talk with you on the telephone. As soon as I'm able to get back to the office—even for a few hours a week—you'll be among the first that I'll see."

I did not feel like telling Christopher any more about my hospitalization. I was too upset about it myself. And it was hard for me to know how he would respond. His mother had always been a hypochondriac who went into long descriptions of her supposed ailments. Christopher would just have to trust that I would continue to be there for him, without me telling him more.

"When you go, I'll feel like there is nothing to keep me here," he said enigmatically. "I've been feeling like running away."

Not now! I thought. I was so exhausted and preoccupied with my own problems that I didn't have it in me to go through a crisis with him. If only he could hang on until I was out of the hospital and able to work! Yet I knew I was Christopher's stability, and that responsibility weighed heavily on me. Systematically, I solicited the help of all the personalities. Cooperation among them was a must now. Even with their agreement to "gang up" on any one of them who might attempt a runaway or suicide, the worry was constantly on my mind. How would he fare in my absence?

10

A GAME OF PRETEND

Nearly three weeks after I returned home from the hospital, while I was still moving about painfully, I got an emergency call from Christopher's roommate. He had had doubts about staying with Christopher when he first learned the truth. Now his doubts had turned into full-blown panic.

"Christopher has just put his fist through the wall," he said fearfully. "He said he was Jackie, whoever that is." He gulped a few breaths and kept going. "He is acting very strangely. I think he must be going from one personality to another," he whispered. "Right now, he is cowering in a corner of the room, doubled up in a kind of fetal position. He looked scared to death."

Timmy, I thought. "Did he tell you about his other personalities?" I asked.

"Yes. Is this one of them I'm seeing right now?"

"I believe you are looking at Timmy. He is just six years old. You can talk to him. He won't hurt you."

"What if he jumps up and says he is Jackie again?" he asked distrustfully.

"I don't think that will happen as long as you are gentle and present no threat to Timmy," I explained. How could any of this make sense to him? "Just tell Timmy that I am on the phone. See if you can get him to talk to me."

"I'll try," he answered bewilderedly. I could hear the roommate's coaxing in the distance, and, finally, a feeble little voice said "hello" into the phone.

"Hi," I said. "Are you feeling bad right now?"

The soft, childlike voice answered a frightened "Yes."

"Timmy, is that you?" I asked, to be sure it wasn't Richard. "You sound awfully scared."

"No." An entirely different voice cut in. "This is James, and I don't feel anything," he replied gruffly. "Nothing at all. Nothing is wrong."

"Oh, I see you've taken charge again, James."

"Had to."

"To keep Jackie under control, no doubt."

"Yes. She has to be kept under control, and I'm getting tired of being the only one who takes charge."

"My sympathies are with you entirely, but there is something I have to tell Timmy."

"I don't know where he went. He's not around anymore," James responded defensively. But I knew it was Timmy's fear that was upsetting Christopher. I had to get through to him.

"James, I think Timmy is near enough that he can hear me." I began to talk through James to Timmy. "You come out, Timmy, the first chance you get."

Sissy answered instead.

She said she and James were tired of Christopher's weakness and Timmy's sorrows. They wanted to go out and tie one on, to drown the problems that were troubling the other two.

"Besides, Dr. LaCalle," she said defiantly, "I'm the one who's keeping Richard from coming out. I'll never let that little creep show his face again. I'm his new babysitter, and he has to do what I tell him."

His new babysitter?

Sissy was interrupted by a small, tearful voice. "They won't let me come out for long." He was now sobbing outright. It was Timmy. This was my chance.

"Timmy, you sound so scared and alone."

"Uh, huh."

"You haven't seen me in almost three weeks. Remember, I told you I'd be fine. I'm at home resting."

"But I didn't think you'd come back."

Damn! If I hadn't been so drugged with painkillers, I could have called him sooner—pain or not! I can't let him down any longer, I thought.

"I'll be seeing you soon, Timmy. I haven't gone away."

"Uh, huh."

Christopher came back with the next sentence.

"What's going on?"

"Is that you, Christopher?"

"Is that you, Dr. LaCalle?"

"Yes, it's me."

"What's happening?" he asked. I could tell he was embarrassed. "Did I black out again? I don't remember dialing your number. Or did you call me?"

"The others were out for a while. Your roommate called me when you dissociated into Timmy and curled up in a corner of the room. And I'm sorry to have to tell you this—Jackie put her fist through the wall."

"Jeez! Jeeeez!" he cried. "What will happen now? He'll move out! How am I going to keep a roommate?"

"It won't be hard if we can get you back to where you were last month. You were doing fine then."

"But I'm not doing well now, am I?"

"No, you're not." I was disheartened at how rapidly Christopher could slip back into his most fragmented state. He must have been even more discouraged than I was.

"I'm sorry to disappoint you," he said. "I tried to pretend you weren't in the hospital, but I guess I just couldn't put it out of my mind. I'm glad you're okay."

"Just go to bed now, Christopher. Some sleep will do you a world of good. Call me in the morning."

I had some time to think over what I was going to do to help Christopher. I could not wait until the following week when I could make it to my office. By that time, he might have lost his roommate or his job or run away impulsively. Timmy had calmed down when I told him I would see him soon, but I knew the reassurance would not last if I had to wait a week or more to see him. And what about Richard? He was in hiding again, with Sissy making sure he stayed there. He was probably hurting as well, but unable to tell me.

By the time Christopher called, I had made up my mind. I decided to meet him the next day at a park near my home. I wasn't supposed to drive, but I could get that far in my car. If I got tired, I could lie back on the grass.

Christopher agreed to meet me as soon as he got off work the following afternoon. He surprised me by being concerned about how I was feeling and whether or not I was up to the visit. He was usually so self-absorbed that he never stepped outside of himself to wonder what was happening to me.

I would feel strange seeing Christopher outside the office or hospital setting. Only once before had I broken my protocol. As I looked back on my visit to Christopher's apartment, I realized I had trusted my intuitions. José would have been furious if he had known I had gone there alone. I had never told him. And now he'd be unhappy if he knew I had left the house when I was supposed to be convalescing. There was no risk involved this time—it was simply the idea that once again I was making Christopher "special." I had to admit to myself that I was treating him differently. After all, I was not planning to meet any of my other patients before my official return to work.

Unique cases call for special tactics, I told myself. I had to get to Richard. As long as the personality of Richard remained unchanged, Christopher would continue to hide away from people or find himself cut off because the other personalities would suppress him. But how was I going to get to Richard? He could not even look at me, he felt so ashamed and dirty. Sissy, the new "babysitter," was now in charge of keeping him hidden.

Babysitter? That was it!

What if I became Richard's babysitter, instead of Sissy? If I took Sissy's place, I could talk to Richard and let Richard out. Role playing could accomplish that. We could play-act an event as if it were actually happening, making the feelings and insights more real.

Then I remembered the role-playing device that one of the hospital's psychiatric technicians had tried with Christopher. He wanted Christopher to take the role of the different personalities by switching personalities each time he took a different chair. This kind of enforced role-taking frightened Christopher. He did not want to do anything that was so confrontational.

I had to think of a method of role-playing that Christopher could slip into spontaneously, almost without realizing he was doing it. More importantly, I had to think of a way to play my role in a manner that would help him to integrate the parts of himself and not dissociate further. If I pretended to be someone I was not, that would confuse him. After all, I had been trying to teach him that he did not have to become someone else in order to cope with life. I wanted him to learn to incorporate his past into his present and to integrate his feelings into a whole person. How could I put on a convincing performance as a babysitter, thus encouraging Richard to come out, and still remain myself?

Then it struck me. Being a babysitter represented a part of my past. Richard represented a part of Christopher's past. If I could show Christopher how I could incorporate my past into my present and how I could accept my "past life," perhaps he would begin to accept the part of his past that was Richard.

I calculated that when I was babysitting at age sixteen, Christopher would have been nine years old. Perfect! All I would have to do would be to play out the 1963 memories, and Christopher would reminisce about the same era with me. More than likely, he would spontaneously regress—hopefully to being Richard at age nine. In that imaginative setting, Richard was more likely to come all the way out and talk to me freely, especially since Sissy could not as easily interfere.

Now I had to find a way to set the stage. What kind of props would be helpful? What did I have from 1963? My high school yearbook, of course. The pictures of the bouffant hairstyles on the girls and the crewcuts on the boys would be enough to help visualize those years. I pulled my yearbook down from the shelf and dusted it off. Finding my class picture caused me to reconsider. Maybe it isn't so easy to accept one's past, I thought. A few of those old days, I'd sooner forget. No, I told myself. Revealing or not, embarrassing or not, this was the easiest way to set the stage and the mood for our age-regression role-playing.

The next day, ready for one of those mild late-spring afternoons, I dressed in baggy jeans, T-shirt, and tennis shoes. I was comfortable in those loose-fitting clothes, and I looked more the part of a teenager. I was feeling pretty good, considering that I had greatly decreased the pain medication so I'd be able to drive.

When I arrived at the park, yearbook in hand, Christopher was there waiting for me—as usual, never failing to appear early for an appointment with me.

We chatted momentarily, and he made no comments about my appearance except to say he was relieved to see me looking so healthy, even though I walked much more slowly than usual. Behind his eyes I could see the childlike loneliness he had felt during my absence.

I told him I had brought something to share with him—my past, a bygone era of nearly twenty years before. I said we would make the "memory trip" together this time. He didn't question this unusual proposal. He was neither reluctant nor enthusiastic, but merely compliant.

The yearbook sparked his interest. He pored over the pages, remembering how people looked and dressed in those days. He laughed when he saw the picture of me in my majorette's outfit. "Gosh, is that really you?" I could see that he was interested when I pointed out my friends. He was impressed that I had had the time and opportunity to participate in so many activities. He had never done such things when he was in high school.

"You sure had to sit funny when you played the cello," he teased.

"Not very ladylike, was it?" I agreed. "I think that's one of the reasons I prefer the flute. Besides, the cello was heavy, and when I carried it in its case, it was bigger than I was."

Christopher was enjoying himself and relishing the chance to see another side of me. He joked at every opportunity.

"What kind of a person do you think I was?" I asked him.

"It seems you were very busy, very active in a lot of things. I think you were probably kinda quiet, though. You looked serious and reserved. Not a party type."

"That's pretty accurate," I said. "I was the perfect type to be a babysitter. Adults always called me responsible." Always too responsible, I thought to myself. "If we had lived near each other in 1963, your mother would have wanted me as your babysitter, especially since she had just gone back to work the year before." Christopher was intent and clearly willing to play along with me. "Just to get into the spirit of '63 a little better, let's pretend that I am your babysitter and I've brought you to this park for the afternoon."

I paused for dramatic effect and then took my role.

"I brought you to this park today because I didn't want to babysit you at your house while your mom takes your brother to the dentist." I listened to my voice, knowing I would have to try to sound more casual and adolescent. "I hope you don't mind, but I don't feel comfortable there. I have gobs of allergies, and I start sneezing and my sinuses swell up in your house."

"I know, there are dust balls all around the furniture." He played into it effortlessly. "*She* thinks it's clean. She's always talking about how dirty everyone else's house is."

"You're kidding," I said with mock surprise.

"No. And most of the time I won't bring my friends to our house. If *she* has company, that's when she makes *me* clean up." Christopher was actively getting into the pretend game.

"Well, the dust was only one reason, really. I didn't want to be there when your father came home. I feel uncomfortable around him. Do you ever feel uncomfortable around him?"

"No."

"Do you like him a lot?"

"No," he said blandly. "I just either hate him or I don't feel anything at all about him."

Christopher had mentally transported himself back in time. The fixed stare and the intensity of his feelings let me know he had regressed in a semi-hypnotic state.

"Grown-ups can be difficult," I said. "Isn't it easier to talk to a teenager sometimes? The kids I babysit talk to me a lot."

"I talk to teenagers," he informed me. "My dad has friends at the base who have kids that babysit me sometimes."

"Good. Then I guess you'll think it's easy to talk to me. You know, I keep lots of secrets—secrets kids tell me. I'll bet you keep other people's secrets, too." Then I changed my voice, making it more playful. "You wouldn't tell a secret of mine, would you?"

"It depends."

"Then maybe I better not tell you anything," I teased.

"Naw. I wouldn't tell stuff that is nobody's else's business."

"And you'd still like me, even if I told you something bad?" I asked.

"Naw. I know how to be a friend."

"Good. So do I. I wouldn't tell on you, either. So tell me a secret." I grinned.

"I'll tell you about the Nasty Club, then. I'm the president," he said seriously.

"Mr. President, is that what I call you?" I lightheartedly inquired.

"No, just call me Richard."

It had worked. Richard was looking me square in the eyes.

We talked for well over an hour. Previously, I had only had glimpses of his character. Richard, as I already knew, was a reclusive sort. Only a portion of his behavior was truly bad, and he knew enough to hide it. He did "nasty" sexual things, but the enjoyment in doing them was not sexual enjoyment. In actuality, he was fearful of sex and did not want to be touched by any of the boys. The enjoyment came from doing hidden, rebellious things to get even with punitive and perverse parents. As the leader of the Nasty Club, he organized other little boys into sexual play. He knew his mother would be horrified if she found out. That was the fun to it. As for the other boys, they, too, found the sex play more fun because it was taboo. Richard thought he was particularly bad for having created the club. I told him that such clubs were not his own invention, that other children did such things.

Then he wanted to know if other boys had babysitters who played the same way. I asked him what he meant. He told me he had been the target of sexual play with teenage girls who would "innocently" want to fondle his penis—which Richard passively accepted, or, possibly, somehow encouraged. It seemed to have happened on several occasions with more than one babysitter, which made me wonder if Richard was not partially responsible.

Richard was uneasy as he talked to me. He was clearly feeling ambivalent about the sex play—guilty and fearful, yet wanting it to continue. He seemed to be uncertain of what I, his new babysitter, would do. He looked at me strangely, and I felt uncomfortable. What was he thinking about me?

I had uncovered a drive in him that I did not expect to find, even though Christopher and I had talked about the possibility of his latent heterosexuality. I had become accustomed to thinking of Christopher as a homosexual and had not prepared myself to deal with any sexual strivings he might have toward me. Now, because of this dual age regression, we were face to face with the awareness of our sexuality, of being male and female, and the connotations that had never been noticed before.

While staying in my babysitter's role, I tried to let him know my intentions and the boundaries of our relationship. "Yeach! Richard!" I exclaimed with adolescent fervor. "Girls my age are not supposed to do that to little boys like you. Don't worry, I would *never* do that to you." I had to make it clear that nothing would happen between us, even if he wanted it to happen. Yet I did not want to reject his heterosexual strivings as unacceptable desires. "Look, Richard," I said. "It's not that things like that between boys and girls are so terrible, but you have to be older, and the girl should be closer to your own age."

"Well, maybe when I'm older. It doesn't bother me now, though."

"You're used to it, aren't you?"

"I'm used to a lot of things—things I guess I shouldn't be used to," he said seriously.

"You have so many serious things to think about."

"I know. People tell me I'm too serious."

"Do you like yourself very much, Richard?"

"I *never* used to like myself." An interval passed while he gave it more thought. "Today, I think I like myself more."

"Good. Then maybe you'll start to come out more. When I grow up and am a psychologist, will you talk to me then?"

"Sure. I'll probably start growing up myself."

"I've got to go back home now, Richard," I said to indicate that our time was coming to an end. I was growing tired and physically uncomfortable. "Don't worry, though. Christopher will be back."

That was all it took to suggest Christopher's return. I closed the yearbook to show that the role-playing had ended. We both straightened up, and instantly, Christopher was back again. He sat still, looking over the grassy slopes of the park. Our free exchange of words was silenced. Christopher was confined to his inner space, brooding over what he had just experienced.

"I'm still doing that—just like with the Nasty Club. I'm still doing the same thing, playing sexual games with other guys . . . not feeling right about it. It's like I'm stuck at that place in time, and I can't grow out of it."

I was pleased to hear how quickly Christopher had integrated his past and Richard's experiences. Stuck in time. What a psychoanalyst would call an arrested latency age, what once was the only explanation for homosexuality. "Well," I said aloud, "that's part of it anyway."

I had made ready to leave, but Christopher's immobility signaled his reluctance. Something was not finished for him. Timmy. I had forgotten about Timmy. I watched Christopher, and I could sense that little boy in him.

"Christopher, I haven't been able to say anything to Timmy."

"Yeah. He's hanging around."

"So let me talk to him. Just look over there, off in the distance for a moment. You don't have to pay attention to anything I'm going to say. Timmy will be listening."

Christopher looked away from me and over his shoulder.

"Timmy, I'm right here. I know you missed me a whole lot."

The head started bobbing in the characteristic gesture of Timmy's. His face turned around to meet me, and tears rimmed his eyes. But he held them back. He was trying to be more grown up now. I told him goodbye, and Timmy made a gesture with his hand as if he were going to touch me. Then he disappeared, and Christopher looked at me in his place.

I could see that Christopher had relaxed. He was finished now. His animated face and movements made his contentment evident. As we walked to the edge of the park, I put out my hand. He ignored it. Instead, he reached toward me with both arms and hugged me. I embraced him in return. My heart danced. For the first time, Christopher had reached out to me. I had never seen him initiate an affectionate gesture toward anyone. This simple expression was his monumental accomplishment. I smiled at him with deep satisfaction, and he smiled back knowingly.

"I'm learning," he quipped confidently.

"You certainly are." I grinned.

11

HOW COULD IT HAPPEN AGAIN?

As soon as I was well enough to return to the office, I scheduled frequent sessions with Christopher. He was experiencing enormous difficulties at work, and he told me his employers shoved more and more responsibility on him. They asked him to hire, train—and fire. Christopher was not up to confrontations with employees. He avoided reprimanding them and also avoided the paperwork that went along with doing their evaluations. Worse, he would sometimes lose an hour or two during blackouts, and he couldn't be sure of important details. Had he already given an order? Had he already paid the vendor?

I kept hoping conditions at his job would improve, but things kept degenerating. Then, on a late Saturday afternoon in July, Christopher called the exchange. In spite of the problems he was having, it had been weeks since he had interrupted me at home. He came right to the point.

"I'm not doing very well. I'm going to have to quit my job."

I knew this was coming, but I could do nothing to prevent it. I felt helpless. We'd explored ways to reduce the stress at work, but it wasn't enough.

"Jeremy will be out soon to take me—I can't quite do it myself. But I have to leave . . . have to get away from here."

This was more than I had expected. I knew he'd quit, but I didn't think he'd run away, too.

"Where will you go?" I asked.

"To San Francisco to live with my brother."

So far? I gulped.

"I'm out of money," he went on. "I spent the little bit I had left on repairing my car. I . . . can't take any more of this."

He sounded distraught.

"Something has got to change. I went to work every day this week. Then I caught myself feeling proud about that. It's terrible to feel proud about something so simple."

I thought Christopher had accomplished a lot, but he didn't think so. He stopped for a moment and then went on.

"It's been almost a year since I started coming apart and couldn't work."

I wanted to correct him. Barely nine months had passed since he first started treatment, but I kept quiet. No point in saying that now. No point in telling him that he expected too much too soon. No point in reminding him that he was being put to extraordinary tests at work. Instead, I said, "I can hear the desperation in your voice."

"Bill collectors are breathing down my neck," he said anxiously. "I feel guilty that I'm not paying you for my therapy. Over the past few months, I haven't been able to live up to any of the standards I used to set for myself."

What can you expect? I thought. You've been in the hospital twice within a year! I tried to comfort him.

"You've only *begun* putting yourself back together," I reminded him. "That takes time. It's a big job to reshape yourself. Don't you think that alone is enough to deplete all your energies?"

"But I can't go on like this. I don't even have the money for next month's rent. I'll live with my brother until I can get some money saved up, then I'll have a chance to get out of this hole I'm in. I'll find a job with less pressure."

"I understand your reasoning, Christopher," I assured him. "But you've made such good progress. You do want to continue in therapy, don't you?"

"Yes. But I can't stay here."

Then he must start with a new therapist, I thought. Without support from a therapist, Christopher wouldn't do at all well in a strange city, living with a brother who'd never been close to him.

"I'm sure there are good therapists in San Francisco who can treat you," I told him. "Once you are there, you can call me. I'll try to have a couple of names for you. You will get started in treatment as soon as possible, won't you?"

I hoped Christopher wouldn't detect my uncertainty. Who would be able to treat him? I worried.

"I promise. I'll call you . . . I'll make an appointment. Listen—" He interrupted himself, and then fell silent. It seemed to me he was mustering his courage. Then he spoke forcefully. "There's something I have to say to you before I go any further."

I was surprised at Christopher's assertiveness. Whatever it was he felt he had to say, it was something very important to him. I caught my breath and waited.

"I love you," he said. "A lot."

I didn't say anything. I *couldn't* say anything. I wasn't breathing.

"You are . . . so . . ." He could not finish the sentence. "I want you to know how much I appreciate you and all that you have given me."

My mind raced ahead of his words. There was something that sounded too final in his voice. Was this a "sign off"—one of those goodbyes that is usually written in a suicide note? Then I chastised myself. How fearful I am, I thought. He just wants to tell me he cares about me. I should just stay quiet and listen to him!

"Sometimes I feel really bad when I call you and bother you," he continued falteringly. "But I have no one else like you." His voice cracked slightly. "I feel so bad to be doing this to you."

My feelings overwhelmed me. I sank deeper into the sofa cushions, trying to sort my emotions and thoughts as rapidly as I could.

Tell him you care about him, too, I thought immediately. No. I won't tell him anything of the sort—that will only confuse him and make it harder for him to separate and leave. He does have to leave. Then, at least, thank him for being considerate of my feelings. . . . Wait! Didn't I hear what he said? This was Christopher himself talking, the person who formerly could not risk experiencing his feelings! Maybe I should point this out to him. I should let him know that these feelings are an acceptable part of himself. But that might distract him from the big risk he just took. I had to acknowledge his need and love, even if it was probably "transference love," the love of a patient for a doctor.

I was stymied.

So many ideas and feelings. How could I reconcile these parts of me pulling in different directions? Yet, I reminded myself, Christopher's struggles with the different parts of himself were even greater. After what seemed to me like an eternity, I found words—at least to begin.

"I . . . don't quite know what to say, except that I'm touched, and, most of all, that I don't want you to feel badly for taking up my time. You haven't taken anything I didn't gladly give."

I paused for a moment and tried to sort through my thoughts. A question came to mind, but I couldn't bring myself to ask it. But Christopher answered my question as if he knew what I was thinking.

"And I didn't tell you what I feel because I thought you wanted to hear it," he said. "I do try to give people what they want to hear—still—but I really meant what I said this time."

"I'm glad you really meant it," I confessed. "You've come to know me pretty well, Christopher. You can even guess what I'm thinking. Either that, or you're psychic."

"I *am* psychic," he said matter of factly. But he didn't give me an opportunity to ask what he meant. "I'll tell you about it someday. Right now, I just want you to know it took me two months to get used to feeling love and appreciation. It's hard, real hard to tell you out loud, but I had to do it."

After we'd finished saying our goodbyes and I'd hung up the phone, I looked at my six-year-old son. I recalled a tender moment after Eddie had outgrown his own egocentric stage. I remembered my delight when he was able to reverse the parenting role. It was after my surgery. "Mommy," he said to me, "I'm sorry you are feeling so bad." He gave me a compassionate hug and adjusted my pillow.

I loved this newfound ability in my son. The self-centered three-year-old in him had given way to a socially sensitive six-year-old. He was growing up to be a caring person.

And so was Christopher.

Following his departure, I worried about Christopher—and missed him. He called me ten days after he arrived in San Francisco to report that he'd already found a job in a home furnishings company. He was driving a delivery truck, which was quite a step down from his previous status as a store manager. But, surprisingly, the pay was not much lower. The two owners of the company were gay, and Christopher felt comfortable around them. And his brother had accepted him into his house without misgivings. Things were looking up for Christopher.

He also reported that his mother and sister lived nearby, and he had been invited over for dinner on two occasions. He had a new stepfather, Jack, for whom he felt no fondness. But he thought he and thirteen-year-old Julie were likely to develop a closer bond. Christopher said he was getting along with his mother, too, better than ever before. But as for Christopher's youngest brother, they did not see much of each other because he lived in Santa Cruz, more than an hour's drive away. The family was able to get together for holidays, if they wished. Yet it never seemed to happen. Although they lived within easy driving distance of each other, there was no closeness between them. I doubted that Christopher would be able to mobilize the family and create the warm feelings he had wanted as a child, and I was concerned that he would become depressed because his efforts and good intentions were not sufficient to pull his family together.

I asked if he had begun looking for a therapist. He had not. I reminded him of his promise and gave him the names of two psychologists. I didn't know these psychologists personally, but I knew they had the proper credentials.

"Do you want me to call them first, Christopher, to be sure they will be able to take your case?"

"No, let me see which one I like best, and you can call after we've had a chance to get to know each other."

I didn't think that was the easiest approach, but I wasn't going to discourage Christopher's independence. Maybe he was right. Perhaps he needed a fresh start, without my influence. But it was hard not to worry.

A few weeks later, Christopher called me again. The frustration of therapist-hunting had unnerved him.

The psychologist he first went to had an office only a few

blocks from Christopher's workplace. Christopher was anxious about their initial meeting but hoped it would work out because of the geographical convenience.

Christopher told the doctor about his psychiatric history of hospitalizations and depression. The doctor carefully took notes. Then Christopher made a tactical error. He diagnosed himself. "I'm a multiple personality," he told the psychologist.

"Oh?" the doctor had scoffed. "Really . . ."

"I *am*," Christopher tried to tell him. "You can call Dr. LaCalle. She'll tell you."

The psychologist said that the phone call would not be necessary. He would make his own diagnosis. Christopher proceeded to tell how he dissociated to James, Jackie, and the others. The psychologist stopped taking notes. He seemed disinterested. He wanted Christopher to tell him more about his depressive symptoms, how he was unable to work, how he had difficulty sleeping. Christopher explained that these symptoms were episodic. Now that he was with his brother, he was feeling depressed but able to work and to sleep at night.

Why, then, the doctor asked, was he seeking treatment?

Christopher explained that he still had blackouts and that he had not yet integrated the thoughts and feelings of the other personalities. The psychologist stopped taking notes again, and Christopher asked him why he stopped taking notes every time the subject of multiple personality came up.

"I'm not going to reinforce that diversionary tactic you use to keep yourself from changing the way you live," the doctor said condescendingly. "If you are talking about your depression and what you can or are doing to change your behavior so the depression will go away, then you will find that I am very interested in what you are saying."

Christopher left the psychologist's office and never returned. He knew that keeping silent about the other personalities would not make them go away. The personalities were a part of him, and they had been disrupting his life long before anyone started talking about them. He was angry with the doctor for implying that the personalities were under his conscious control and that he could simply choose not to use them as a "diversionary tactic" any longer.

When Christopher called to tell me what had happened, he

said he was not going to call the second psychologist, as I didn't know the doctor and couldn't recommend him from personal experience. He wanted to prevent the same situation from happening again. He had already had one other bad experience. He had met a man in a gay bar who said he was being treated by a psychiatrist. Christopher became curious and asked the man how long he had been in treatment and if the psychiatrist had helped him. The man said he had been in treatment for over ten years, with several psychiatrists. But this psychiatrist was the best. Christopher took the psychiatrist's name and called for an appointment.

The doctor's office was spacious and luxurious. The psychiatrist sat behind his desk with a pen in his hand. Christopher repeated the information he had given the psychologist. The psychiatrist seemed unimpressed, but Christopher was relieved to see that he took notes without stopping. Then, at the end of forty minutes, the doctor looked up from the notepad and told Christopher that further diagnostic tests would have to be given.

Christopher told him that the hospital records and his psychologist's records were available. The psychiatrist said that the symptoms suggested a neurological disorder and that Christopher would have to have a brain scan or, at least, an electroencephalograph. Christopher told him that he had been examined by a neurologist while in the hospital and that nothing was wrong with his brain. The psychiatrist then suggested that Christopher be admitted to a nearby hospital for a few days of observation.

Christopher told him that he was feeling well enough to work and that he did not want to go into a hospital unless he became severely depressed or suicidal. He then told the doctor of his financial problems and that tests and hospitals were more than he could afford.

The doctor stopped taking notes and handed Christopher the name and address of the local mental-health clinic. "They don't have many psychiatrists there," the doctor said, "but you should be able to find something you can afford."

Christopher wanted to give up, but he had promised himself that he would make at least three attempts at seeking treatment. When he walked into the mental-health clinic, he immediately disliked the impersonal feeling there and the overflowing waiting room, but he was relieved that the treatment would cost so little.

The intake officer was a woman who had been trained as a clinical social worker, and Christopher liked her from the first moment. She listened. She took notes only during the pauses. She accepted what Christopher was telling her. She asked the right questions. She seemed concerned. She did not suggest medication, hospitalization, or tests. Christopher told her he was surprised at how comfortable he felt with her, and she responded that she had once treated someone with multiple personalities.

Christopher was taken very much by surprise. How could he have been so lucky to find this woman, who had the experience and understanding he needed? But then she told him her job was to evaluate and assign the cases that came into the clinic. She would not be his therapist.

Christopher could not hide his disappointment. The social worker told him that she would turn him over to a therapist who was interested in his disorder. A case distribution meeting would be held that week, and his therapist would be assigned at that time. She promised she would also call me to gather further information.

When I talked with the clinical social worker on the telephone, I, too, liked her instantly. She was warm, quick to grasp the situation, and systematic in her approach. I felt saddened that she would not be treating Christopher. She assured me that she would do the best she could to get Christopher what he needed.

Within a few days, Christopher was given an appointment with a psychiatric resident—a young man. Christopher attended several sessions but never formed a strong therapeutic alliance with the doctor. After several weeks, Christopher called and told me he was frustrated because he thought the sessions were pleasant but superficial. The psychiatrist did not seem to know how to use the information about the other personalities.

I asked if the doctor had seen any of the other personalities. No, and Christopher was unsure how the young doctor would react when it happened. He might frighten his doctor. Christopher was about to give up on the therapy. I reminded him he needed a therapist to call in the event of a psychiatric emergency.

"Christopher," I told him, "these feelings and misgivings you are having about the sessions are things you need to be telling your psychiatrist. I cannot treat you long distance."

That was my last conversation with him for several weeks. Had I said the wrong thing? Although I wondered about him frequently, I thought it best not to call. If he could make a clean break from me, he was more likely to put effort into a therapeutic relationship with his psychiatrist.

Because of Christopher's absence, I now had the time to take on another multiple. For some time, I had been wondering what it would be like to treat another case. I had learned a great deal, but how well could I apply my knowledge with a new patient?

I put the word out among the therapists in the study group that I was available to take someone else. Since the study group had become a clearinghouse for multiples to make contacts with therapists in this field, I soon received a call from a woman who had been seeking treatment.

"I've been working with a male therapist for six years," Ruth said during our first appointment. "I've done a lot of uncovering and analyzing, but I'm not integrating."

I was intrigued and offered to help. But this time, I said to myself, I'd set my limits from the very start. All the therapy could reasonably take place inside an office or hospital. And we'd have to agree that phone calls after hours would be for absolute emergencies only. Although I knew I wouldn't be as confused, uncertain, or unknowing as I was with Christopher, I had to prepare myself to be intensely drawn into Ruth's situation. To keep myself from being completely drained, our extended sessions would be limited to two hours. If I didn't take this more self-protective stance, I told myself, I'd burn out and be of no use to Ruth, or Christopher, or any other multiple in the future.

After talking with Ruth, I could see why she hadn't been improving. Her personalities had not learned to communicate among themselves, and mutual cooperation was nonexistent. She was—in Christopher's words—stuck in time, continually reliving the traumas of her past. This was going to be an even more difficult case than Christopher's. Ruth had at least twenty-six personalities, maybe more. And, as far as I could tell, she also had a secondary diagnosis of borderline personality disorder, a disorder that made the problems of "splitting" and interpersonal relationships even more complex.

Meanwhile, I was beginning to get calls from other therapists in the community who wanted to know more about multiple personality disorder. I talked with them, sent them reprints in the mail, and referred to the study group those who were currently treating a multiple. I was becoming aware that I had learned more than I realized.

My study of multiplicity had grown to be an ongoing interest. But it was one that I didn't share with my husband. Not sharing was foreign to me—to us. Before Christopher, we had always shared everything. We graduated from the same university. I did my internship in the clinic where José worked. We read together, wrote together, lectured together, practiced together, suffered together, rejoiced together. Now I felt separate. And growing more separate. How could this happen?

But maybe it wasn't a bad thing. In fact, in some ways, I knew that it was better this way. I was thirty-five years old. Christopher had provided me a chance to test my ability to act according to my own standards—even if it meant being shunned, even if it meant being alone. At last I had learned to be firm in my own beliefs. I knew I had to gain the respect of the psychiatric old guard at the hospital. And José couldn't do that for me or with me. I had to stand alone.

And I did it.

With time, I swayed them—the skeptics, the ones who were as closed-minded about multiplicity as José had been at first. Now they not only considered the possibility that multiplicity existed but accepted that it wasn't as rare as they'd thought. It was only a matter of time before one of them would encounter a multiple himself. Already, José had begun to consider the possible diagnosis of multiple personality whenever a patient presented enough of the symptoms.

The only problem was that I was so caught up in the rewards of my efforts and my growing independence that I hadn't had time to think through the negative effect it was having on my marriage. I was so focused on my own pursuits, I hadn't noticed José was still feeling excluded. So José was pressed to begin drawing attention to the feelings he was having, to his mounting anxiety over the way we were relating to each other.

"It's bad enough when I scarcely see you at home, but you're gone from the office for hours," José complained, "and I don't even know where you are."

"Just taking care of business," I said. I wasn't doing any more than my usual running around with shopping, errands, and the like. I simply wasn't checking in with him each time I made a move. "I didn't realize it was a problem. If I'm going somewhere that I can be reached, I always give Liz a number where she can call me for emergencies. Or I tell the housekeeper where I am when I check in at home."

"But you don't tell *me*. Everyone seems to know more about my wife than I do!"

I was surprised at his overreaction. It wasn't like José to feel unimportant. "I can always carry a pager if it gets to be a problem for my practice." I was skirting his issue, and I knew it. "So far, it isn't necessary . . . unless you want to *always* be able to reach me."

Warning flashes came from his eyes. "We'll talk more about it at dinner," he responded coolly.

I didn't really want to go out to dinner with José. Not that I wouldn't enjoy the veal at Pierre's French Cafe, as we had planned earlier in the week. But he wanted to talk. And I wished I could put it off.

I wasn't ready to work on our marriage. I had been sliding along on a distant but comfortable enough level since Christopher's departure. I was just getting used to this new kind of independence, and the status quo was fine for me—at least, for right now. I was enjoying giving my uninterrupted attention to my own personal and internal challenges. So I was dreading seven o'clock, the dinner hour.

I managed to avoid the issue, but only for a short while after we arrived at the restaurant. José soon began to challenge my armor of indifference.

"We should talk, shouldn't we?" he said as we looked at the menu. "We've become pretty distant the last few months."

"Yes, we have." I nodded slightly and then fell silent. My guard was up.

The waiter interrupted. I was glad that I had a moment to

think. What did I want from José right now? The problem was I wanted nothing. Not anything. Not criticisms, not approval, not support . . .

"What's happening with you, Trula?" He looked at me intently. "You've cut yourself off from me." His face was strained.

His earnestness distressed me. And I'd have to respond. "Yes, I suppose I have."

"Why?"

"I don't know why. I've been going through . . . some sort of change." I was stumbling. "I'm not sure what it's all about yet."

I kept my gaze cast downward. I was protecting myself from his need to know.

"Well, what . . . what sort of change?" He shrugged his shoulders and paused significantly. "Who?"

The word hung in the air, suspended in silence. Of course, I thought. That's classic. Isn't it just like a man to think his competitor would be another man—not my work, or anything else, for that matter?

"It's not still that Christopher case, is it? He hasn't been calling you after hours anymore . . ."

"And you haven't seen him in the office either," I interrupted. "He's moved away," I added flatly.

"Oh!" He smiled.

"You needn't seem so pleased," I said. As José's smile vanished, I quickly went on. "You know he's not the problem. And you needn't worry about anyone else."

"I wasn't implying—"

"You weren't?"

"No. I wasn't. I'm just trying to—"

"Look, José, it's something more fundamental to our relationship."

"Then why won't you talk about it?"

He really was trying. His eyes were tender, and he reached across the table to take my hand.

"I don't know." I felt myself thaw out a little, but then I drew up the barriers again, despite twinges of misgiving. This was a role reversal, and I appreciated how hard this was on his pride. But I couldn't make myself feel something that didn't exist for me in the moment.

"I just don't feel like being close."

He looked hurt, orphaned. He slowly withdrew his hand. "I don't understand," he said, his voice low.

"I know this isn't like me. Maybe I just want to be left on my own for a while. I've gotten kind of used to having to rely on my own resources."

"I feel like I'm being blamed for something," he said defensively.

"No—well, maybe I am blaming you a little."

I should stop now, I told myself. I'm really not ready to talk, even if he is. But I felt cornered. He was getting to me again.

"It started with me not being able to tell you everything. I'd always told you everything on my mind, every move I made. But when it came to Christopher, you didn't treat with respect something that was important to me. I learned to hold back to avoid conflict."

"Is that what's happening? You're holding back to avoid conflict?"

"We haven't quarreled for a while. That's not all the problem . . . I wish I could tell you. But I don't understand what is happening to me, yet. And I want to work it out myself. I need time to do that—alone."

I'd never shut him out before. He looked wounded. Then he sat up straight and looked around as if he were eager to leave.

"I've hurt you," I said. I regretted having wounded him.

"You might say that," he said, his face closed and cold. Now neither one of us wanted to talk, and the silence settled in like a winter frost.

Weeks went by. José and I kept a wary distance. I thought of Christopher frequently, and I missed that unique relationship I had developed with him, even though the hours were now filled with other patients. I kept hoping he had taken my advice and discussed his misgivings and uncertainties directly with his psychiatrist at the mental-health clinic. Then, two months later, my exchange put through a call to my home at about 9:00 P.M.

"There's someone on the line crying so hard I can't understand him. He says his name is Timmy, and he wants to talk with you."

Timmy? I hadn't talked with Timmy in months. The dissociation was a bad sign, and I was fearful of what could have happened to Christopher.

"Help me," a small voice pleaded. "I'm scared. I'm really scared."

"What is the matter, Timmy?"

"Jackie wants to kill him."

"Kill who?"

"Mommy's husband."

"Christopher's stepfather? Why?"

Timmy began sobbing so hard he could not talk. I heard the telephone receiver drop on some hard surface. Then I heard someone pick up the phone, and an unfamiliar male voice addressed me.

"Dr. LaCalle, this is Christopher's brother. He left the phone, and now he's sitting on the couch and staring into space."

"What is going on with your stepfather?"

"Christopher and I just found out this morning. Last night, Mom caught Jack, our stepfather, in bed with our thirteen-year-old sister. Julie said he has been having sex with her for almost two years."

"Where is Jack now?"

"He's in jail. Mom called the police right away, and they came and picked him up."

She had to take action on this one, I thought grimly. It wasn't easy to look the other way this time.

"It's better that your stepfather is in jail. Christopher is probably not the only one who is experiencing homicidal rage right now."

"Yeah. Mom has gone completely crazy. We called a doctor to give her a sedative. We're also pretty worried about my sister."

"Have you called Christopher's psychiatrist?"

"I didn't know his name or how to reach him. Christopher has talked about you, and I knew he had your phone number written inside the phone book cover. He was crying and said he wanted to talk to you. So I called you because I didn't know who else to ask for help. Then he took the phone away from me. I thought he wanted to talk to you, but he dropped the phone. Now I don't know what to do." His voice was getting shaky. "I've never seen the other personalities before. He has told me about them, but I kinda didn't believe him. Now I can see them, and it's unreal! One of them is really angry and threatening to kill Jack. I think I'm going to flip out, too, if this keeps up."

"What is Christopher doing now?"

"He's down on the floor playing with my three-year-old son—like nothing's happening," he responded, dumbfounded. "He never plays with his nephew. I don't understand. Why is he doing that *now?*"

"Has Christopher told you about Timmy?"

"Yes. I heard him call himself Timmy when he talked to you. Is he being Timmy right now?"

"Probably, since he's doing what a little boy would do. If he stays in the Timmy personality, he will be safe until you can get hold of his psychiatrist. Start calling him by the name Timmy, and he is more likely to stay in that personality for a while. Be kind and reassuring to him. Tell him that you are going to take care of things and that you talked to me and will be talking to his psychiatrist."

I gave Christopher's brother the phone number of the clinic and the name of the psychiatrist who had been attending Christopher.

"Christopher could probably use a sedative himself. The psychiatrist can hospitalize him, if need be." I listened to the confident, calm way I was advising him, but inside I was distressed. "On the other hand," I went on, "if he falls asleep, he may be back to being Christopher in the morning."

I was tempted to call Christopher the next morning to find out what happened, but, with effort, I resisted the impulse. Christopher had a psychiatrist in San Francisco, and I was four hundred miles away. I was certain I couldn't let my personal need to be in touch with Christopher interfere with the available—albeit tenuous—connection Christopher had developed with his psychiatrist.

Two days later, Christopher called me. He was back to being himself again and had pulled together remarkably well. I was greatly relieved. He remembered nothing from two nights before. By the time his brother had gotten through to his psychiatrist that night it was 10:30, and Christopher had fallen asleep on the floor. The next morning, his brother found him curled up in a fetal position. His pants were wet. He woke up grumpy, he told me, and felt Jackie's presence as he removed his clothing and took a shower.

"I felt like my past was happening all over again. It happened to my little sister just like it did to me. My mom—" Christopher's voice cracked. "How could she not know?" he asked desperately. "She even admitted she had suspicions about my father. And she said she had suspicions about my stepfather, too."

Over the telephone, I could hear even more anguish in his voice.

"My mom let it happen *again*. How could she?"

Chapter

12

MAKING HEADWAY

"Yes, she's done it again, Christopher," I told him.

It had to have happened to him as a child, just as he remembered through Richard, and I knew he must be numb with the shock of history repeating itself. He could no longer wish away the incest with his father, no longer pretend that the memories were not real. And now I was sure of his mother's role in the incest.

"She's subconsciously set up another child as a victim," I said to Christopher. "You know she doesn't do it on purpose."

"I know. I see how sick she is. That's why I can't hate her anymore." I could hear the resignation in his voice. "I don't remember much of the last two days," he added, "because I was splitting constantly."

"It's important, Christopher, that your other parts help you remember later."

"They will," he said, not sounding pleased about it.

"You need to integrate all that's just happened. Have you talked with your psychiatrist?"

"No." He sounded apologetic. "I'd have to explain the whole thing to him, and I'm not up to doing that."

"Do you want me to talk to him?"

"No. I'm not going to stay here in San Francisco much longer—just long enough to make sure my little sister will be okay, and then I'm getting out."

"You're coming back here?" I hoped he was returning.

"Yes. I'll be back where at least a few people really care about me."

We concluded our phone conversation then. I was expecting to see Christopher within a few weeks, but he didn't show up for two months. I felt as if I had been put on hold, not just in waiting for Christopher, but in waiting for my personal life somehow to reach a more definitive outcome. Then, when Christopher finally did come to keep another appointment, I was dismayed. It was Jeremy who strode through my office door—by this time, I'd know that proud walk of his anywhere.

"It sure is good to see you," he said, settling himself in the chair. To me, the soft hint of Jeremy's accent was unmistakable. "I feel like I've just come home, even though San Francisco is actually my home."

"Does that mean you plan to stay awhile, Jeremy?"

"You never miss a thing, do you, Dr. LaCalle?" His drawl became more pronounced. "I haven't been called by my name since I left here . . . feels kind of strange hearing it again."

"Didn't you come out while you were with your psychiatrist?"

"No. I was around a lot, but Christopher was the one who was out most of the time, except for those few days when his stepfather was thrown into jail. But now I've come out—since San Francisco. I have to find a place down here, and I'll have to find a job."

"Are you ready to start back into therapy?"

"I don't need to. But Christopher does," he said genuinely. "He's sure been a wreck. Those doctors up there didn't help him much. To my way of thinking, all the therapy was just on the surface."

As I listened to Jeremy's emphatic words, I thought he described the situation well. By this time, I was convinced that no therapist could help Christopher unless a deep trust had been established first. And certainly no one would be able to manage a crisis unless the therapist knew the personalities and had formed a close relationship with the most vulnerable part of Christopher—Timmy.

"There's a lot Christopher has to work on in therapy," Jeremy went on, his voice slow and thoughtful. "He'd never like to be close to anyone before he knew you. But he felt close to his sister, and there are people here he wants to know better. He's glad to be home, too."

Christopher's reappearance was like a homecoming for me, as well. I realized the special rapport was still there, even with Jeremy. Though Christopher had been hundreds of miles away, I had been kept part of his life.

"Tell me more about Christopher feeling close to his sister."

We were back into therapy again.

Jeremy led into the story, but soon switched back into Christopher. I had heard the compassion well up within him when he spoke of his sister and knew this was what brought Christopher forth. Love between Christopher and his little sister had grown, mostly because of his fatherly protectiveness, and he had discovered that he learned to be a nurturing person. He was thrilled, he told me, that he could be so significant a figure at this critical point in his young sister's life.

By helping his sister, Christopher was also helping himself. When she described to him what happened to her with her stepfather, he felt drained. But as she talked, he was able to work through some of his own feelings. He had, out of his need, created Jackie when he was a child. Jackie took care of him, was sad for him, protected him, was angry for him. Now Christopher could be to his sister what Jackie had been to him, and—in a way—undo some of his past. Christopher helped his sister talk about her rage toward their stepfather. He helped her not to feel guilty or responsible for what happened. Now, he himself was the supportive person. Accepting and working through his part in this way was an important turning point for Christopher. And these events strengthened my belief that there is some good that can come out of almost any tragedy if only we'll look for the lesson to be learned.

As our session drew to a close, Christopher wanted to know how I had been doing. I took this as further evidence of his healing. I told him that during the months he had been away I had continued attending the monthly study meetings on multiple personality and was still collecting articles on the subject. Then, confident that he would be able to benefit from the reading, I gave him copies of the most helpful material. I knew his comments would be useful to me, so I asked him to let me know what he thought.

"Why do you continue to spend so much time studying this?" he asked. "Do you ever expect to see another person like me?"

"I already have."

Astonishment was plain on his face. "Coming to see you in your office?"

"One woman came here. I'm seeing her until her therapist returns." I thought of Ruth and how different she was from Christopher—unattractive and demanding in a confrontational way. "Others I've seen in hospitals—four multiples, to be exact." With Christopher's incredulous look, I wondered if he found these numbers hard to believe. "And then there is one more, a man. I'm not sure of him yet. He may turn out not to be a multiple personality."

"You must be worn out! Do all of them take as much time as I have taken?"

"They probably would if they were my patients. I've seen all but one of the people for diagnostic purposes only. I've been consulting for attorneys and other therapists."

He was still wide-eyed. "I can't believe there are so many people like me around here."

"You're not the only one who doesn't believe that, Christopher," I said, laughing at the thought that he, too, could be a skeptic. "Most people have a hard time believing the figures that Dr. Slater and others like me are collecting. Dr. Slater keeps a record of all the calls that come to him and to other therapists of multiples in our group. He's made a rough estimate. He thinks that out of the two million residents of our area, about one hundred multiple personality cases are in treatment of some sort—most of them, as yet, misdiagnosed and undiscovered. But even with those figures, that still makes your disorder relatively rare."

"Well, whether I'm rare or not, I've still got to go out and find me a job." He'd perked up—and I heard that familiar slight drawl. Jeremy was back. "A plain ol' ordinary job. Nothing fancy."

But it was Christopher, mainly, who looked for a job. Jeremy had disappeared after the first couple of employment interviews.

Fortunately, Christopher had been able to save a little money while living with his brother, but he was still pressured to go out job hunting daily. The remainder of his time he spent working intensively in therapy.

Finally, a breakthrough occurred in the way Christopher remembered things. Up until this time, most of his memories had come through the other personalities. Gradually, Christopher was able to recall the same events himself. With the amnesia barrier broken, he would know of events experienced by the others. But he had the memory as if he were distant from it, almost as if he were watching it on a movie screen. Christopher described this as seeing himself from the outside, detached and depersonalized.

"These memories don't seem real," he had told me. "They are like shadows."

The breakthrough came while he was talking about his father. He made a psychic shift, and the memory became real.

"What is it, Christopher?" I asked when I saw the astonished look on his face.

"There was a picture that came in, but it was different. It felt clear, not hazy. It felt real!" he said in amazement. "Real, like you are to me right now."

"What was it you saw?"

"I saw a hairy chest over me. I didn't see a face, just the chest." He groped for words. "But I could feel its warmth, and I could feel my own body. It's hard to explain. It's kind of like I stayed inside my own skin."

I understood what he was telling me. Most people are able to remember an event and recall the sensations and emotions that accompanied it. But this experience—a part of human existence that the rest of us take for granted—was revolutionary for him.

With Christopher, nothing could be taken for granted. For example, I had come to take for granted that Christopher would always seem to call in a timely way. It was always just when I had a cancellation and could work an extra hour with him into my schedule. Or he'd call when there was something I needed to tell him.

Just good timing, I'd thought, but too many coincidences occurred. I would be calling him on one line and Liz would buzz me on the intercom to say there was a call from him on another line. It had happened once too often, and so this time I said something.

"Christopher, did you install a bug in my phone?" I asked jokingly. "How is it you always seem to call at the right time—even at the right minute!"

"It's hard to explain," he said seriously. "I can tell what people are thinking or feeling about me when they aren't saying it with words. I can tell even when they aren't with me and are miles away."

What had started as one of my offhand remarks had opened up something more serious.

"You're talking about mental telepathy, a sort of extrasensory perception?"

"Yes."

"Have you ever felt me thinking about you?"

"No. I don't think so." Christopher stopped to consider it. "But you're on my mind so much, it's hard to tell. I get the feeling with some people and not with others, or I get it with certain people but not all of the time. It's like being tuned into someone—I can tune into their minds and make them do things, or make things happen."

The wishful thinking of an otherwise helpless child, I thought. But Christopher was an adult. Did he still believe he could influence others by remote control? Perhaps, I thought, if we examine or refute something specific, something I could validate with my own reality . . .

"Have you ever been able to influence my behavior by sending a thought to me?"

"I don't think so. Sometimes I'd be wishing you would phone me, and you would. But that's not the same thing. The feeling is someplace between wishing and trying for it to happen and not trying or thinking about it at all."

Now that he had opened up on this subject, Christopher explained it all to me in a rush. "It's kind of like being in a trance—aware but not aware at the same time. I'm a part of what is going on around me, but I'm separate and distant at the same time. It's hard to explain. It's like a *knowing*, a knowledge that I feel everywhere, not just in my thoughts. I just *know* something. I'm sure of it, and it *is*. This knowing comes to me when I'm not looking for it, when I don't expect it. But I've also noticed it more when I'm tuned in to it, when I'm not pushing it out of my head by keeping busy. It's really strong when I'm depressed and sitting around a lot. That's also when I'm more likely to think bad thoughts, and I can make bad things happen to people. The messages I send back are angry and hurtful ones, and I know that someone will be hurt."

I thought his fear of his sixth sense stemmed from his uncertainty regarding the side of himself that was at times unfeeling or full of homicidal rage. But I listened to Christopher and kept silent about my own beliefs and opinions.

Christopher was frightened by his "powers," and he would have been even more frightened if I had given the concept of his extrasensory perception or other powers any further credence.

"I understand your fear, Christopher. But, so far, we haven't even established that you can do something as simple as make me call you." It seemed to me that Christopher was hoping I'd be a conservative voice of reason. "Don't you think it's jumping the gun a little to assume that you can make bad things happen to people?"

"Yeah." He conceded the point, but still sounded doubtful. "You've told me before that bad thoughts don't mean I'm really going to *do* something bad."

"That's right. You've been full of rage before but, as an adult, you've never harmed anyone or even attempted any damage. We need to discuss this further, but it will have to wait until our next session." My mind had suddenly gone back to why I had dialed him. "I'm going to have to change our appointment time, though."

"That's why I'm calling you!" He sounded surprised.

I asked if he had to change the time, too.

"Yes. I can't make it because I got a job."

"Congratulations! Where?"

"A bathhouse in L.A."

"A bathhouse!" I groaned. "Oh, no, Christopher, not *you* working in a bathhouse! That's absolutely the wrong job for you!"

But he had spent a month searching for work, Christopher told me. He was relieved to find a job—any job. And Jeremy's influence, strong at first, had vanished. The last time I had seen

Jeremy was when he came back from San Francisco. Yet strong traces of his influence remained. Christopher sometimes would deliberately put a mild Southern lilt into his voice to add flair to a conversation. Christopher felt he could do and feel all of Jeremy's thoughts and actions. Since Jeremy was the most recent personality to be "born," I reasoned that he had been the first and easiest to integrate. In any event, Jeremy was no longer to be found. Christopher now encompassed Jeremy's values and exhibited more of Jeremy's pride in himself.

I winced at the thought of Christopher overseeing patrons at an establishment where homosexuals gather for casual sexual encounters. The steam rooms and spas were only an excuse, the same sort of public ruse that is used by massage parlors for heterosexual males.

"I've only been a bathhouse customer twice in my life," Christopher told me. "It makes being gay disgustingly cheap. I hate that sort of thing."

"I know you hate it. So why are you there?"

"I'm out of money. It's the only job I could find."

Christopher suffered through his work at the bathhouse. James could have adapted to the job much more readily. The atmosphere of casual sex would not have bothered him, but Christopher no longer had James to rely on. In developing a more callous outlook himself, he took on James's role and, thus, prevented switching to James.

He had hoped he would be able to tolerate the job without dissociating again, but with each stressful week at work, he became fearful that James would reappear. Painstakingly, he kept what normalcy he could in his life outside of work. In spite of his taxing schedule, he continued to look for a better job and was determined to keep up with regular psychotherapy.

I was trying simply to help Christopher remain stable because he was under such stress. I did not feel that further gains would be made in his therapy. Because of my expectations, I failed to notice a quiet but significant change that had taken place. I became aware of it only when I realized I was feeling less maternal toward Christopher. The protective, countertransference feelings had diminished. At first I thought my feelings had changed because Christopher was acting responsibly and had stabilized briefly, and so I no longer had to be as concerned about his welfare. As a matter of fact, I had not seen or heard from the other personalities in weeks, and I had not talked with Timmy since the long-distance phone call from San Francisco.

Timmy, I thought—it was Timmy! I missed him and did not know why. Up until recently, even when Timmy was not out, his presence could be felt now and again. I sensed that it was not only that Timmy was feeling safe and secure. Something had changed. A timid, needy, clinging quality in Christopher had been lost.

"How is Timmy these days?" I asked.

"I don't know. I feel very out of touch with the others."

"Please see if you can get in touch just enough to let me know how that part of you is doing."

Christopher sat quietly and took on a glazed, trancelike expression. His eyes darted back and forth in a way I recognized. He was listening. After a long silence, he said, "He's fine." I waited, but he said no more.

"Well, can you tell me something about him?"

"He's seven years old and going on eight. He's very busy and has been feeling pretty good."

Seven and going on eight . . . past the oedipal stage. No wonder I felt differently. The little boy, Timmy, did not need me in the way he had before. That was good, the way it was supposed to be.

Also, Christopher had become accustomed to the work at the bathhouse. His routine, and the stress of his job, had lessened. Soon he began to discover feelings and experience what others consider commonplace—for instance, anger.

I had never seen Christopher angry. I had seen James cold and hostile, and I knew of Jackie's outright aggressiveness. But Christopher himself had always been passive and meek. What most of us call anger, Christopher would label "violence." And he hated violence. He had always dissociated from it by letting Jackie encompass his most aggressive feelings.

He told me he had gotten into a quarrel with his new roommate, and Jackie had come out and become violent. Jackie's violence turned out to be nothing more than her act of throwing an empty glass to the kitchen floor. No one had been hurt. Nothing but the glass had been broken. And his roommate had already left the apartment and did not even know about the angry gesture. Still, Christopher had been petrified by Jackie's outburst. I tried to explain to him that normal people get angry and even break things now and then. He was not convinced. I knew he had to discover for himself the truth of what I was saying.

Christopher and his roommate had been struggling to make peace between them, and one evening, after a particularly grueling afternoon, the two of them began to bicker over housekeeping duties.

"He's such a slob," Christopher told me afterward. "I picked up the pillow he left on the floor and threw it on the bed. Then I walked out of the room and slammed the door."

"Sounds like you were really angry," I commented. I kept my voice as bland as I could, given the excitement I was feeling inside. Christopher was using the word "I" to describe his angry feelings.

"Angry? Yeah. I sure was!" Christopher said, the anger still lingering in his voice.

"Say that again."

"What? You mean, 'I sure was angry!' "

"That's right. Now, say it again with more feeling."

"I sure was angry!"

I was delighted at the gusto in his voice. "Great! How does it feel when you say that?"

Christopher shrugged his shoulders. "Fine," he said.

"You don't feel violent?"

"Sort of." He scratched his forehead. "I felt kind of violent when it happened, but I didn't *do* anything violent."

"So you could control it."

"Yes."

"Jackie didn't have to be angry for you, and James didn't have to come out to control it."

Christopher's face lit up. "No," he said excitedly. "I did it myself!"

This was progress, really promising progress. But I sometimes thought it would have been easier for Christopher to stay inside the safe, empty shell of himself, the waking personality. Step by step, he was incorporating all the memories, feelings, and attitudes that had once been a part of the other personalities. Discovering these feelings was a slow, painful process, relieved only by occasional lulls when the growth reached a plateau. And

Christopher often asked me how he would feel in the final stage, when the empty shell of his waking self was filled. I could not promise him anything. I could not tell him what complete self-hood would mean for him. So I told him what being a whole person meant to me. He listened carefully while I shared my philosophy.

First of all, being a whole person meant for me being aware—aware of all parts of myself, not shutting down feelings, not oper-ating solely on intellect, but maintaining a balance with emo-tions. It meant self-trust. It meant utilizing all my natural ele-ments: reason, passion, lust, survival instincts, spirituality, curi-osity, sociability, protectiveness, possessiveness . . . the list was long. And for me to be a whole human being meant I had to live in the present, accepting my past as part of myself and knowing the future would come in its own time—and I would deal with it as it came.

Then I explained to him that for years he had cut himself off from his past. And in doing so, he had cut out parts of himself. Now he was integrating yesterday with today. He had feared the future, but now he was learning that if he took care of today, tomorrow would be taken care of when the time came. As he learned to live in the present, in the here and now, he would begin to discover he had feelings he never knew he had. Some-times, I told him, the discovery would be pleasant, perhaps even joyful. But often it would be painful. And I could only promise him that at each crossroad in his life, each new challenge would bring more of the same.

But all the while I was telling Christopher about becoming a whole person, I felt like a hypocrite. I had a challenge of my own to face, and I wasn't doing a very good job of it. What had I done to integrate all the new feelings and perceptions I had developed? I had been shelving my feelings, putting off confronting myself, putting off looking at my marriage.

I had to take time to think about *me*, about what I had done and what I'd become. I had to do it soon. What if I waited too long to get a handle on myself? It had already been months. The dis-tance between José and me had become habitual. All I knew for certain was that I had taken my time, time I needed. But where would José be at the end of this time?

He had pulled into himself, just as I had. Already we were

living on two separate islands. He had tried to bring us back together, but I hadn't been ready. It was time for me to make the next move—it had been for quite a while—but I wasn't pulling myself together.

I could delay no longer. I was glad the weekend had arrived and I could get away from the office and the house for a while. The beach was a good place to think, so that's where I went. It was early springtime, too cool to do anything but walk to keep warm. It was quiet. The diehard surfers were there in their wetsuits, but everyone else was still at home waiting for summer.

It had been eighteen months since I started with Christopher, and although his integration was nearing its final stages, we still had a long way to go. And postintegration therapy was just as important as any of the rest of it. At that point, I thought, he would have just achieved the unity that most people have when they begin therapy.

Then I stopped short. Darn! I was at it again! Thinking about Christopher and not myself. I looked at the movement of the waves and let the rhythms still my thoughts. After a while, a peacefulness slowly settled in.

Something had changed within me. I closed my eyes to try to focus in on what it was. What was the feeling? The little girl is gone—no, that's not quite right. There are two little girls. One is . . . I imagined myself, still, spontaneously kicking off my shoes and running through the sand with complete abandon. That was the small-town childlike enthusiasm and genuineness of my youth, and it was closer than ever. No. It's the other little girl, the frightened one. She was the one, the source of that nagging insecurity I always tried to tune out. Was she completely gone? I didn't think so. But I'd have to work to tune in to her now and then, rather than frequently work to tune her out. Now, how did this translate into my life?

That was finally obvious. I didn't feel alone . . . abandoned. There was a newness to this feeling. It was okay if I had to face problems on my own without support, or even understanding. I enjoyed the sense of freedom—and confidence—that this new feeling gave me.

But where did this leave José?

Wasn't it his role to protect me, take care of me, advise me, help me make decisions? Head of the household! That was certainly the way he was raised. The oldest son, taught to be responsible, especially to his little sister. But in recent months I had stripped him of all that sort of influence.

Where *did* that leave him? Us?

He wasn't a male chauvinist. He had changed his thinking as he became "modern" and Americanized. And, certainly, I had made sure he knew all about women's rights. Still, if he couldn't gain my attention and fill my needs as he always had, he'd be feeling as abandoned as I once felt. I had to let him know he was important in my life—even if it wasn't in the same way as before.

I would feel lonely without him. I loved him. I began to miss him as I thought about him. How could I have remained distant from him for so many months? I was ready to go back home and talk.

"Where have you been all afternoon?" José asked as soon as I came in the house. "I was home early with the kids."

"I played hooky so that I could go down to the beach and think."

He looked at me as if I'd said something strange. "Uh-oh. What does *that* mean?" I could hear the note of nervous anticipation in his voice.

"Nothing to worry about, but we do have to talk."

"How about now?"

It was a perfect time. I was ready. He was in a good mood, relaxed. Eddie was at the neighbor's, and Carmen was taking a nap. He poured us each a glass of wine, and we sat down in the living room. I liked the way he was preparing to listen.

"I'm feeling like I have some explaining to do." I stopped and looked at my glass. "I know you've been wondering when I would get around to this." I hesitated again. "I don't think this talk will resolve everything, but I want it to be a start."

He sat quietly, waiting for me to go on.

"What it all boils down to sounds . . . so simple. Too simple." I was mumbling, feeling awkward. "I'm afraid you won't understand."

"Give me a chance."

"In the last year and a half, a lot has happened to me—personally and professionally—complex and subtle changes." I was faltering again. "Maybe if I could write it all down, you'd know

219

what the experience with Christopher has meant to me."

"Christopher again?" I could tell he was pulling back—but only slightly.

"I don't want to talk about Christopher," I assured him quickly. "I'm just telling you how I came to what I am about to say." How could I put it simply without sounding simplistic? I'd just have to plunge in. "What I've learned is that you can't always be there to advise me or protect me or to make things easier on me. In fact"—this was the important part—"I don't *want* that anymore." I went on quickly. "That's a childish notion, a girlish romantic fantasy, and I've hung on to it too long. I've learned not to be afraid anymore of real independence."

"Are you kidding? I've always thought of you as independent."

"Stubborn and willful, maybe—like you—but not independent. I can see that now. And it's so easy to rely on help and understanding from someone like you. You've accepted that responsibility so readily."

"But," he said in amazement, "you've never asked my permission for anything. And do you have a mind of your own!"

"I thought you'd have trouble understanding this."

"But, Trula, I don't think I'm the only one who sees you as independent." He did sound genuinely surprised. "I think our friends would laugh if they could hear you now. Look at all the things you do completely on your own. Haven't I told you the comments other people make about your accomplishments?"

"Yes, but that's not what I'm talking about. What you're seeing is all on the surface—things I *do*, how I *act*. Not how I feel on the inside."

"And so much of the time," he interrupted me, "you need so much to have things go your way that you seem fiercely independent to me."

I wasn't offended. He was stating a fact both of us were already aware of. How was I to make him understand? Was he seeing only what he wanted to see? Was he too close to me to perceive me accurately? Could a *man* understand this? Somehow, I didn't think I would have nearly as much trouble explaining this to one of my women friends.

"If I were so independent," I attempted again, "then why did I need your agreement and approval? What do you think all our arguments over Christopher were about? I wanted your support and was angry when I didn't get it."

"But I did support you, even if it wasn't in the way you wanted. I've always believed in *you*. I just couldn't agree with the way you weren't setting enough limits with that case. You were too involved, tense, strained—absent from us."

"I agree. I knew that then, but I couldn't stop it. I've learned from my study group that an overreaction like that is not unusual for therapists treating their first multiple. At least I didn't do what some do and retreat from the painful emotions by becoming clinical and intellectualized."

"That's probably what I would have done—*did* do!" José seemed surprised at his own insight. "Even though it wasn't my case, your emotions were enough to make me very skeptical."

"Here we are talking about Christopher again!" I said. "I wanted to talk about us."

"We are talking about us, about how I did or did not support you. But I'm confused. What do you want from me?"

I paused and weighed my words. This was the crucial part. "I like it when you support me, but it's no longer essential that you do." He looked at me rather blankly, as if the words hadn't sunk in. "I'm sorry I had to become so distant from you for a few months." Now guilt was creeping up on me. "But I think it was the only way I could experience my aloneness in a way that I could gain strength from it. I had to grow up inside."

"Grow up? Or not need me anymore?"

The conversation had taken a perilous turn. I could sense the vulnerability in him.

"I was afraid that's how you'd feel." I had a sinking feeling. "But please don't take it that way. I do need you, but not in the role you've always taken—more of a big brother than a friend." I looked at him. Would he understand? "Let's try not to worry about it," I said, hoping fervently that this renewed closeness wouldn't be lost. "We'll work it out with time."

"You're not going to pull away from me again?"

"No. Oh, no! I want to be close to you. I've really missed you."

I reached over to touch his face, and he pulled me into his arms

. . . warm and gentle . . . I snuggled closer. My head was nestled under his chin. "Mmmmm," I purred, "I'm always going to need this."

The following week was a tough one for me. Eddie was sick. My housekeeper had quit. Hospital consultations were piled up after office hours. And, to top it off, my other multiple, Ruth, was in crisis. By Friday, I was dragging. When I looked at my schedule I was grateful that all of the day's appointments were with patients who were doing well—Christopher included. I smiled, thinking of the progress we had both made.

That day, Christopher had some concerns about his integration into one personality. "But how will I do it all alone?" he asked.

"Alone?"

"Yes. I've always had the others there to help."

I saw what he meant. "You're right," I said. "Doing it alone won't be easy. You'll have to take full responsibility for everything. And whatever happens, for good or for bad, you will feel it."

Christopher was not sure he wanted to take all that upon himself.

"Look, Christopher, don't you think there are times when I wish I didn't have to own up to my feelings?"

"You?"

"Yes, of course, me. It's hard to be responsible for myself all the time. Sometimes I think it would be nice if I didn't have to be responsible for my own anger, for example. Maybe I could just have an hysterical fit and pretend I couldn't control myself. Trouble is, I'd know it was a lie."

"Yeah, I think I know what you mean. The other day at work, I had to manipulate a situation so that I could get what I wanted out of my boss. I'm not used to doing things like that. I wouldn't do it even if I heard James's voice telling me to do it. Usually, then I'd have a blackout. And I'd just find that somehow it had been done. Well, this time it was like James never existed—or as if he became me and I became him. Sometimes I'm so confused I don't know who is taking control or if all of it is just me alone." Christopher looked away from me pensively. "Sometimes I feel lonely inside. I get lonely for the others who became so much a part of me after I found out they existed. Now they seem to have faded away as I learn to do what they have done. It's kind of like someone has died, but I know they aren't really dead. They're just gone."

"Loneliness must be a new feeling for you." I was thinking of Timmy, the lost, lonely little Timmy I had first met.

"Yeah. I never was close to anyone, but I never felt lonely either. Lonely isn't a good feeling."

I wondered if Christopher had been better off before—no, of course he hadn't. He just needed to have someone near him to love. And he needed to be loved in return.

"Christopher, it's important that you are able to be alone and rely on your own internal resources. But you must also be able to strike a balance between being on your own and relying on other people. I think you need closer friends, true intimacy."

"Well . . ." He looked a little sheepish. "I have you, and I know Diane and Sylvia really care about me."

"But it's not enough, is it?"

"No."

"Then what are you going to do?"

"I guess I'll just have to let someone else get close to me. I've been wanting to do that. But I haven't found anyone I can trust enough to become a big part of my life. I'm ready, but still a little afraid."

It wasn't long after this that Christopher told me he'd found Carl, a new friend. Carl, Christopher said, was special, the kind of gay man that Jeremy had always admired. Carl was educated and refined, handsome and well dressed, and he had an executive position with a reputable accounting firm. He had accepted his homosexuality but knew how to succeed in the heterosexual business world by keeping his private life to himself and his sexual preferences unknown to his fellow employees. Carl was near Christopher's age, but more mature. Christopher told me that Carl had experienced all sides of the gay world and had "settled down" to a more conservative lifestyle. He made a good income, lived in a well-furnished condominium, and had established long-term friendships.

And Carl had told Christopher that when he met him, it turned his life upside down. He did not know why, but he was instantly drawn to Christopher.

Christopher's recital made this sound like he was quite taken with Carl, yet Christopher was cautious. He said he wanted to get to know Carl slowly, that Carl was moving too fast for him.

"I want to be sure he's a good choice."

I smiled inwardly, hearing those echoes of Ernest's reasonable approach. "You sure have nice things to say about him, Christopher. What's causing you to have doubts?"

"He's not like anyone I've known before. He'd let me take advantage of him."

There was a hint of James—always aware of another's vulnerabilities and tempted to profit from them.

"But I wouldn't want to do that—take advantage." Christopher had spoken with a quiet forcefulness, as if countering the temptation within him.

"Anything else bothering you?"

"Yes. I'm afraid he'll get too emotionally involved. I mean, what if we get involved with each other? What if something happens and I get sick again? I've only been integrated a couple of months—and that's after almost two years of therapy!"

Christopher made it sound like a long time, I thought, when he'd made excellent progress in a relatively short period. Yet he was right. He had every reason to be concerned about a relapse. In an acute period of stress or crisis, he could go into personality splitting again. Other integrated multiples had been known to dissociate.

"If you did get sick again, Christopher," I assured him, "it wouldn't be like before. You've learned too much. I think you'd pull yourself back together quickly. And I seriously doubt if we'll ever see the other personalities out as clearly as they once were."

"If I told him I am a multiple," Christopher said anxiously, "I don't think he could handle it." Christopher's distress was evident. "And if I got sick, that would be even worse."

"Then don't tell him. You have that option."

"No, I have to," he said resolutely. "It wouldn't be fair to him to hide something as important as that."

Christopher looked worried but determined. I had confidence that whatever he decided to do, he would do what was best for him—all parts of him.

Chapter
13

FACING THE UNTHINKABLE

It was not long before Christopher told me he would bring Carl in to meet me. He'd explained to Carl about his psychiatric hospitalizations and that he'd tried to kill himself. Then, when he'd told him about the other personalities, Carl was incredulous. Christopher, at a loss to know what else to say to his friend, had arranged the visit with me. And so the two of them sat in my office, looking to me for answers.

I studied Carl quickly to see if I could get a clue as to how to approach him. He was as attractive as Christopher had described him—tall, lean, and intelligent-looking. He'd come directly from his office, dressed in his business suit. But he'd taken off his jacket, loosened his tie, and rolled up his sleeves. The white shirt set off his deep tan, and he looked rather laid back. Friendly enough, I thought, but definitely awkward in this unusual situation.

Carl still seemed a bit stunned as we began to talk. And Christopher's discomfort was painfully obvious.

"I think he'll take it better if it comes from you," Christopher said. "Tell him anything he wants to know. Tell him"—he turned to look at Carl, then turned back to me—"anything that might make him change his mind about getting involved with me." There was a long awkward pause. "I don't want him to get hurt," Christopher blurted.

I started explaining the situation to Carl, but then Christopher interrupted me. "I think it would be better if I leave the room," he said. With the same hurried awkwardness, he got up and left.

Christopher had said he wanted us to talk freely. More than that, I realized, he didn't want to have to listen to what I might say. And, as he closed the door, I resolved to proceed as cautiously as possible. Carl, however, took the lead and started right in.

"I don't know what to think," he said, shaking his head. "This whole thing is so bizarre. He talked about other personalities. What does he mean, 'other personalities'? How many are there, Dr. LaCalle?"

"Seven," I said with reserve and matter of factness, and then watched for his response.

"Then it's true!" Carl gasped.

"Yes, it's true," I said calmly. I'd have to reach for words of reassurance. "I don't think Christopher will ever again be as mentally ill as he once was. Although, I must say, he has integrated all of the personalities so recently . . ." I paused, concentrating on observing Carl's reaction as much as on my own words. "I don't know when or if he might have a relapse and split again."

"I think that's already happened—at least, Christopher said I was talking to the James part of him when he was telling me about his multiple personalities."

"Oh!" I sighed, disheartened by the news.

"But he didn't look or sound much different, so I didn't know what to believe."

"That's a relief to hear. If James had been out in full, believe me, you would have noticed! There would have been a sharp change in Christopher. The personalities have been fading away, becoming so weak that Christopher is unable to retrieve them fully—even under hypnosis."

I went on, explaining that Christopher and I weren't using hypnosis anymore. I also told him that James had lingered on longer than the others.

"He doesn't really come out, Carl. Christopher just feels as James felt when it comes time to be assertive or handle difficult situations, although recently with you he must have had a slight relapse."

"This is very confusing, but I'll just have to learn to understand it," Carl responded. "I've got no choice. I'm already involved with him emotionally."

"Aren't you fearful?"

"To be honest with you, I am—a little. But there's something about Christopher. I trust him—don't ask me why."

We were both silent, reflecting on what Carl had said.

"I trust him, too." I was saying aloud what had first struck me as a private thought.

Carl told me he wanted to know about the personalities. I briefly named and described each one, watching for Carl's responses. It was obvious that he had quickly become more intrigued than afraid. He listened quietly as I explained how the splitting of personalities began in early childhood, how amnesia barriers had developed, and how Christopher had regained those split-off parts of himself since he began treatment. I knew I could not explain everything. And, in spite of Christopher's request to "tell all" to Carl, I was not going to reveal Christopher's traumatic past—especially how his father had sodomized him. My thoughts were of Christopher, sitting anxiously in the waiting room. Christopher could share this with Carl if and when a time came that it was important for Carl to know.

"It sounds like his sexual orientation is mixed up," Carl said, "but he sure seems gay to me. There isn't any chance that one of those personalities—like Ernest or Sissy—could, uh, mess up our love life, is there, Dr. LaCalle?"

"That's something I've thought about. I don't have the answer, but I do know it wouldn't be Sissy or Ernest who would cause any changes."

"Then who?"

"It's not really a 'who,' Carl. Those personalities have become a thing of the past."

Carl was looking at me intensely, wanting the best answer I could give. I wanted to respond to Carl's question honestly, just as Christopher had requested. I knew Christopher didn't want Carl to be hurt, and I didn't want to jeopardize the most significant relationship Christopher had ever had. I tapped my knee, thinking.

"Christopher should be hearing this," I said at last. "Would you mind?"

With Christopher in the room, I repeated Carl's question about whether Christopher's sexual orientation might change.

"Let me try to explain it this way," I said, weighing my words carefully. "Christopher has had two young male personalities, their sexual orientation not fully developed. Both could have been heterosexual. As he continues to integrate feelings in himself, these latent tendencies could influence his sexual behavior. Of course," I said, now looking at Christopher, "what I am saying is highly speculative. I have no other cases to compare you with, Christopher. And you have integrated so much already, it's possible that no change will occur in your sexual feelings."

"I really doubt that I'd change," he said, and then shrugged. "I guess you never know."

"But," Carl asked me, "do you think there *could* be a conflict, a sexual problem later on?" He seemed more puzzled than anxious.

"There's a remote possibility," I responded. "Can you be prepared for the unexpected?"

"Sure. I usually am," he said confidently. "So, if that happens—well, it happens." He looked at Christopher. "I already care about him enough to want whatever is best for him."

His words brought me a sense of relief. I felt Carl's sincerity. I respected his courage, and I couldn't help but be pleased that Christopher had taken a liking to a man with such fortitude and maturity. I reflected as well on the strength and maturity that was required from José, to have been able to cope with the changes between us. I was deeply thankful I had married a man like him because I knew our marriage had a good chance of enduring for a lifetime.

Following our meeting, the relationship between Carl and Christopher developed rapidly. Christopher was encouraged by Carl's acceptance and optimism, and within two weeks Christopher had moved into Carl's home. Carl told him it was foolish for Christopher to live hand to mouth when there was plenty of room at his place.

"I can't believe how he turns everything over to me," Christopher said to me soon after he'd moved in. "He's so giving and trusting. I wish I had more money so I could share expenses equally. I'd like to be as good to him as he is to me."

Christopher's job at the bathhouse stood in sharp contrast to the conservative life he and Carl shared together. Soon, as might be expected, Christopher's working environment became even more distasteful to him. He wanted a white-collar job, one in which he could earn more money. Carl wanted him out of the bathhouse, too, but he was not sure what he could do to help Christopher. Carl didn't want to put pressure on Christopher, but, after weighing the risks carefully, he decided to assist Christopher in finding a position within his own company.

"He says he likes math," Carl told me when he came along on one of Christopher's appointments. "I'm teaching him how to handle the type of accounts we have at our company so that he can apply for a position at one of our branch offices. Christopher is smart, and he catches on fast. I can tell him who to contact for an interview, what they'll be asking him, and what to write on his application."

With Carl's instruction and support, Christopher readied himself for his new career. Carl saw to it that the right people in the right places met with Christopher, and Christopher landed a job on his first try. Feeling positive and confident, he had gone through the job interview just as any other person would. He no longer needed Jeremy around to help out. Christopher joyously quit his job at the bathhouse, vowing never to return to such an establishment. He thanked Carl profusely and was determined to show his appreciation by succeeding right from the first day at the office.

The work was challenging and stimulating, and Christopher was trying terribly hard to excel at everything he did. In fact, he became anxious as he tried so hard to please his new boss, and soon found he was losing a few minutes at a time.

"My boss doesn't understand why I can have something explained to me, do the job perfectly for that day, and then come back the next day and have to have it explained to me all over again. I'm dissociating again—kind of spacing out, but not switching. It's embarrassing because it makes me look stupid."

"If you will just relax and stop trying so hard to be perfect, you'll probably stop 'spacing out,' as you put it."

"I can't relax with my boss around." The tension was evident on Christopher's face. "She is always complaining about how much work she has to do and how tired she is and how it is getting her down. I feel like I have to do things for her or everything will fall apart."

"You have a woman boss? I didn't know that."

I contemplated the dynamics of the situation a moment, and then it struck me. Christopher got along well with women—all kinds of women—except for one kind.

"I think you may have a negative transference operating," I told him. "Who does she remind you of?" I knew the answer to my question would be obvious.

Christopher drew his brows together, but only for the briefest of moments. "My mother!" he said with absolute certainty. "I feel the same way around my boss that I feel around my mother when she starts moaning and complaining about how hard life is. I feel like I have to take care of her." He looked at me resolutely. "But I don't have to take care of her, do I? Those are her problems, not mine."

Having gained the insight quickly, he resolved to change his attitude at work immediately. He soon managed to let his boss's complaints go unattended while he channeled himself into learning how to do the standard procedures that were set before him. The brief memory lapses ceased.

Christopher was making progress on all fronts. He had learned to take full responsibility for his actions, his abilities, his feelings, and his dissociation. He allowed himself to be wrong and to be imperfect. He learned to accept the sides of himself that he had heretofore found unacceptable.

"I really got angry at Carl last night when he turned the stereo up too loud when I wanted to read," Christopher told me. "I went and shut the thing off, stomped out, and slammed the door behind me."

"*You* did that, Christopher?"

"Yes, *I* did that. Then I felt a little childish about pouting so long afterward, and I came back in and apologized for taking off like that."

"*You* felt childish?" I emphasized.

"Uh, huh." He grinned back at me sheepishly, but with a comprehending twinkle in his eye. "Have you ever done anything like that with your husband, Dr. LaCalle?"

"Who, me?" I responded, with an impish lilt. "Why, I *never* overreact or act like a child. I'm too mature for that, don't you know?"

I was enjoying my tongue-in-cheek commentary, having regained my sense of humor about myself now that I felt more clear about my relationship with José, but then my thoughts drifted away. I reflected that the months of intensive work— daily hospital visits; extended, biweekly outpatient sessions; hours of telephone conversations day and night; personal contacts with Christopher's friends, family, employers, and therapists; consultations with respected colleagues and monthly seminars; and Saturday afternoon study trips to the university library—at long last the efforts had paid off. And here we were now, comfortably bantering about how I handled my own life! This was something I could never have foreseen at the start. Now I could rest, I thought. Christopher was a whole person. To my greatest satisfaction, I knew why.

Christopher had progressed to the point of needing to know how to solve commonplace problems. He wanted to know about "normal" relationships and how people could be committed to each other and concerned about each other. Since Carl had come into his life, words like "compassion," "attachment," and "love" had taken on new meaning for him. Love no longer meant fickle romanticism and idealized expectations. With love came a sense of responsibility for the welfare of the other person. He was committed to Carl, just as Carl was committed to Christopher's well being.

Only four months after meeting Carl, Christopher's life had become uneventful. For him, routine and predictability constituted a major success. After a lifetime of chaos, trauma, disappointments, bitterness, rage, and loneliness, Christopher was experiencing a more mundane and emotionally balanced way of life. His life had become predictable. With Christopher, stability was tantamount to success.

Just when I was about to suggest spacing out our appointments to every four weeks, Christopher presented a new problem. This new difficulty came as a surprise.

"Carl has been sitting around a lot lately," he told me with a worried expression. "He doesn't want to get out as much as usual. He says he's tired, but I don't think that's it."

"You seem really troubled, Christopher." I was puzzled. "It doesn't sound like such a big problem."

"Dr. LaCalle, I think he's not telling me something. I don't always have a chance to see what he does, but I think he's been drinking too much."

"What makes you think so?"

"He seems depressed. He can hardly get out of bed in the morning."

Certainly, I thought, Christopher knew firsthand what depression can do to a person.

"Maybe he is depressed," I said, "but that doesn't have to mean he's been drinking."

"But he doesn't have anything going wrong in his life, and he does have friends that I think are alcoholics. Listen, believe me. I've been there myself. I know. He's acting guilty or angry about something. He's more moody."

Christopher's speech was pressured.

"I hear you," I said to quiet him. "What are you going to do?"

"I'm going to tell him what I think, and I'm going to ask him to come to you for help. I'm sure he'd rather talk to you."

I explained to Christopher some reasons why it might not be the best idea for him and Carl to have the same psychologist, but I told him I would be willing to help them both if I could see no conflicts and if I was sure I could do Carl some good.

To my surprise, I heard from Carl the very next day. He wasn't avoiding his problems, but instead was eager to talk. He took the first hour I had open.

"I have been drinking too much—almost every night. I don't think Christopher sees how much I drink, or maybe he does. I'm not an alcoholic, though. I can stop drinking, and I will."

I'd heard that line many times before from alcoholics. I didn't believe Carl and wished he'd be honest with himself. Yet, if he wasn't ready to admit it, I thought I could still begin slowly to help him see how alcohol was interfering with his life. I hoped he'd come to recognize his problem.

"Is this kind of drinking pattern something that happens every once in a while?"

"No, Dr. LaCalle, it's not like me. I think what's happening is that loving Christopher the way I do has brought up some old pain, memories of my last lover. This is a hurt that I thought I'd put to rest."

"And alcohol will help take care of that pain?"

"Of course not. I told you. I've decided to stop drinking and to get over this thing with Paul once and for all."

This was one of those times I enjoyed being proven wrong. In the coming four weeks, Carl lived up to his commitment to himself. He explained to Christopher about Paul, and then brought Christopher into one of his sessions. Christopher was very supportive and listened with composure while Carl went on and on about his ex-lover. Carl was allowing himself to finish his grieving—and Christopher understood.

The drinking had stopped, and the grieving was over. Yet Christopher soon told me that Carl was still lethargic. Carl was depressed, Christopher insisted, and so something else had to be wrong. And, tragically, Christopher was right. Something else was wrong, but it was nothing that Christopher could have expected, nothing that Christopher could have understood or have experienced. The chain of events that brought the problem to light started with one of Carl's visits to me.

"Why do you think I should go see my family doctor?" Carl asked me.

"Because your life is going along beautifully, yet you are looking down and feeling tired."

"So you think it could be something physically wrong with me?"

I suspected Carl knew the answer to his question. "It wouldn't hurt to get a checkup, would it?" I asked.

"I should. I haven't had one in a long time. And I have something on my chest—a purplish-brown spot, about the size of a quarter. Another has started showing near it. It's been worrying me a little."

A little? Didn't Carl know, I thought, about malignant melanoma? It was fast-spreading and often lethal. I was alarmed. Of course, it could be something less dangerous, but he'd better have it checked right away.

"Darn it, Carl! You'd better get it looked at. If nothing else, it could be the worry about this spot that's getting you down." I was going to be adamant about this one. "Promise me you'll call your doctor right away."

233

The next time I saw Carl, he had been to several doctors. The purplish-brown spots weren't common to men his age, his doctor told him. And so he'd had to go to the UCLA Medical Center, where experts confirmed the diagnosis.

"It's called Kaposi's sarcoma," Carl said almost nonchalantly.

I breathed a sign of relief and leaned back in my chair. At least it wasn't malignant melanoma. But I'd never heard of Kaposi's sarcoma. Was it a dangerous malignancy?

"What is it that you have, Carl?"

"It's a skin cancer that comes with AIDS."

"AIDS?" Again I was ignorant, but I thought there was something about it in the back of my head. "Is that the disease that breaks down the immune system? I thought I read—"

"Yes. Acquired Immune Deficiency Syndrome," Carl explained. "I didn't know much about it either until I went to UCLA. The gays have started to talk about it some. At UCLA, they told me five hundred cases have been recorded since 1979, mostly gay men." Carl's tone was detached, unemotional. "And—are you ready for this? You asked me once if I could be prepared for the unexpected . . ." His mouth turned up in a bitter grin at the irony of what I had said. "They told me over half of those people are dead now." Slowly, all expression drained from his face, and he sat silently staring past me.

I was in shock. And I thought Carl might be, too. I looked at him dumbfoundedly, as if he could make what he said mean something different. Half of the men dead—in only three years? Could it be true he had a fatal disease? He seemed so healthy, in his prime.

He was looking out the window behind me, yet not really looking at all. He gave no indication of what he was feeling.

"I don't think any of them at UCLA really know what they're doing," Carl said flatly. "Nobody could give me a straight answer. All they said was they were still learning about AIDS." He looked back at me, but his expression remained blunted. "I don't have any confidence in what they tell me. So what am I supposed to believe? I asked them if I was going to die, and they said they didn't know. They want me to participate in a study of a new drug. It seems to me they're all worked up and ready to experiment with anything."

"You're going to go back to UCLA, aren't you?"

"If I want any treatment at all, I'll have to." His energy seemed to be steadily depleting as he talked, as his voice wound down. "But I sure don't like the idea—being a guinea pig."

"How are you feeling about this, Carl? How are you taking it?" My direct question about his emotional state seemed to spark some response in him. He sat up and repositioned himself in the chair.

"I'm just going to put it out of my mind," Carl told me, firmly now. "I'll take their treatments as long as they don't make me worse. And I'll go on with my life."

I suspected Carl was denying the seriousness of the situation. I wondered what his prognosis really was and what he should be doing to take care of himself.

"Would it be okay with you if I talk to the doctors at UCLA?"

"Oh, sure. In fact, I already asked Dr. Williamson to call you. I figured he might tell you more than he's told me."

"And Christopher? Have you told him?"

"Yes."

In the silence that followed, Carl's expression became grave.

"And . . . how is he handling it?"

"I'm not sure. He said he thinks we should take this calmly and rationally. He said he wants to do some research on AIDS, and he wants to talk to you." Hints of what used to be Ernest, I thought. Thank goodness, Christopher himself could now keep a level head.

Before I met with Christopher, I found an article on AIDS in the latest *Time* magazine that was delivered to our house. That evening, I kicked off my slippers and curled up on the sofa next to José while he watched television. The title, "The Deadly Spread of AIDS," gripped me, but I was still unprepared for what I would learn. For sixteen months, the Centers for Disease Control in Atlanta had been compiling statistics on AIDS. Carl fit the category of AIDS victims: Caucasian homosexual males in their thirties and forties. And 20 percent of the cases occurred in California. I couldn't help but consider the outrageous unlikelihood that this could be happening the way it was: an AIDS victim living with an integrated multiple. Carl and Christopher, each with a rare illness—but together? Fate is unbelievable at

235

times, I thought. I turned my thoughts back to the article. Interferon, an experimental drug, held promise. That was probably what the UCLA doctors wanted to use with Carl. Hope. There was hope!

Then I was struck a blow. The disease, the article said, was probably transmitted sexually. Christopher! Oh, no! Not Christopher, too! I had a terrible sinking feeling. I knew I wasn't visibly shaking, but I could feel myself shaking nonetheless. I must have been staring into space.

José noticed my stillness.

"What's the matter?" he asked.

"Nothing. I'm fine." There was no need to go into this with him, I thought. I'm fine on my own.

"What are you reading?" He looked over my shoulder to the magazine. "AIDS? Why is that upsetting you?"

There was no use in denying I was upset. He knew me too well. "One of my patients has been diagnosed with it."

"You aren't going to keep seeing him, are you?"

"Of course! Why not?" I knew that the day before, José had already read *Time* from cover to cover. He knew I wasn't going to catch AIDS from just being near Carl.

"Trula, I know that I'm not supposed to be protective of you anymore, but—"

"But?"

He was going to advise me anyway. "Couldn't you . . ."

Here it comes, I thought, and how am I going to deal with it this time? But he stopped himself.

"I worry about you, that's all. You have such difficult cases. I can tell, just by overhearing conversations in the waiting room."

"Yes, I do," I admitted. "But I also have several people with the easier, everyday-living sorts of problems."

"So, you're not going to get really upset over this case?"

"I can't promise you that. If you knew the circumstances, you'd understand why I can't say I won't be very upset. But, in any event, I'll take care of it myself. I'll be fine."

I hadn't convinced him. He held back from saying anything more and looked a little perplexed. I hadn't wanted to talk about the case, yet José wanted to take care of me and didn't know how to do it in a way acceptable to the "new" me.

"You know, José, maybe I *could* use a break," I said to show him I appreciated his concern about my welfare—even though I didn't need him to shelter me. "How about planning a four-day weekend this month? Wouldn't the kids love a trip up north?"

He smiled.

"You do the driving, of course," I teased.

He pinched me and grinned with delight. This was good. I needed a little lightheartedness and a bit of rest, considering the tough times ahead.

A few days later, a white-faced Christopher came to the office. He handed me two journal articles on AIDS—scientific and reputable studies he had located at UCLA. He couldn't refute what was written. He had to accept the reality.

"What a dumb one I am!" Christopher said. "I thought he was depressed!" He was chastising himself. "I feel so guilty about getting on his case, now that I know he's sick."

"Christopher . . ." What could I say? "Try to look at it this way. It took a certain series of events to get him to a physician." I was thinking that Christopher had so much to worry about. He had to let himself off the hook on this one.

"The people at UCLA said I've been exposed to AIDS, too," Christopher went on, "but there's no way of knowing if I'll get it. They don't know yet what the odds are."

"Scared?"

"No. Not for myself." His shoulders drooped. "I'm really worried over Carl." The burden on Christopher appeared overwhelming. "You know, Dr. LaCalle, I can't believe how well he's taking it. He's braver than I am!"

I didn't want to dispute our differing perceptions of Carl's mental attitude. Carl's denial would break through soon enough, and then they'd both have to deal with this crisis differently. With that kind of stress in Christopher's life, I was fearful he wouldn't hold up.

"What do you think will happen to Carl?" I asked.

"He's going to be fine. Just fine. I'll make sure of it."

If only what Christopher said could be true, I thought. It would be nice to believe that Carl would be well, and that they'd both go on with the contented life they had been building together. I, too, wanted to deny the possibility that Christopher, or Carl—or both—could die. And I wouldn't let myself think about it or anticipate the pain.

That's probably why I felt myself getting angry when I talked with Dr. Williamson on the phone. What a pompous one! I thought. He rattled off statistics as if it were all old hat to him. I knew it was an irrational thought, but I felt like he was being overly confident. How can he be so damned sure of the prognosis? Carl has a 40 percent chance of being dead a year from now? And a 70 percent chance of dying within two years?

I had a hard time listening to what he was saying. Celibacy. Carl would have to be celibate. That was his best recommendation. Christopher was at high risk if they weren't celibate. And Christopher should be careful with other sexual partners, practice what Dr. Williamson called "safe sex." I found out that for a while Carl would go into a dormant phase. He'd be able to work. And then . . . I found myself shutting out his voice. I could barely listen to more. Dr. Williamson sounded cold, factual, clinical. What did I expect? He was talking as one professional to another. Damn! I was feeling angry. He was breaking down my defenses. This hurt. This hurt too damn much!

I thought of Carl. Young. Healthy looking. Bright. Hard working. Attractive. Socially active. Physically adept. How could this be a man who would die? I understood now why Christopher was approaching the crisis as if tender loving care would make the problem go away.

"He's not taking care of himself," Christopher said with exasperation a few weeks later.

"What do you think he should be doing?"

"Not working too hard—those long hours he's been keeping."

"Can he get out of the overtime he's putting in?"

"I think he can, but he says the company is pressuring him."

Carl had already told me that he wasn't able to concentrate at work and that he felt tired all the time. Since his work wasn't up to par, he put in extra hours to compensate. He was terrified of being fired, of finding himself both sick and unemployed. Christopher knew the situation, but, in his way, he was trying to help.

"Maybe you should let Carl decide for himself if the work is too much for him," I suggested gently. "You know, it just might be a way for him to keep his mind busy so he won't dwell on his illness."

"But he's so tired when he gets home!" Christopher looked distressed. "He's going to lose his strength. He won't go out for walks in the evening because he's too tired. And he's not eating right."

"Who is preparing the meals?" I asked, wondering if Christopher had been following any contamination precautions. The scientists weren't yet altogether positive that AIDS spread only through intimate, direct contact.

"I am. One of *their* rules, you know. But I can't live like that, by all those restrictions. No. I fix the meals now because I *want* to. Carl's a better cook, but he's too tired. I fix lots of fresh fruits and vegetables. I make him take vitamins, too."

"You really are trying, aren't you?"

Christopher was close to tears. "Yes, but it makes me so angry that he won't cooperate."

"Christopher, everyone has his own way of coping with serious illness. Carl has told you he wants to do a good job at work. He needs to feel productive. Sure, he could do more for himself in other ways, but . . ."

"He's got me to take care of him."

"Well, that's the way it is." I shrugged. "Do you want to throw in the towel?"

"No."

"Well, then?"

"I'll do it his way, but it won't be easy."

When has it ever been easy for Christopher? I thought.

"Diane and Sylvia don't understand why I'm staying."

"They don't?" I was surprised. They had had dinner with Carl and Christopher on several occasions. I knew they liked Carl. They had told Christopher they were happy for him. Surely, they—because of their own long-term relationship—would understand Christopher's commitment to Carl.

"They knew someone who had Kaposi's sarcoma. The lesions took over his internal organs, and he died. They're afraid I'll get it from Carl."

Well, I thought, I guess I do understand. And Christopher put my thoughts into words.

"They like him a lot, but they love me."

"Your friends think you're risking your life. Are you?"

"Not me." He said it with a weak grin. "I'm a survivor. I'll get by."

Chapter 14

DON'T SAY GOODBYE

Carl continued his visits with me. And he'd made up his mind to throw himself into his work. Work was something he could control when everything else in his life was so uncertain. By this time, he'd even become unsure of Christopher and agonized over whether Christopher would stay with him. He had bouts of depression, but most of the time he was able to fight off the melancholy.

"All I have to do is worry about making enough money, investing it, saving it," he told me on one of his visits. "I'm going to need it for treatments."

But before long, the trips to the many doctors who wanted to examine Carl filled him with despair. He didn't want to talk about it—in fact, he soon didn't want to see the doctors anymore.

"I'm no hero," he kept saying. "I can't keep up with this."

He decided he wouldn't make any more appointments until after the first of the year. The holidays were coming up. He'd give himself a break for a couple of months. I was pleased that he made that decision, because immediately he again felt somewhat in control of his life. But nonetheless his uncertainties about Christopher came to the fore again. He had to face that dilemma, too. Would the two of them really be able to work things out together?

Carl had a hard time asking Christopher about their relationship. He was afraid he'd hear the worst, that Christopher didn't care enough to get through the tough times with him, so Carl asked Christopher in front of me. He needed my support, and he thought Christopher was sure to be honest if I was listening.

As Christopher answered Carl, I studied him to determine if he was sincere, and I felt he was in earnest. "All I want from you is for you to maintain a positive, hopeful attitude, and not give in to the disease."

This he could do, Carl responded. Yes, he could keep a stiff upper lip. "Christopher won't have to live with a drudge," Carl told me. "I'll have more fun in life." Then he turned to Christopher. "We'll figure out a way to do it together."

I had reservations about this "solution." First Carl resolved to work, then to be good company . . . pretty soon there would be something else. I could see they were refusing to deal with the ultimate outcome. I knew they weren't handling it all, that maybe they couldn't. At least they were coping day to day.

But as I expected, Carl's resolve wasn't enough. His depression kept creeping in. And Christopher wanted to go out—do things, be with people—while Carl wanted to stay home. Carl was too fearful of socializing, I thought. Quarrels erupted. I worried they'd get out of hand, that Christopher would not be able to tolerate the conflict. Even the joint counseling sessions on a frequent basis didn't help.

"What if someone could tell that I am sick—that I have AIDS?" Carl lamented.

At the same time he kept wondering aloud if Christopher might meet someone "wonderful" and begin to find him a bore. So Christopher felt he couldn't leave the house. Certainly, he couldn't go out without Carl. He'd feel too guilty leaving him at home, and Carl would be too threatened. So their condo—a refuge for Carl—became a jail to Christopher.

All the while, Christopher continued to cope. He kept on with his job, visited Sylvia and Diane, and came to my office for joint sessions with Carl. He sought new ways to alleviate their misery, too. He joined a health club. Carl wouldn't mind if he went there, Christopher explained to me, and maybe Carl could even come along. Next, Christopher looked into evening classes. There was nothing he could sign up for—he couldn't attend regularly. Sometimes he really needed to stay home with Carl.

They were becoming desperate in their search for ways to ease their woes. Their next idea was something they felt would keep them both busy and active, get them out and looking around: they'd leave the city and buy a home in the suburbs. The house payments would be only a little more. There would be clean air, quiet streets, a garden—even space for Carl to do his work at home. They could buy a computer.

Carl caught on to the idea with enthusiasm. And for a while it worked. They enjoyed going out house hunting with the realtor. Carl's mind was busy thinking of how they could turn a quick profit by selling the house in a couple of years, after they'd put some work into it. He was excited. Christopher was delighted with his enthusiasm.

For the next few months, they worked side by side. Christopher didn't have to stay home weekend after weekend. There were trips to the paint store, the lumber yard, the furniture auctions. Carl would sometimes get discouraged because he lacked the strength to do much of the heavy work, but Christopher didn't mind. He was happy to be busy and productive. Occasional joint sessions were enough, and I decided not to see Christopher individually. He needed a chance to work this out on his own. And for a time, during their visits to me they talked about the future as if tomorrows were plentiful.

Then the house was complete.

What was there left to do? Now was the time, they decided, to get the piano Carl had always wanted. That cheered him up for a few days. Then it was pets. Christopher thought this would add a little fun to the house. A bird . . . a dog . . . next he went shopping for an aquarium, all to make Carl happy. They knew they were spending too much money, but it didn't seem to matter. All that mattered was for Carl to feel good, to have a diversion.

In the midst of all this, Carl lost his job. He was fired—flat out fired—for inefficiency.

He'd never told them he was sick. What good would it have done? It wasn't as if he could promise them that he would take a few weeks off and his problems would be solved. This was a double blow. It wasn't just that he'd lost his job. He was reminded of the deadly reality that no cure was in sight. The interferon treatments hadn't helped; he was sick, and he wasn't going to get better.

Carl now sat home, alone during the days, steeped in depression, immobilized. Christopher came home to clean and cook, all the while watching Carl sit zombielike in front of the television. Antidepressants were too risky for his immune system—Carl would have to tough this out, without anything to alleviate either the physical or the emotional pain.

Christopher knew about depression. "You can't give in to it," he told Carl. "You have to make yourself *do* something. If you sit, you'll get even more depressed."

Christopher came to see me.

"If he sits, he'll die. He'll die soon."

So Christopher stopped cleaning, except for the most strenuous work. He stopped cooking. He stopped paying the bills. He went to work in the mornings and told Carl, "You're home now, so you do it!"

I had to admire Christopher's wisdom. Carl did do the work. It took him all day to finish the simplest chores, but he got them done. Christopher was pleased.

Now Christopher took it upon himself to help Carl look for another job. "You can still work." Christopher explained his latest idea to Carl. "Take an easier job—one you can do without trying."

But Carl's self esteem was crushed. Angry for having been fired, he raged at himself, convincing himself of his own worthlessness.

Christopher argued with him. "If anything," he told Carl, "you're worth too much."

In this, Christopher was right, but not as he had expected. As Christopher helped Carl prepare and send out his resume, Carl's pessimistic belief that no one would hire him for a lesser position than the one he'd had was confirmed. And he couldn't lie, either. He couldn't hide that many years with the same company.

Thus, Carl became even more depressed, as he saw Christopher leave for work day after day and make a living with the company that had "betrayed" him. Before long, his thinking became muddled. He wasn't his reasonable self any longer. He let the housework go. He refused to go out. He stopped calling his friends. He stopped receiving visitors. Carl went into total isolation, except for the occasional visits to me, and Christopher's love and patience were being tested to the limits.

One night, Christopher didn't come home from work. He called Carl from a bar to say he'd be home later. But he never arrived; he was out all night. And when he did make his appearance at 6:00 A.M., he claimed he had no memories of the night's events. He didn't even remember making the phone call, and he couldn't answer Carl's interrogation about where he had been and with whom he'd been.

"If you don't remember what you did," Carl screamed, "then who does?"

"Martin might."

"You told me you didn't remember who you were with! Who in the hell is Martin—a fresh trick?"

"No." Christopher was being his usual honest, thoughtful self. "I've been feeling like there's a Martin around lately."

"You're talking multiple personality garbage!" Carl threw back at him. "You think I'll believe it! You really are crazy!"

Christopher was stymied; Carl's righteous anger was unrelenting.

"Isn't it too damn convenient that you're talking like that now?" Carl's voice was heavy with sarcasm. "I haven't heard about any of the other personalities in a year."

Christopher withdrew from the argument. His strength was gone. He called me from work that day, sounding as frightened as he had two years before. "I need to come in to see you as soon as possible, Dr. LaCalle."

He told me briefly on the phone what had happened and that he felt as if he had nothing left to give. Carl was so self-absorbed in his own plight. He had been unable to see how depressed Christopher was becoming. The stress had finally become unbearable. Christopher had exhausted all the ways to cope that he knew. His new defenses wouldn't hold up, and so the old defense—dissociation—had returned like a familiar ghost.

I quickly resigned myself to the fact that Christopher had experienced the relapse I had been expecting. I was amazed that he had held up under so much stress for as long as he did.

"Because there's a new part—this Martin—I'll need to start seeing you regularly again," Christopher told me. I could hear the embarrassment in his voice.

I knew I'd better act on this right away. "Martin" was a new split, probably not well formulated. I was almost certain he was a special-purpose fragment—an ego state rather than a full personality. Christopher was beginning to create him to take care of tasks and cope with feelings that he could not tolerate.

I had arranged to see Christopher the next day and lost no time confronting the issue directly.

First, I had to make sure Christopher's night out wasn't another of the pranks Sissy used to pull—thoughtless, but not the end of the world.

"So you went out and had fun, even stayed out all night, did you, Christopher?" I said.

"Yes. I know it was me, but it doesn't feel like me. I could never do that to Carl."

"Wait a minute, Christopher. You certainly have parts of you that can be wild, party all night, be self-centered."

"I know. I know I can be that way, but not like *this*. Not me!"

"What is it then? What is it that only Martin could do?"

"Leave." Christopher looked bleak with the honesty.

"Leave?" I pursued. "For a while or permanently?"

"Move out." Christopher was shame-faced. "I just couldn't do that."

"No? You've walked out on lovers before," I countered unrelentingly. I had to be sure this was not an old pattern.

"Never like this! I didn't care about the others." He looked hurt by my confrontation. "Carl deserves everything he wants from me. I'd feel too guilty if I moved out."

"Well, I guess you'll just have to stay then. You're strong enough to put up with the increasing stress. You won't get more depressed . . . start splitting . . . creating more crises for Carl." I wanted Christopher to hear the impossibility of what I had just said.

"But how *could* I leave?" Christopher wailed. "I couldn't do that to him! He'd be crushed!"

"He would feel terribly abandoned, wouldn't he?"

"Yes—he's already been abandoned by most of his friends." There was anguish in Christopher's voice. "Except for the AIDS Project volunteers, I'm the only company he has."

"And," I kept on relentlessly, "I suppose that if you moved out, you wouldn't come around anymore. You'd be too busy with

246

your own life, just like Carl's friends who don't come to see him anymore."

"That's not true!" Christopher protested. "I'd come as often as I could, and I'd call every day."

"But that wouldn't be much good, would it?" I asked, falling into the role of devil's advocate.

"Sure it would! I'd be getting a better night's sleep, for one thing. I'd be more rested, so I could take him out on the weekends."

"That's fine for you," I followed, "but you don't expect Carl to take care of himself at night, do you? Sometimes he needs to get hooked up to the oxygen tank, or he needs help up and down the stairs. You told me so yourself."

"I know. But volunteers can come on rotation, and I could take my turn spending the night there, too."

"Oh."

I paused to let Christopher reflect on his own arguments. We sat looking at each other silently. I recalled for a moment words I'd heard on television—what Mother Teresa had said about how it's not how *much* we give but how much *love* we put into giving. Those words seemed to apply to Christopher and how he could give to Carl.

"I really won't be much good to him if I stay, will I?" he asked sadly.

I didn't feel I needed to respond. I was waiting for him to come around to his own conclusions.

"It's really been getting me down, watching him getting sicker, weaker, more depressed. It's so hard to come home to it every night, without any break. If I go out—even for a little while—he gets jealous and upset, so I stay home. But I get depressed, too. I wish I were stronger! Why can't I be stronger?"

"I think you are stronger—every day," I disagreed quietly.

"But not strong enough for handling this right now."

"You *could* let Martin have the courage to move out for you. Of course, moving out is probably not the kind of strength you're thinking of."

"No, I wouldn't think of that as strength. It's the coward's way out."

"So, would you let Martin do it?"

"You're right. If I continue the way I've been going, that's

247

probably what would happen. No matter how much I *should* stay, I won't."

"So?"

"So I better accept my weakness and have the courage to move out on my own, without splitting," he said sadly. "But it won't be easy."

Again, I thought, nothing is easy for Christopher.

When Christopher moved out, Carl felt angry and bitter. He felt abandoned and betrayed. His funds were running out, and with Christopher living elsewhere, the house payments would be impossible for the two of them to make. At the rate his money was dwindling, he wouldn't be able to live there another year.

Nonetheless, Christopher moved out of the suburban home he'd shared with Carl and back to the city. In addition to all the stress of living with Carl, he'd been wasting too much time each day on the freeway. That had tired him as well. And as soon as the move was complete, he realized how much better he felt—and he remembered the entire move, including the pain that went with it. The dissociation had ceased.

Christopher drove to see Carl every other evening; on alternate days he called two or three times. By now he'd made friends with a volunteer from the AIDS Project and appreciated the much-needed support he was receiving for his decision to move out. Within a few weeks, Carl could see that Christopher was feeling better. He had to admit that their relationship had improved. Christopher could be more loving and giving than ever. And Carl, because he did care about Christopher, was glad to see his dearest friend looking more relaxed.

Left alone, and no longer preoccupied with Christopher's comings and goings, Carl had time to face himself and his circumstances. There was nothing to distract him from his personal crisis: denial first, depression, isolation . . . and now? He had to confront the inevitability of his own death.

Carl could still make his way to my office unassisted. When he came after I hadn't seen him in three months, I had to work to conceal the shock I felt when I saw how much he had changed. Lesions were now visible on his face and neck. His tan, healthy look and energetic style were distant memories; the lesions were even more striking against his pallid skin. His pants bagged, looking uncharacteristically slovenly where he'd drawn them up with his belt.

It pained me to see him like this, as he shuffled into my office and slowly lowered himself onto my sofa. I thought of Christopher's anguish—living with Carl and watching him go down hill day by day.

"It's been a year and a half since I was diagnosed," Carl reminded me. "You know what that means."

I knew. His time was running out.

"I'm getting really sick." He heaved a deep sigh. His breathing was labored. "The lesions are spreading throughout my lungs, I think, but I'm afraid to find out. Those doctors will probably want to cut me open or put something down my throat so they can look around." He stopped to breathe again. "I'm no good to anybody." He weakly brushed his hand in the air and let it drop in his lap. Resting his chin on his chest, he mumbled feebly, "Why don't I just die?"

It pained me to hear him talk this way about himself, feeling so worthless. Yet, I found I had to pause to think of what contribution Carl was still making to life.

"It's not true that you aren't good for anything, Carl. You're sharing with me, and that's helping me become a better psychologist—and a better person."

Carl sat slumped on the sofa, his shoulders hunched over his chest in the characteristic posture of patients with respiratory obstruction.

"But look what I've done to Christopher." He was totally deflated.

"You've taught him a lot, that's what you've done."

"And made him miserable. I'm a burden."

"Christopher is being made stronger by these difficult times. Without the challenge you've met together, he'd never have known he was capable of such loyalty and devotion."

"Do you think he has held up okay? He seemed pretty confused for a while."

"Not just okay, Carl," I said firmly. "He's done astoundingly well. If you had known him as long as I have, you'd see a remarkable change."

"I do see how he's held on," Carl acknowledged. "I never

thought Christopher was the type who could have stayed with me this long." His lower lip trembled slightly. "Especially when I have nothing . . . nothing left to give." His voice trailed off.

"Except your love," I said firmly.

"Yes, that." There were tears in his eyes. "At least I have that to give." Carl reached for a Kleenex and tried to regain his composure.

He was very quiet, I thought, as if there was some important reason why he'd come—and yet he couldn't seem to get to it.

"Is there anything I can do for you, Carl?" I asked as gently as I could.

"I . . . need to talk with someone."

I wondered what it was he couldn't talk about with Christopher.

"You need to talk with someone about—" I led him.

"Dying."

Of course. That was what Christopher wasn't ready to talk about, but Carl had now begun to accept. It's time, I thought, perhaps a final stage of growth.

"Sure, Carl," I said warmly, without hesitation. "Let's talk about dying."

By the grace of God, I didn't have a terminal illness, yet I felt a kinship with Carl. I'd been through this before—dealing with my own fears because of a couple of medical crises in previous years that had forced me to consider the real possibility of my own death, and in my clinical practice I'd often helped others with their concerns about dying. "It's something we've got in common. You're just a little ahead of me, that's all. Or, then again, maybe you're not. One never knows."

Carl came to see me several times after that to talk about death and dying. Since neither of us knew for certain what was on "the other side," we simply shared our views and listened to each other. Carl had no religion, no faith, no belief in an afterlife. He wanted to hear how I coped with the idea of death. He wasn't sure what he thought about God. He was interested, but he found greater comfort in thinking that for him death would simply mean that life was finished—no more suffering, no more pain. Yes, he could accept that. He could accept the end.

What held greater meaning for him now was how he was going to carry out the end. He wanted to be as free of pain as possible, and he asked if hypnosis would help. I was sure it would, and it did. Carl wanted so badly to be free of pain that he readily went into a trance and felt quite comfortable. Encouraged by this, we made cassette tape recordings of his sessions, and he used these at home. With this method, the posthypnotic suggestions helped him reduce the pain even when he wasn't in a trance.

For Carl, the acceptance of his death had brought a certain kind of dignity and peace—a composure that was both striking and humbling. I was inspired by his determination to carry on the best he could.

Christopher appreciated the turn Carl had taken. The old expectations that Carl had once put on Christopher were gone. He now encouraged Christopher to have friends and to take some time for himself. Christopher took the chance to bring his friend, Wayne, along for a visit. This was the first time Carl had seem them together, although Carl knew Wayne as a volunteer for the AIDS Project, and Christopher had talked about Wayne.

"It was hard to see them together," Carl told me. "Hard to know that Wayne will still get to be with him after I'm gone. But I know it's what's best for Christopher. He needs to have someone."

"But they're just friends, aren't they?"

"For now, but I can tell they are good for each other. It will become more."

Not long after that, Christopher stopped by my office at midday.

"Can I take you out to lunch?" he asked.

This was an unusual request, in fact, unprecedented. I must have looked surprised because Christopher seemed to know what I was thinking.

"I want to thank you for helping Carl."

"That's a very nice gesture, Christopher, but you don't have to thank me."

"Well, I know you've been seeing him for free since he has so little money, and he won't ever be able to repay you."

"It doesn't matter."

"You know, you've really been a good friend, Trula."

His use of my first name slipped quite naturally into the conversation. He'd never used it before, but it sounded right.

251

"You've been a darned good friend yourself, Christopher." I smiled at him. "Carl is really going to need his friends now more than ever."

"He really relies on you, you know."

I nodded.

"But don't feel bad if you can't take all his calls," Christopher counseled me. "He has other people he can call if he needs to."

"I'll keep that in mind," I said, touched by Christopher's consideration.

"And don't worry about me," Christopher advised. "I'm doing fine."

"I'm glad you're okay. I'd thought you were."

"Now . . . can't I take you to lunch?"

I hesitated.

One of the cardinal rules of the therapist-patient relationship—at least in traditional circles—is that the therapist does not socialize with the patient. But was Christopher still my patient? We had stopped regular sessions months before, and his last visit was when he moved out of Carl's home.

"I'm not seeing you for therapy anymore," Christopher said. Again, it was as if he were reading my mind.

"You're right," I admitted. "But before we make any more changes—and we certainly have been doing that—why don't we postpone the lunch for a while, just to be sure."

"That's all right. I understand." He looked at ease with the idea. "I better wait. If I do need a psychologist before this is over with Carl, I don't want to have to go looking for a new one."

I was pleased he understood my intent.

The coming months were catastrophic. I was glad I was still supporting Carl and also waiting in the wings for Christopher in case he should need me. During this time, Carl's mother died of cancer. He'd known she was near death. She couldn't help but say to him that she wanted to be the first to die. And she did.

Carl grieved deeply. He'd loved his mother.

By this time, the bank had foreclosed on the house Carl and Christopher had purchased. They couldn't keep up the payments, but Carl had protected Christopher's credit by taking over full ownership. He then moved to his mother's house, and in doing so moved closer geographically to Christopher. Living among his mother's things was hard on Carl, but dwelling on the happy childhood memories there comforted him. Moreover, he no longer had to worry that he'd be out on the street before he died.

Carl was still able to move about with assistance, slowly and painfully. He made arrangements to come see me once more. I knew he was determined to do it. Without saying anything directly, he implied it might be the last chance for us to talk face to face.

I wasn't prepared for what I saw. The door to the waiting room was opened by the AIDS Project volunteer who had brought Carl, a quiet but amiable-looking old gentleman who showed saintly patience as Carl took all of five minutes to pass over the threshold. I saw the wheel-equipped green oxygen tank get pulled in first, and it banged on the metal floor plate so hard I thought it would loosen the tubes that dangled to the floor and then found their way upward.

Then Carl painstakingly shuffled through the vestibule. The tubes were inserted in each nostril and were taped to Carl's chalk-white face. I caught my breath and held it, searching that face for the Carl I once knew. He looked like he had just been taken from a Nazi concentration camp—the hollow cheeks, the sparse hair, the vacant eyes, the look of having seen unspeakable horrors. And Christopher had lived with seeing this deterioration, day by day.

Liz straightened up in her secretarial chair and didn't hide an unforgivable gaping stare. Carl's posture was bent as he continued his old-man's shuffle to my office. His companion took a seat, picked up a magazine, and prepared to wait. Then, when Carl was nearly into my office—all the while never having said a word—he straightened himself as tall as he could.

At that moment, José opened the door to his office and looked around. The unfamiliar banging and shuffling sounds had brought him out to check on what was happening, and he stood still, taken aback at what he saw. I was glad Carl's back was to José. I prayed my face did not betray me and hoped at the same time that Carl would not turn to see José. Carl greeted me in a weak and gasping voice, and then, moving even more slowly than before, found his way to a chair and positioned his tank in front of him. Once he was settled, I was glad to be able to shut the door and spare Carl any more wide-eyed looks.

Carl had come again to talk about death. He had accepted it, he said, but he believed Christopher hadn't.

He wanted to die soon, he told me, in his sleep. He was tired, so tired. Pain was what he knew best, I thought. Yes, the hypnosis had helped, Carl told me. He used the tapes religiously, but couldn't we do more hypnosis over the phone? Yes, of course we could. And I told him I'd make some new tapes and send them to him. He told me he didn't want to take any more Percodan; he thought it was making him act strangely. "I want to be clear until the end," he told me. No, he wasn't afraid of dying. He was only afraid of the pain getting worse. He didn't think he could stand it if it were worse—but dying? The thought brought him peace.

But Christopher didn't want to hear about it when Carl mentioned dying.

"Christopher isn't ready to lose you," I said.

"I know. My time is coming . . . soon." He spoke in gasps, but with equanimity. "You'll help Christopher . . . when I go. Won't you?

"Of course, Carl, of course I will. I promise."

"I still have some time left . . . have to get my affairs in order. I haven't been able to finish my mother's estate . . . even if it's so small. Already I'm thinking . . . my own . . ."

I wanted to tell him there was still time. He was still able to be up and about, even if it was extraordinarily difficult.

But Carl spoke abruptly. "Time to go. I think something's . . . wrong with my oxygen tank. The gauge . . . I'm almost out. We put on a fresh tank . . . before I left the house."

I panicked, and I knew he read my face.

"Don't worry. The hospital across the street . . . I'll use the emergency room. They have oxygen there."

I was astounded at his composure. Obviously, he had thought about such problems before.

"Next time," he said as he prepared to leave, "I won't be so anxious to leave my house. I'll remember . . . to put an extra tank in the trunk."

Hearing him talk about a next time felt good.

"Are you sure you have enough in there to make it across the street?" I was remembering how long it took him to come in and estimating how long it would take him to leave.

"I'm sure . . . at least twenty minutes left. Sorry for having to be so abrupt."

I couldn't believe he was apologizing.

"Don't think of me, Carl," I said hurriedly. "What can I do to help you?"

"Tell Bob, the person I came with, to get the car . . . bring it up to the door. I can handle the tank myself."

I did Carl's bidding and helplessly watched him go about the business of leaving. Thank goodness the waiting room was empty, I thought, and that Liz had left for an early lunch. José came out of his office and saw me standing pale-faced, staring at the door as it closed behind Carl.

"Are you okay?" He spoke gently, putting his arm around me.

"Not really."

"Isn't that the man I'd seen come in with Christopher? I could barely recognize him."

"Yes, that's him." I didn't feel like elaborating.

"What's wrong with him?"

"He has AIDS." The words caught in my throat.

"Oh . . ." José quickly put the story together. "So *he's* the one! Oh, my gosh!" He was quiet. I knew he was thinking of the impact this was having on me. "Oh, my gosh," he said again.

I looked into his eyes and I could see he understood. "You'll be all right, won't you?" he asked tenderly.

His compassion touched me. I held rein on the painful sadness his sensitivity brought to the surface.

"I'm a big girl," I said, "but I appreciate the concern. Just give me a hug. That's all I need right now."

After I waited a couple of minutes, I called the emergency room to see if Carl had arrived. He was there.

Carl had been right. That was to be the last time I'd see him in my office. After that, we kept in touch by telephone. I wanted to see him again, but couldn't reconcile my schedule and the two-hour round trip to his house. I'd wait for a three-day weekend, I thought, Labor Day, if not sooner.

There were no phone calls from Christopher, which I took as a positive sign. Weeks passed. But, as is often the case with people who put things off, I had waited too long. Christopher called. Carl was hospitalized at the City of Hope. Now the drive would take three hours, but I had to go. I'd just have to take the time that Saturday; time was no longer something I could count on.

I told Christopher my plans, but he wanted to talk to me before I went. He said there were things Carl hadn't told me, legal troubles over his mother's estate that Carl was likely to mention.

"He's been getting delusional," Christopher told me. "So it's hard sometimes to sort through the truth of what he says. I think you better know the story before you go up there."

I told him I appreciated the warning. "If I don't know what's going on," I said, "I won't be able to help him as well. I might even say something wrong."

"Oh, I don't think you'd do that. But I am hoping you can help him calm down. He's been quite worked up and . . ." Christopher cut himself short. "Listen, I'll tell you all about it when I see you."

"Okay, let's do it soon."

"How about lunch tomorrow? Is it all right this time?"

"Sure, Christopher, sure." I'd said the words quickly, then stopped to think. Yes, my feelings were genuine. There really was no reason I shouldn't have lunch with Christopher. "In fact," I told him, "I'll really look forward to it."

Christopher came by at noon the next day. We walked to a restaurant near my office, strolling under sunny skies and talking like friends. We were in no hurry. Christopher wanted to be sociable and not serious for a while. His steady grin let me know he was enjoying my company—the informality—and our light conversation.

"So tell me what's new with you." He spoke as if he'd asked that question often. I was delighted.

"Well, what do you want to know?"

"How are your children?"

"They're doing great." I beamed spontaneously, but then I did that when anyone mentioned Eddie and Carmen. "Eddie is going into the fourth grade, and Carmen is in kindergarten."

"Already?" he asked with surprise. "Time goes so fast!" He

shook his head. Then he asked if I was still attending the study group on multiple personality.

"I go faithfully," I told him. "In a few weeks I'll be in Chicago, meeting with mental health professionals from all over the world. We need to compare our experience and share our research and learning with each other. This will be the 'First International Conference on Multiple Personality and Dissociative States.' I'm really looking forward to it."

"Do you think many people will be there?"

"I've heard they're anticipating three to four hundred conferees."

"That's incredible!"

"Isn't it though? The last four years have sure changed things in this field."

I knew Christopher was unaware of how little was understood about his disorder when I first started treating him. But he knew enough to recognize that times had changed; he'd found newspaper and magazine articles on the subject. He knew that multiplicity was being discussed by mental health professionals more than ever before.

"And do you know what else is exciting, Christopher? I'm part of a new association called The International Society for the Study of Multiple Personality and Dissociation."

"What a title!"

"For short, we call it ISSMP and D."

"Even that's a whopper!" he said, laughing.

We rounded the corner and made our way into the Cajun restaurant. I knew as soon as we were settled that Christopher would get around to telling me about Carl. I'd enjoyed the pleasant chat with Christopher; I was sorry the mood couldn't continue. But I knew he'd been living on a daily basis with life-and-death issues, and I told myself a little lightheartedness had been good for us both.

I was the one to start in. "So, tell me about Carl. How is he doing?"

"Actually, he's doing pretty well, considering." Christopher didn't seem too downcast. "It's been real hard for him, of course. I go to the hospital every evening after work. It's so far—after eleven when I get home. Wayne goes with me when he can. It's good to know Wayne will be there, all the way . . . to . . ."

I finished the sentence silently for him: "To the end."

"Tell me," I said, "how is Carl handling seeing you and Wayne together?"

"Really well. He's over all his jealousy. He's not hanging on to feelings like that anymore." Christopher paused to reflect. "I can't believe how peaceful he seems now, in spite of how physically uncomfortable he is."

"But you said on the phone that there's something I should know about."

"Yeah." Christopher swallowed hard. "It's not easy for me to tell even you. I'm feeling so disgusted—Carl's father is trying to get possession of Carl's inheritance. His mother left the house to him, but it seems it was owned by his father as well at the time of their divorce. They'd agreed to let her live in it as long as she wanted. Now, with Carl's mother dead, his father is claiming the house is his. He's gotten an attorney to force Carl out."

"But why is he troubling Carl with this now? In a while this will all be over. His father could have the house."

"The man is afraid Carl will leave his half of the house to me— one of those 'dirty faggots,' as he calls us."

"The house is all Carl really has to his name, isn't it?"

"That's all, and just a few personal possessions and some furniture—and he wants me to keep them or dispose of them after he's gone."

"What would you do with his share of the house if he left it to you?"

"I'd easily let his father have it if he wasn't acting this way. I really don't want it. The idea of making a profit off of Carl's death makes me sick."

The phrase "dirty faggots" kept coming back to me. How could a man who would rob his dying son be contemptuous about someone else's so-called morality? The father's behavior was despicable. I had a hard time imagining a nice man like Carl having a father who could be so extremely bitter and selfish.

"What will Carl do?"

"I don't know. He's talked with his attorney, but he has no strength to fight. No money either."

"So he might want to talk about it?"

"I'm sure of it," Christopher said. "He's not surprised his

father would do something like that. They've never liked each other. Still, it hurts."

"I appreciate you letting me know about this ahead of time, Christopher. I need to get over being angry about it. I don't want Carl to have to cope with my feelings, too."

Saturday turned out to be an excellent day for the long drive. The San Gabriel Valley air was crisp, cool, and unusually clear. I was enjoying the first touch of autumn and opened my sunroof and turned up the stereo. I was being a typical Southern Californian, I thought, but for a short while I wanted to relax and put my mission out of my head.

The signs for the City of Hope caught my attention when I headed into Duarte. I was happy the hospital had accepted Carl, even if it was so far away. Here, Carl would get the very best care available. I pulled into the parking lot, admiring the aesthetic look of the grounds. Then I took a deep breath and walked in.

It had been a long while since I had been in a hospital as an unofficial visitor. I'd forgotten that I'd have to observe visiting hours. What time was it? I checked my watch: a reasonable hour, I thought, but only if they had afternoon visiting hours. I should have called ahead to check. I approached the nursing station to ask.

"Hello," I said quietly. I didn't want to startle the nurse, who was in the midst of deep concentration. "I'm Dr. LaCalle. I'm here unofficially to see a patient of mine, Carl . . ."

"Oh, yes! We've been expecting you," she said, in what I thought was a surprisingly familiar manner. "Dr. Chu wanted me to page him as soon as you arrived. He wanted to speak with you first. Won't you please have a seat?"

I didn't wait long. Dr. Chu responded immediately. A young doctor, perhaps a resident, I thought, as we shook hands.

"I've looked forward to meeting you. Carl has talked a lot about you, Dr. LaCalle," he said with open admiration. I felt embarrassed. I had done nothing to deserve this special recognition.

"How is Carl doing?" I asked. It was Carl I wanted to talk about.

Dr. Chu gave me a long description of Carl's medical status and drug treatment. I wondered if he knew I was a psychologist and not a physician, but I appreciated being treated as if I understood all the terminology he was using. "Sometime I'd like to hear about your pain-management approach with hypnosis," Dr. Chu said when he'd finished describing Carl's treatment.

So he did know who I was.

We walked toward Carl's room, and I knew it without asking. A warning was posted: BLOOD AND SECRETION PRECAUTIONS. WASH HANDS BEFORE AND AFTER CONTACT. An infectious waste bin stood outside the door. A nurse had entered just ahead of us, covered in a white gown and wearing surgical gloves.

"Why don't we wait?" Dr. Chu suggested. "She'll be done in just a minute."

It all seemed mysterious, if not frightening. But Dr. Chu was smiling. I felt myself getting increasingly nervous about what I'd see on the other side of that door.

"I haven't been in yet today," Dr. Chu said, "so I don't know what kind of a day he's having. Yesterday he was very disoriented and confused. He just drifts in and out."

The nurse came out. She'd taken off her gown. Now she pulled off her gloves and dropped them into the bin.

"We can go in now," Dr. Chu said.

By this time, I was none too eager.

Carl was sitting up with his head resting on a pillow. He was caught in a web of tiny plastic tubes that were taped into his nostrils and on his arms and ended in bottles, tanks, and monitors. I could see he was too weak to raise his head up to look at me, but when I moved into his view he smiled faintly.

"Do you know who is here to see you?" Dr. Chu asked him.

"It's . . . Dr. LaCalle," Carl said. He struggled to smile again.

"How are you feeling today, Carl?" Dr. Chu asked.

Carl turned to look at Dr. Chu, who was standing on the other side of the bed. The movement of his head was painfully slow.

"Much better, today." Carl's answer was weak. "Doing fine. It must be . . . Saturday . . . Dr. LaCalle's here."

"Yes, it's Saturday. Listen, Carl, I'll come back to see you later." Dr. Chu seemed satisfied that Carl was clear-headed and able to have a visitor. "It's been a pleasure to meet you, Dr. LaCalle," he said as he turned to leave.

"Have a seat," Carl gasped again. "Make yourself . . . comfortable." His hospitality seemed out of place in the situation, but nonetheless so characteristic of him.

I moved a few papers off the chair, sat down, and pulled up closer to him.

"You changed your hair," he said. "It looks nice."

"Thank you."

"You look younger."

"Thanks again! It's part of a new me."

"New you?"

"Yes," I joked. "You know what happens when women get close to forty."

"Oh." He grinned weakly, but I could see a twinkle in his eye. "You, too?" he said then. "I . . . thought you'd be different."

"Nope. I'm just a plain ordinary human—given to the same vanities."

"How disappointing."

He hadn't lost his sense of humor. I enjoyed it. But I wanted to be sure to have enough time to talk to Carl, to get to the things that really mattered to him. I knew he'd tire quickly.

"Tell me how you are doing, Carl," I said, moving to a serious tone.

"Well . . . I don't like being in this room. Look out the window now and then . . . all I can do."

"Are you comfortable otherwise?"

"They treat me well here . . . kind people." He stopped an unusually long time for breath. "I can't complain."

"And Christopher?"

"He comes every evening. Sometimes I think I . . . fall asleep when he's here. I don't always remember."

"And Wayne?"

"He comes often. I like him—he's a good person."

Carl's expression then changed. He looked depressed. I couldn't altogether discount the possibility that the thought of Wayne with Christopher disturbed him. But Wayne wasn't on Carl's mind anymore.

"My father isn't a good person," Carl said.

"I know. Christopher told me."

"He told you about the house? That's . . . pretty bad, isn't it."

261

"Yes. I think so, too."

"What should I do?" Carl asked helplessly. "I shouldn't let him . . . do a thing like that, should I? My mother . . . wanted *me* to have the house."

"What do *you* want, Carl?"

"Just want to let it go . . . be done with it."

"Then you wouldn't worry about it anymore?"

"No. It would be finished."

"Then?" I pursued.

"You think it would . . . upset Christopher?"

"Not a chance," I reassured him.

"Then that's what I want," he said, relieved. "I'm going to sign . . . the papers."

He'd been trying to hold his head up a bit, but he gave up the effort now and relaxed into his pillow. I could see the tension had left his body. He'd closed his eyes, so I sat quietly and waited to see if he had fallen asleep.

Carl opened his eyes again. "Thank you," he said. "I needed to know it was okay . . . to not fight anymore."

Something about his tone made me think he didn't want to fight for life anymore, either. But now he changed the subject.

"Tell me . . . something about you," he said.

"Well, let's see." I tried to think of news that would interest Carl. "In a couple of weeks I'm getting a new car."

"Let me guess—a BMW?"

"No. A Nissan 300ZX sports car—in red, no less!"

He tried to laugh. His choking attempt turned into a cough that I thought would bring the nurses running.

"Are you okay?" I asked.

He nodded slightly, and I waited while he got another breath. "I love the Z," he said. "Always wanted one. But don't you drive . . . a silver Peugeot sedan?"

"Uh, huh. I thought it was about time I loosened up a little."

"Conservative Dr. LaCalle?"

"It'll still be the same old me, even after I get through my midlife crisis."

Carl was grinning in spite of the tubes and tape pulling at his mouth. But his mood soon changed again.

"I won't see you . . . in your new car," he said seriously.

"Who says you won't? The next time I drive up here, I'll park it under your window."

"Next time?"

"Next time. I promise."

There never was a next time. Carl died before the car was delivered.

Christopher was the only real "family" Carl left behind. He was the one to arrange for the cremation, the memorial service, the distribution of Carl's meager belongings. Christopher handled it all with sensitivity, strength, and respect for Carl. No one could ever want a better "family" than Christopher was to Carl.

After everything had settled down and Christopher had had a chance to rest, I called him.

"You know, Christopher," I confided, "I have a feeling that something has been left unfinished. It's silly, but it has to do with my new car." My voice was choking; I couldn't hold back the tears. I hadn't anticipated this sudden rush of emotion. I was glad Christopher couldn't see me, but he must have known I was crying. "I . . . need to go to the cemetery and drive by his place there. I know it's only his ashes and a marker, but it's all I have left of Carl."

I couldn't hear Christopher, but knew he was listening intently.

"The problem is," I went on, "I don't know where the marker has been placed, and the cemetery is too big to find it easily."

"I'll go with you."

"Will you?"

"Sure. I go there myself sometimes."

"Can we go this Saturday?"

We agreed when and where to meet. When Saturday came, I cut some roses from my garden. The late fall blooms looked beautiful, and I remembered that Carl always liked the large yellow roses when I had them in my office.

When I arrived at the cemetery, Christopher was waiting. He'd come early. I pulled up next to him; he got out of his car and walked over.

"Is it far from here?" I asked.

"A little too far to walk, unless you have lots of time."

"Then why don't you get in?"

Christopher slid into the leather seat of my new car.

"Mmmm . . . nice," he said, looking around at the interior.

"This is the car I promised to show Carl the last time I saw him. I never got to do that." I felt awkward. "I suppose this seems a bit strange, trying to do it now."

"No," he said reassuringly, "I understand."

"How have you been?" I asked, rolling down the windows to let in a fresh breeze.

"Pretty good, I guess." He heaved a sigh. "Just really sad—a big void. It's like I don't know what to do with myself."

"How is Wayne?"

"Really good. I'm so glad he's there for me now," he said. "Wayne sends his regards."

"Carl really liked Wayne—and I haven't even met him."

"Maybe you could come over for dinner. Or, if it's easier, we'll come by one day and take you to lunch so you can get to know each other."

"I'd like that, but give me a little time, will you?"

Christopher looked at me blankly.

"I'm used to seeing you with Carl, remember?"

"That's right," Christopher said with sudden comprehension.

I started up the engine, and Christopher pointed the way. It was a magnificently serene memorial park. Rolling green hills, weeping willows, flower beds, and stone walks. I stopped the car where Christopher indicated and pulled over. Roses in hand, I followed Christopher along the shaded walkway to an interior courtyard to where Carl's name was chiseled in stone on the wall. *Carl Williams.* I stared at it. How strange to see his name like that, among dozens of others—cold, impersonal, so unlike Carl. It didn't seem right.

Christopher looked around for an empty bronze flower vase, found one, and inserted it in the holder next to Carl's name. I placed the flowers in it and stepped back. We stood there awhile, then wordlessly turned to leave.

We walked slowly, side by side, neither of us caring to shatter the stillness of the moment with words. When we were back at my car, Christopher pulled something out of his pocket.

"I have something for you," he said quietly. "My favorite picture of Carl."

He unfolded the paper that protected it. Carefully, he put it in my hand.

I looked at it. There was Carl, leaning back on a sofa, his feet up, a wide toothy smile beaming his warmth. Tan, healthy, whole. Just as I wanted to remember him. Christopher could not have said or done anything else that would have meant as much. I appreciated who Carl was. And, even more, I appreciated who Christopher had become. I didn't know I was crying until I felt a drip on my hand. A tear was brimming in the corner of my eye, and I reached quickly to wipe my face with my hand. Christopher noticed.

"It's okay," he said soothingly. "It's okay to cry. We loved him."

"Yes, we did, didn't we?"

My tears were flowing now. I tried to wipe my nose on my wrist, and then looked down, still embarrassed. Christopher leaned toward me and put his hand on my shoulder. He patted me softly and waited for my tears to subside. I set Carl's photo down and shuffled through my purse for some tissue. I couldn't yet look at Christopher. I knew I'd cry more if I did.

"You've been a good friend, Christopher, to Carl . . ." I was still looking at my lap. I pulled myself together, mustering my courage. I turned to Christopher. "And to me."

Christopher looked at me steadily and openly and smiled. I didn't look away. Our transition was complete. We'd come so far—friends now, not doctor and patient.

I took Christopher back to his car. We didn't say goodbye. He got out, and I waved to him as I drove off.

"Don't say goodbye," I said to myself. "Don't say goodbye."

INDEX